AMERICAN WELFARE CAPITALISM

AMERICAN WELFARE CAPITALISM

1880-1940

Stuart D. Brandes

THE UNIVERSITY OF CHICAGO PRESS
Chicago and London

The University of Chicago Press, Chicago 60637
The University of Chicago Press, Ltd., London

80 79 78 77 76 987654321

Stuart D. Brandes received his Ph.D. from the University of Wisconsin at Madison and is associate professor of history at the University of Wisconsin, Center-Rock County.

Library of Congress Cataloging in Publication Data

Brandes, Stuart D.
American welfare capitalism, 1880-1940.

Bibliography: p.
Includes index.
1. Industrial relations—United States—History.
2. Welfare work in industry—United States—History.
I. Title.
HD8072.B7 331'.0973 75-20886
ISBN 0-226-07121-9

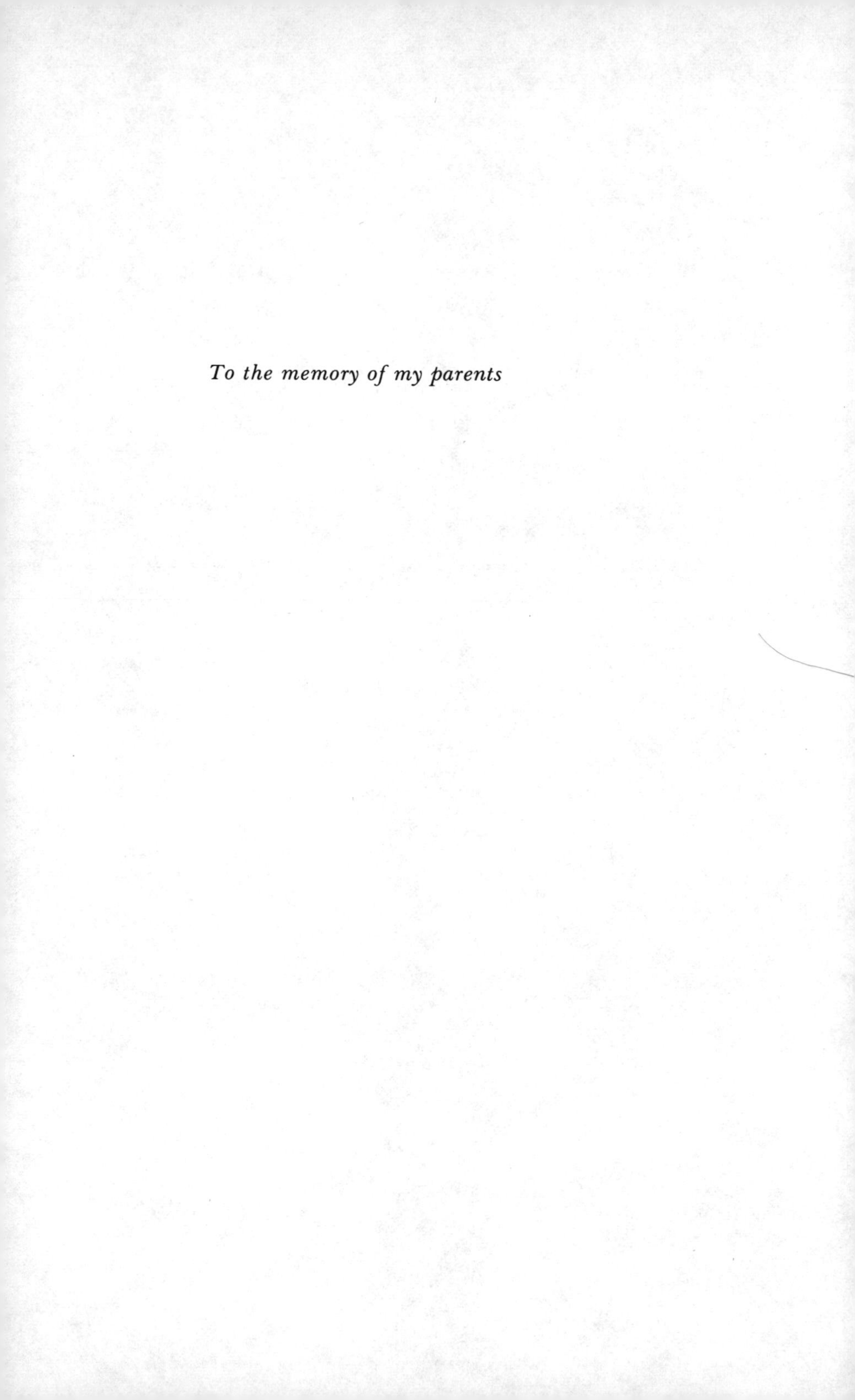

To the memory of my parents

Contents

Preface

Although the moving songs to which labor once marched now seem as quaintly anachronistic as the defiant jut of a businessman's jaw, the labor struggle of the early twentieth century commanded men's loyalties as have few others in American history. Perhaps it is not surprising that its literature has not been known for its impartiality. In the case of welfare capitalism, the unavoidable choice of language precludes from the very outset an entirely neutral posture toward the subject. "Welfare capitalism" is itself a probusiness term; "industrial paternalism" is its pro-unionist counterpart. Similarly, the student must choose between the synonyms "industrial village" or "company town" and "representation plan" or "company union." Each refers to the same thing but conveys different impressions. In the interest of scholarly detachment (if not colorful prose) the terms I use are those which seem to be least emotional in tone.

Dozens of librarians, typists, students, friends, family, and colleagues have contributed materially to this study. Many businessmen patiently and generously aided me in my searches. I would like to express my particular gratitude to Professor E. David Cronon of the University of Wisconsin, who directed the dissertation on which this manuscript is based, and to W. Elliott Brownlee, Jr., Dan Carter, Paul Conkin, Carl Harris, and Rogers Hollingsworth, who helped in various ways. I owe a very special debt to Richard Berke for his aid in revising the original manuscript. The enthusiasm, encouragement, and equanimity of Polly Powrie Brandes were indispensable ingredients. The errors and deficiencies are my own.

The Crisis of Industrial Relations

Given the traditional American attitude toward economic progress, the latter part of the nineteenth century provided a basis for immense satisfaction: having already matched its rivals in industrial production, the United States was riding a continually climbing output. If ever there was a time for good old American optimism, one might have thought, this was certainly it. But optimism was inappropriate—for the deeply held American belief in the natural tie between material gain and human progress was being severely shaken. The very people who were supposed to be bringing about the Golden Age seemed to be locked in an accelerating struggle that made fearful doubt quite as reasonable as heady optimism.

There was abundant evidence to suggest that the American working man was not happy. Individual rejections of working conditions, while difficult to measure, were perhaps the most economically costly of all the forms of dissatisfaction. An unhappy worker had the option of expressing his displeasure in a variety of ways. He might, for example, make a pretense of effort while accomplishing only enough to avoid punishment. He might malinger. He might drink. He might leave his job. In extreme cases, he might even purposely sabotage production. And workers did all those things in large measure. Lethargy, absenteeism, insobriety, and rapid job turnover endlessly vexed most cost-conscious businessmen. These factors alone would have made industrial relations, by 1900, a social and economic problem of the first magnitude.

But they were not the only factors. If economically less costly, perhaps, there was a form of worker dissatisfaction that was far more ominous—the strike. Between 1880 and 1900, nearly 23,000 strikes affected more than 117,000 establishments.[1] That was an average of three new strikes a day for twenty years. Like the other forms of opposition, strikes were both an inconvenience and a serious economic cost. What made them particularly disturbing, no doubt, was the accompanying violence, frequently answered by even greater violence. Just who was responsible for initiating the violence is a subject of continuing argument, but there is no question that both sides had the capacity and the requisite attitudes.

On the one hand, some companies favored, as a "solution" for strikes, the "big stick" system, admirably described by Georgia textile-maker Oscar Elsas. Asked what he could do if his employees struck for higher wages, Elsas replied that "in an acute situation where I had only men to deal with I'd just as soon get a gun and mow 'em down as not." Companies did get guns, all kinds, along with an armory of other weapons: "We have machine guns, riot guns, and rifles. We have tear bombs loaded with tear gas and we have ferry pistols, relics of [World War I], which shoot gas shells, and star bombs." So spoke R. L. Ireland, Jr., general manager of five coal mining companies. Colorado Fuel and Iron built an armored car in its shops and christened it the "Death Special." In the Paint Creek district of West Virginia, mine operators ran a special train to bring in strikebreakers—the sides and roof of one car were plated with boiler steel, and slits cut in the doors allowed two machine guns to fire simultaneously. Not uncommonly armored forts protected company property.[2]

Along with the armories came the armies. In 1923 Pennsylvania Governor Gifford Pinchot estimated that police employed by coal and iron companies outnumbered state-employed police by twenty to one. The Pittsburgh Terminal Coal Company organized its force by rank—colonels, captains, sergeants, privates, and so forth. In 1914, evidence indicates, Colorado Fuel and Iron employed men specifically to organize militia in its company towns. At Berwind, Tobasco, Sopris, and Primero, Colorado, there were infantry units; at Hastings and Deluga (owned by the Victor-American Coal Company) there were cavalry units; and Walsenburg had an artillery unit commanded by a former officer in the British Army.

A variation of the big stick policy was the practice of hiring a force when the need arose. Large numbers of temporary plant guards, commonly described by workers as "finks," "missionaries," or "busters," could be found waiting for employment in the lobby of the Mills Hotel in New York City, at the Salvation Army Hotel in the Bowery, and elsewhere in the country through "private detective" agencies. On duty, many such strikebreakers carried a foot-long lead pipe in addition to their sidearms, giving the big stick policy a literal meaning. Like all armies, these were costly. During a long strike in Pennsylvania in 1911, a county sheriff pocketed a fee of $42,641 simply as his commission for furnishing deputies to protect coal mines, and the Pittsburgh Coal Company, which employed up to 308 police at one time, spent over $670,000 on "defense" in just two years.[3]

The workers responded in kind, of course. At Cripple Creek, Colorado, in 1893, miners under the command of a former West Point cadet invented perhaps the first Molotov cocktail—a beer bottle filled with dynamite which could be catapulted at company agents by a huge bow gun. In 1922 miners at Penobscot, West Virginia, built a makeshift cannon from a four-inch-wide steel casing, filled it with powder and iron, and fired on company property.[4]

Bloodshed was inevitable. During the great railroad strikes of 1877, aside from the millions of dollars lost in property damage, hundreds of people were wounded and many killed. Nine were killed in Martinsburg, West Virginia; thirteen in Chicago; twenty-six in Pittsburgh. According to one estimate, state troops were called out to quell strike violence roughly 500 times between 1875 and 1910.[5]

The transformation of economic conflict into actual military confrontation nearly reached its logical conclusion in the coal fields of West Virginia in 1919, where labor relations deteriorated virtually into overt warfare. In September of that year a group of 5,000 union miners assembled with the purpose of marching on Logan County and unionizing it forcibly. About 900 men, armed to the teeth, marched forty-one miles before Governor John J. Cornwell convinced them to return to their homes. "It was dark and the moon was shining and the camp fires were there," recalled one unionist who heard Cornwell's speech, "and there were in that crowd about 5,000 rifles. It looked more like Dante's Inferno than anything I can think of, with the moonlight shining on the rifles."[6]

Were capital and labor on a collision course? Was there to be a social revolution? What was to become of the economic progress which Americans valued so highly? Could America's liberal traditions withstand the impact of a technostructure imposed on them? These and similar questions troubled thoughtful Americans. Frequently they leveled their criticism at business. Unless business was reformed, many thought, a just and humane system could never be built.

Business leaders were seldom given to abstract thought about the proper shape of a new and more humane industrial order. They did, however, devote a great deal of attention to building their own individual enterprises. In order to do so, each had to manage an often sizeable labor force which could, as we have seen, become intractable and even dangerous. Though many would probably have preferred it otherwise, this involved more than just a question of wages. Business leaders found that workers had to be housed and fed and had other needs as well. Social problems inevitably impinged on American businessmen, commanding their attention and involving them directly if they hoped to make their businesses successful. Business leaders became more and more concerned with areas of endeavor which extended beyond the more normal realms of production, commerce, and wage scales.

One of the most important social problems was the acculturation of young persons to the industrial society. By 1900 various American firms operated every form of school short of a college or university. Toddlers could attend company kindergartens, children could attend company grammar schools, and in some cases company high schools were available. The educational endeavor of Colorado Fuel and Iron Company was so well developed, in fact, that it subsidized a normal school where teachers trained for its company schools.[7] Workers' wives could attend company-sponsored cooking and sewing classes. Workers themselves could learn to speak English or improve their job skills at company schools. Beyond that, they could improve their minds by reading books from a company library or pick up wisdom from a company magazine.

Even the most basic problems of food and shelter often aroused the attention of American executives. Many employees dined at company restaurants. Company stores proliferated, and many companies provided milk for their employees from a company dairy. One company even had an eighteen-acre truck farm from which it supplied its employees with milk, fresh vegetables, eggs, and chickens.[8] The United States Steel Corporation once owned more than 28,000 houses in which its employees lived. The Pelzer Manufacturing Company owned and governed the entire town of Pelzer, South Carolina, where 6,000 people lived. Hundreds of other company towns dotted the landscape from coast to coast.[9]

The mills and factories of America were dangerous places, and companies sometimes aided in case of sickness or accident. Company doctors were sometimes available to tend ill or injured workers, and patients were sometimes nursed back to health by company nurses in company hospitals. If an employee's wife fell ill, some companies provided visiting housekeepers who would clean his house.[10] In the blackest circumstance a United States Steel employee's remains could be taken to the company morgue at Gary, Indiana. Company funeral parlors existed in some southern cotton mill towns, and at Alabama City, Alabama, the Dwight Manufacturing Company purchased land for use as a company cemetery. Lest widows and orphans be left shiftless, some companies sponsored company orphanages or industrial homes where dependents could live.[11]

Some companies sought to mitigate the boredom and monotony of factory work. An employee of the National Cash Register Company, for example, might pass his leisure time playing tennis, golf, croquet, basketball, pool, or quoits, all in the company park. Others could bowl at a company bowling alley, swim in a company pool (U.S. Steel owned nineteen of them), bathe in a company bathhouse, or enjoy a film at a company moving-picture house. There were even clubs for balloonists and rifle marksmen. If an employee's tastes were more culturally oriented, he might attend a concert by a company band, or (if he worked for the Colorado Fuel and Iron Company) visit the company circulating art collection. Hershey Chocolate Company employees could visit a company museum and zoological garden.[12]

Employees often became disconsolate from the changes in their lives arising from moving from farms to cities, and some employers took steps to help their employees adjust to city life. Some companies, accordingly, made it possible for employees to keep cows or chickens, and one maintained a company bird sanctuary. Company gardens were very popular with many employers, and floral displays (perhaps picked from a company greenhouse) graced many factories and houses, recalling misty memories of an agricultural past. Urban living required more attention to grooming than had farm life, and company manicurists cleaned fingernails while company shoe polishers blackened boots. In case employees ran afoul of the many regulations established by community living, free legal advice was sometimes available.[13]

Taken together, these practices compose what is known as welfare capitalism; by definition, any service provided for the comfort or improvement of employees which was neither a necessity of the industry nor required by law. Welfare capitalism constituted one solution offered by American businessmen to the crisis of labor-management relations of the early twentieth century. Ultimately, it proved to be an unacceptable one. Americans rejected the big stick policy, the idea of a social revolution, and welfare capitalism as well in favor of the now-familiar tripartite system—a continuing tug of war between big labor and big business with government seeking to prevent either side from gaining predominance. Some Americans accepted tripartism only by coercion, to be sure, and it did not extend to all sectors of the economy or to all sections of the country. But though the decades since the Great Depression have seen many labor struggles, the debate has largely concerned the stewardship of the system and the development of its complex administrative machinery; its basic features have remained intact. The issue of the means of allocating resources in an industrial society has been largely decided, and the violence which had plagued American industry early in the century has decreased.

Most students of recent American history have regarded the tripartite system as a great victory for social justice, an achievement which adds much luster to the record of the New Deal. Most also feel that the coercive means by which it was achieved were fully justified. According to the prevailing view of recent American history—the school of thought sometimes termed "progressive history"—early twentieth-century businessmen had scant regard for the needs of others. The rather low public morality of the Civil War and postbellum years continued to characterize the business community well into the twentieth century. Employment of women, children, convicts, and immigrants, for example, was ample evidence to many that businessmen cared little for the needs of working people. Unsafe and unpleasant mines and factories further contributed to the squalid lot of workers. In light of this demonstrated insensitivity, intervention and coercion by public-spirited reformers seemed fully justified.

An important aspect of the indictment of businessmen was their attitude toward union men. According to this view, the techniques used by businessmen when dealing with unionists were highly questionable. Practices like blacklisting, hiring thugs and strikebreakers, and using yellow-dog contracts were prime candidates for criticism. Taken together, they amounted to nothing less than intransigent resistance. Combined with insensitivity, this intransigence was the root of much of the violence that characterized American industrial relations. If these attitudes had been allowed to persist, years of strife and stagnation, perhaps even revolution, would have resulted. Indeed, so the reasoning goes, the perceptiveness and concern of the reformers of the thirties saved businessmen from their own folly.

The critics of business found evidence to support their case in the history of welfare capitalism. Irving Bernstein, who presented perhaps the broadest examination of welfare capitalism, argued that "the central purpose of welfare capitalism [was] avoidance of trade unionism." Robert Ozanne, who wrote the most extensive discussion of welfarism in a single company, declared that "welfare measures . . . were evolved as substitutes for unionism." Milton Derber, the most recent student, reached much the same conclusion. By implication this analysis added the charge of duplicity to the indictment of businessmen—rather than sincerely trying to help workers, they were instead pursuing their own aims. Another line of argument emphasized the dearth of welfare activities in industry. The implication was that only a handful of employers had any desire whatsoever to ameliorate the conditions of working men; most cared not at all.[14]

Neither the general interpretation of the history of industrial relations nor the place of welfare capitalism in it has gone unchallenged, however. In the 1950s a small but vocal band of scholars, known as the "business revisionists," sought with some success to redress the balance. Led by Allan Nevins and others, they argued that the positive contributions businessmen made far outweighed their occasionally predatory tactics. Welfare capitalism offered the revisionists an ideal opportunity to buttress their defense of business, but with one exception they failed to seize it. In their massive study of the Ford Motor Company, Nevins and Frank Ernest Hill called welfare capitalism a "bright dream" and described its era at Ford as "the brief golden age of the company, the . . . era of social conscience."[15]

In the 1960s a series of studies by historians even more critical of American business than the progressive historians argued that the system of industrial relations left by the New Deal was quite unsatisfactory. The chief benefactor, argued the spokesmen of the New Left, was business itself. Since business had gained so much from the system, they found it hard to accept the argument that the system had evolved in opposition to businessmen's wishes.

On investigation these historians came to believe that businessmen not only had made important contributions to the development of the system but indeed had devised it themselves. In this view businessmen were not shortsighted but instead remarkably perceptive. They correctly understood that their dominance of American society faced serious challenge in the form of radical labor groups like the Socialist Party and the Industrial Workers of the World, and this awareness led them to seek an accord with an acceptable kind of unionism. Their leader was Mark Hanna, the industrialist and adviser to President William McKinley, and their instrument for achieving this accord was the National Civic Federation. Their efforts continued until they met success during the 1930s. Thus, rather than being a departure from the past, the New Deal was the fulfillment of the corporate state, its chief result being the entrenchment of business hegemony. As William A. Williams, the leading exponent of this version of recent American history, asserted, "although their power was more hedged around with legal checks, and by the increased strength of labor and agriculture, the large corporation leaders clearly exercised the most power, authority, and influence in the system."[16]

Welfare capitalism also occupied a place in this interpretation of the past. One suggestion held that welfare work was a means used by enlightened businessmen to win the confidence of their shortsighted, stubbornly anti-union colleagues. Another held that welfare work was a way of assuring the industrial stability at home which in turn would lead to victory in the race for economic expansion abroad. Above all, according to this view, welfarism was a means of indoctrinating workers into accepting corporations as the central institution of modern American life. "Part of the process of integrating the lives of workers with that of the corporation involved the assumption by corporations of many functions now seen as government responsibilities," wrote James Weinstein. Welfare work, added Stephen Scheinberg, "helped to transform the corporation itself, from solely an economic institution into the basic social unit of American society."[17]

Particularly after the publication of Robert Wiebe's *The Search for Order* (1967), a new interpretation of recent American history began to take shape. This school asserted that the most important occurrence in the early twentieth century was the appearance of large modern organizations—the bureaucratization of American life. This synthesis has been alternately described by Louis Galambos as "organizational history" and by John Higham as the "bureaucratic orientation." Ellis W. Hawley has found in the 1920s the appearance of an "associative state," while James Gilbert suggests that the era is marked by the rise of "collectivism."[18]

Welfare capitalism has yet to be fully integrated into the organizational or bureaucratic synthesis, although it has been observed that welfare capitalism contributed to the appearance of modern personnel management.[19] Nevertheless, just as have spokesmen of progressive history, business revisionism, and the New Left, advocates of the organizational synthesis will undoubtedly find much in the record of welfare capitalism to buttress their case. While it is interesting to view welfare capitalism from these varied perspectives, however, it would be unwise to make welfare capitalism the chief foundation of any interpretation. Welfare capitalism did contribute to the making of a modern labor management system, but it was only one of several elements which did so. Similarly, the modernization of industrial relations was but one facet in the making of a modern America. It may well be, furthermore, that Higham was correct when he asserted that "in a long-term perspective, the distinctive feature of the period from 1898 to 1918 is not the preeminence of democratic ideals or of bureaucratic techniques, but rather a fertile amalgamation of the two."[20] Welfare capitalism was an important test of whether an amalgamation of democratic ideals and bureaucratic techniques was possible, and if so, of what form such a combination should take.

2 The Early Days of Modern Welfarism

"A new day has dawned in industry." The year was 1914, the speaker John D. Rockefeller, Jr. And from the highest seat in American industry, U.S. Steel president Elbert H. Gary affirmed repeatedly that the American businessman had indeed undergone "a great awakening."[1] These lords of business were proclaiming the gospel of the "service department," of "mutual interest work," "sociological work," "fellowship work," or "advance work," better known as "welfare work" or "industrial betterment"—in short, of American welfare capitalism.[2] They were putting their imprimatur on the quasi-productive business activities which came under these heads, activities like rental of housing, profit sharing, provision of libraries, garden planting and beautification, various forms of schooling, and the organization of ball teams and other kinds of sports and recreational activities.

There is, of course, nothing like public approval of the man at the top for bestowing legitimacy, but welfarism's coming of age had been marked as early as 1905. Studies of welfare capitalism were being published then, studies made not only by newspapers but by scholars, some of them advocating welfare activities. Prominent economists such as Richard Ely and John R. Commons published studies of welfare work in particular factories. Moreover, government studies appeared with greater frequency, most of them made at the federal level but some made by state agencies as well. Welfare capitalists themselves began to organize into groups to discuss and promote their programs.[3]

Actually, like most ideas whose time had come, welfare capitalism was not new; it was in fact as old as American industry itself. And like many grand works of men, its beginning was something less than grandiose; it was a school, made up of five Webster spelling books for texts, three New Testaments for library, and a faculty of one: a twenty-two-year-old part-time teacher of the three R's. His name was

Samuel Slater, and for his introduction in 1790 of machine methods of cotton spinning, Andrew Jackson would later dub him the "Father of American Manufactures." In order to recruit boys for his mill at Pawtucket, Rhode Island, Slater offered to keep a Sunday School where they could learn on their day off—the idea worked well, and so did the mill, well enough that six years later, in 1796, Slater felt prosperous enough to hire a full-time teacher. Thus began American welfare capitalism.[4]

Though a first step, Slater's program was no mere anachronism; welfarism grew with the flourishing of cotton textile milling in New England. Constructing mills near the sources of water power which were sometimes not close to population centers, New England industrialists provided dormitories for the farm girls they hoped to attract. In addition to dormitories, other accoutrements were sometimes offered: the Merrimack Manufacturing Company, together with other companies in Lowell, Massachusetts, constructed a school, an Episcopal church, and a hospital. They also sponsored the *Lowell Offering*, a magazine written by mill girls, probably the first employees' magazine in the United States.[5]

Writings on welfare capitalism began to appear in the 1830s. The first crude statement of theory appeared in an influential treatise on the technique of cotton manufacture published in 1832. In *The Carding and Spinning Master's Assistant: or the Theory and Practice of Cotton Spinning*, James Montgomery warned mill owners that labor relations was "a very tender point," a "delicate subject," and cautioned them "to avoid all severity." "I do not hesitate to assert," wrote Montgomery, "that a Spinning factory can never be managed more profitably, and more to the satisfaction of the proprietors, than when there exists a good feeling and good understanding between the managers and workers."[6] It would take some eighty years before men like Gary and Rockefeller could announce with confidence the victory of this philosophy over that known as the big stick system.

Welfare activities during the mid-nineteenth century were concentrated mainly on housing for workers. For example, between 1860 and 1884, the Waltham Watch Company increased by tenfold its expenditures for employee housing. A program of wider scope was undertaken by the Ludlow Manufacturing Company of Ludlow, Massachusetts, as it increased its investments in the town's community services and built streets, a sewage system, water works, gas works, a church school, and a masonic hall. Taken all in all, however, the period constitutes the calm before the surge of modern welfare capitalism.[7]

A number of factors were at work in preparation for the surge. For instance, some companies would find that if they established housing, they might not be able to limit themselves simply to providing the homes if they wanted to keep the homes properly maintained. One company, for example, would find that its employees converted bath tubs to coal bins. Another would discover that its employees practiced the peasant method of cleaning floors—dousing with water and swabbing with a broom—with highly undesirable effects on the ceiling of the apartment below. A third company, employing many European immigrants, would face the problem of involuntary de-wallpapering—the steaming of paper off the walls by concentrated boiling of foods.[8]

The heavy influx of immigrant workers would lead inevitably to employers' desire to change their ways. Sometimes these habits were not so much destructive as simply obnoxious to a society which would never be greatly tolerant of differences. Thus a leader in the welfare movement would support cooking schools because she was irked by the strange Lithuanian sausages, dark Slovak bread, and "uncouth Polack pickles" eaten by factory workers. Sometimes, as in the cases of the doused floors and the boiling of food, the habits could be costly. Among the most serious were drinking habits, and welfarism was one form of combat. For instance, when President John H. Patterson of the National Cash Register Company learned that a man planned to open a saloon across from the factory, he purchased the cottage himself and began a kindergarten instead.[9]

The growth of mass production would carry with it growing pressures on the employee and therefore on the employer. Employees developed a kind of ennui from performing the same operations day after day, or from performing tasks so specialized that they bore little relationship to the finished product. Asked how she managed to make it through the day, one young woman who performed the same operation over and over again at International Harvester replied, "I marry a duke in the morning and the rest of the day takes care of itself." It took no special insight to see that such daydreaming could be costly in terms of productivity and could raise the probability of accidents. It was equally obvious that employees who did not daydream were not necessarily happily productive. "My recollection goes vividly back," wrote B. Preston Clark, vice-president of the

Plymouth Cordage Company, "to the impatience with which one waited for the whistle to blow. The doing of one monotonous thing time after time seemed unendurable, and I did it for but a fraction of a lifetime." Again, employers would come to see welfarism as a possible solution, in various forms, such as recreation or beautification. Explaining why he beautified his factory, one New Hampshire cutlery manufacturer would remark that "work is many times wearisome and monotonous, and the more beauty that is thrown around the worker the better spirit he can put into his work."[10]

This growing sense of impersonality would develop not only out of the direct circumstances of mass production but out of bigness itself, where it would be felt not only by the employee but by the employer as well. As individual businesses grew, employee and employer lost contact with one another, and the problems which arose could no longer be handled by the boss on an ad hoc basis. Macy's department store in New York, for instance, frequently responded to the special problems of its employees: a clerk who was starving herself to support her widowed mother was provided meals at the store; a girl whose father had committed suicide was given funeral expenses; the company interceded when a reluctant, fearful mother refused to allow her daughter to have a tumor removed from her eye—the mother relented and the eye was saved; the company worked to help a girl who had paralyzed her writing hand in a suicide attempt.[11] Obviously, with a company as large as Macy's, the frequency of such events forced the bureaucratization of its humanitarian responses.

Largeness and the resulting loss of contact between employer and employee could itself create or exacerbate labor problems, for it was easier, perhaps, to carry out destructive acts against a large, faceless authority than against someone you knew personally. This might have been the case when acid was poured on a shipment of cash registers at National Cash Register Company. At least John Patterson, company president, thought so, and he moved his desk onto the factory floor in order to determine what pleased his employees. But S. Thurston Ballard, a Louisville miller, saw the essential futility of the personal approach in a large organization: "I tried faithfully to make up for this want by infusing my own personality into the work, but I was too busy, and was called here and there and could not, and did not, get in touch with the men as I had hoped—it was impossible." Ballard gave up the direct approach and resorted to welfare work.[12]

The problems engendered by largeness would multiply, for the nineteenth century would be an age of immense industrial growth. The Firestone Tire and Rubber Company went from twelve employees in 1902 to ten thousand in 1917, and in the last two decades of the century, the average labor force in the steel mills rose from 220 to 412.[13] A special form of bigness was represented by the trusts, whose peculiarities made them particularly prone to be influenced toward welfarism. Not only were they very large, they were also very profitable, and thus had two important ingredients for a positive attitude toward welfare: a large enough number of employees to justify a systematized welfare program, and the wherewithal to pay for it quite comfortably. Trusts were also less competitive than other companies, so they could afford to provide quasi-productive programs without the necessity for close scrutiny of results.

All of these factors, then—mass production, growth, immigration, the special problems introduced by existing programs—along with the particular situations of individual industries and added to the central ingredient of labor unrest, were creating the milieu in which welfare capitalism would blossom.

It should not be surprising that the first modern industry to adopt welfare practices was also among the largest. The rise of welfarism in the railroad industry well illustrates the interplay of events. By 1877 railroads had become the predominant form of land transportation in the United States; all through the seventies, demand was heavy and track was being laid at a prodigious rate. This meant, of course, that construction of track and equipment were far in advance of facilities for employees. As a result, transient trainmen often slept cramped in their engines, in empty freight cars, or along the track. The luckier ones frequented cheap hotels. Eating places and sources of recreation were also limited.

A popular answer was the saloon; one Indiana terminal town with a population of nine hundred was afloat with thirteen saloons. Tired workers who had a better-than-nodding acquaintance with demon rum were not an attractive prospect in an industry where expensive goods and many lives depended on close control of large and powerful high-speed engines. As alternatives to this unwholesome situation, railroads encouraged the growth of a special railroad branch of the Young Men's Christian Association and occasionally built their own rest houses. The first railroad YMCA was established in Cleveland in 1872; the Pennsylvania Railroad built what was probably the first railroad rest house in 1875. Railroad executives preferred the YMCA facilities to their own (one reason was that employees bore part of the expense), and by 1879 there were thirty-nine railroad YMCAs with twenty full-time secretaries.[14]

Important as the YMCA was as an alternative to the boxcar, the hotel, and the saloon, that was not the only reason for its subsidization by railroads. In 1877 a series of strikes tied up all five American trunk lines and all the major rail centers. Shaken by these disruptions, which continued sporadically thereafter, railroad executives sought to avoid their repetition by improving their workers' general conditions. Accordingly, railroad YMCAs provided more than just food and shelter. They also typically housed baths, libraries, athletic facilities, classes on railroad work, and, significantly, Bible classes and religious meetings. The underlying theory was that well-housed, well-fed, clean, properly educated Christians do not strike, or at least were less likely to than those with different life-styles. More than that, according to Cornelius Vanderbilt, Jr., the YMCA "educates and spiritualizes; it promotes economy and thrift; it brings railroad men together with surroundings and discussions which produce the happiest results to themselves, their families, and their employers." The rail magnate was not indulging himself in empty rhetorical flourish; in 1888 he donated $225,000 for YMCA facilities along his New York Central line.[15]

The labor troubles of the seventies gave impetus to several influential developments, particularized in the lives and works of two men, a minister and a manufacturer. The minister was Washington Gladden, a Congregationalist and, more important, a member of the Social Gospel movement in American religion, which taught that ministers and churches ought to concern themselves not simply with the spiritual well-being of God's children but with their material circumstances as well. As a pastor in the small factory town of North Adams, Massachusetts, Gladden became involved in a labor dispute when local shoemakers formed a union and one manufacturer retaliated by importing Chinese scabs. In fact, Gladden had no high regard for union leaders, referring to them as "noisy, crazy, crack-brained creatures, whose capital stock of political philosophy consists of one or two half-truths, and a full assortment of lies." But he did believe that capital's share of wealth was too large, his half-brother's death in the Civil War had given him a constitutional abhorrence of violence, and he was, after all, a Social Gospeler and man of God.

Thus as the conflict edged toward violence, Gladden forcefully proposed that Christianity be applied to the labor situation, that employers become more altruistic, and that they apply the golden rule in their relations with employees. Gladden was not very clear about the mechanics when he first spoke of the matter in 1876, but he impressed businessmen and over the years he would bestow his approval as they developed specific programs. Thus, invited to address an 1896 meeting of Procter and Gamble stockholders, he remarked that their factory was "the kind of a thing about which I have thought and dreamed and prophesied a great deal." One of the great exponents of welfare capitalism, Gladden was influential in the development of the American Institute of Social Service, which became a kind of institutionalized form of the social gospel and a staunch advocate of welfarism.[16]

The manufacturer George M. Pullman was moved enough by the strike of 1877 to help organize and lead a "Citizens' Law and Order League." But as a man of grand designs and large ambitions, Pullman was also about to embark on a project which was intended to do much more than combat strikes. He would build a town designed in such a way as to "exclude all baneful influences," as he put it. Nor would it end there; by providing decent homes, good education, and beautiful, closely ordered surroundings for his workers, Pullman would not simply mitigate the "necessary" labor evils of modern industry, but make working in industry a positive and glorious good.[17] If the YMCAs could do what Vanderbilt claimed, then how much more could a whole town, properly designed, do? Pullman, Illinois, site of the Pullman Palace Car Company, would be the utopia of the Industrial Age, the home of the "New Capitalist Man."

If anyone could, George Pullman would see to it that the town was properly designed. It was not an empty slogan that, in railroad transportation, going first class meant riding a Pullman car; he would make sure that working for the Pullman Company meant going absolutely first class. Begun in 1880 and occupied in 1881, the town was a completely integrated manufacturing community. Besides the new factory for the production of sleeping cars, it encompassed houses for employees, a hotel, a church, and an arcade building with shops, a library, and a theater. Pullman owned and controlled everything, overlooking matters with such meticulous concern, such dedication to efficiency and integration, that the pipes which carried human waste from the houses funneled it not to sewers or septic tanks but to the company farm, to fertilize vegetables sold in the town's shops. Little wonder that, besides creating the New Capitalist Man, the town was designed to return a six percent profit on the investment. Little wonder that it became a curiosity and showplace, attracting a heavy stream of visitors. And little wonder, finally, that it became a milestone in the development of American welfare capitalism, embodying in such attractive and magnificent form profit and panaceas for the businessman's troubles.[18]

A source of great controversy and conversation, the Pullman experiment was a guiding beacon for many businessmen in the 1880s, as labor disturbances continued and grew. One example was that of N. O. Nelson, a manufacturer of plumbing fixtures, who in 1886 joined a committee to seek settlement of a strike that paralyzed railroad transportation in Saint Louis, the site of his plant. Nelson approached the manager of several railroads controlled by speculator Jay Gould, but Gould's lieutenant refused even to meet with him. The refusal caused Nelson to think more deeply about labor problems, and, impressed with the Pullman experiment, he built a smaller-scale Pullman-type town near Edwardsville, Illinois, twenty miles east of Saint Louis.[19]

The year 1886 was a year of particularly intense labor distress, culminating in Chicago's bloody Haymarket Affair. It was also, not coincidentally, a year in which several of the most prominent welfare capitalists (in addition to Nelson) began their programs. The Solvay Process Company began a sewing class that year, the first step in a program of welfarism which by 1890 had expanded to include a commodious clubhouse with a six-hundred-seat auditorium. The same year saw Procter and Gamble hit by no fewer than fourteen strikes, leading the makers of Ivory Soap to introduce a profit sharing plan. Between 1886 and 1888 perhaps two dozen firms initiated welfare programs, and by 1890 welfare capitalism was well under way.[20]

Along with the labor troubles, and in part because of them, actions by public officials and governmental groups helped to pave the way for welfarism. Realizing the controversial aspects of labor relations, most politicians were wary of getting involved, but some government labor bureaus offered encouragement. Labor bureaus seldom dared praise it openly, but they did study welfare capitalism and thereby represented it as advanced or enlightened practice. As early as 1887, the Pennsylvania Bureau of Industrial Statistics conducted a survey of welfarism, and Carroll D. Wright's tenure as U.S. Commissioner of Labor enhanced the movement even more, for he was a long-time advocate of welfarism. Under Wright's direction a steady stream of reports on welfare programs emanated from the U.S. Bureau of Labor Statistics.[21]

Then of course there was the matter of direct public interference—through legislation or the threat of legislation—in the business of business. As the idea of public control grew more prominent, the need for cultivating an attractive public image became a more central company concern. The passage of the Sherman Anti-Trust Act in 1890 thus made the trusts even more welfare-oriented than they had been before. Technically, they had been outlawed by the legislation, but the act was toothless and welfarism could help keep it so: welfare work gave the appearance, at least, of social responsibility and thereby improved the image of the great combinations. Standard Oil of New Jersey (formed 1899), United States Steel (organized 1901), and International Harvester (organized 1902) all became leading exponents of welfare theories.

Yet in spite of these propitious trends, the rise of welfarism was slowed in the early 1890s as a result of two factors, one major, one minor. The less important was the more dramatic, being laced with irony and presented on the front pages of America's newspapers as a national drama of violence which required the intervention of the president. It was a strike which happened in the one place where it was not supposed to happen—Pullman. Starting as a reaction to Pullman's cutting wages, in bad times, without making a corresponding cut in the town's rents, the 1894 walkout was quite mild for a time, and although after about a month good will began to grow strained, relations between employer and employee were generally friendly. The strike became a major matter, however, when Eugene Debs's American Railway Union refused to handle Pullman cars. American Railway locals soon turned the boycott into strikes against their own employers, turning the Pullman strike into a national issue when President Grover Cleveland ordered out troops in effect to break the strike.

It was only natural that a breakdown in labor-management relations at Pullman suggested to some that the ideology was bankrupt. But insofar as the violence of the strike involved American Railway Union men and their adversaries, rather than Pullman workers, the criticism was off the mark. It was also true that part of the problem lay not in the philosophy but in the philosopher: the adamant stance of the Pullman Company was related to George Pullman's pique over what he considered his employees' lack of appreciation for the facilities provided. But regardless of personalities, paternalism was an intrinsic element of welfarism, and the charge that the town's paternalism bore much of the blame for the strike—a charge made by the U.S. Strike Commission, which had investigated the incident—constituted a significant and influential setback.[22]

Compounding the situation was the larger, overriding issue: the business depression of 1893-97. Always to be considered marginal activities, welfare programs would consistently be among the first areas to feel the pinch when companies tightened their belts. Throughout its history, welfarism would decline when unfavorable business conditions set in. Moreover, insofar as welfarism was directed against strikes, there might even be an inclination on the part of the businessman to regard its success, in such times, as a rather dubious reward, for in bad times, strikes could even be useful to business—a form of layoff whereby the employer was relieved of the responsibility to pay unwanted labor as well as the responsibility to call the layoff. Thus the first federal survey of welfarism, published in 1900, stated that no company had initiated welfare programs during 1893-94. Although inaccurate (some companies did initiate programs in 1893), this reflects the moribund state of welfarism in the early nineties.[23]

But it was a temporary state. In spite of the Pullman affair, by 1897 there was renewed interest in welfare measures, for prosperity had returned—and labor troubles continued. For instance, the National Cash Register Company experienced several strikes and lockouts in the early nineties, and the factory was set afire three times, apparently by disgruntled employees. As soon as business conditions permitted, the company, which would become as fervently devoted to welfarism as was William Jennings Bryan to free silver, embarked on a welfare program unparalleled in ambition. In 1897 and 1898 a series of companies took up welfare programs, and expansion continued into the first decade of the twentieth century, in step with the rising level of labor militancy, which saw the number of trade unions more than triple between 1899-1904, with more and more unionists going on strike, and more and more strikes being won by unions. Not until 1905, in fact, did the rise in union membership, in strikers, and in the frequency of labor successes begin to level off.[24]

Spreading the Gospel

The gospel of welfarism found a variety of instruments for the propagation of the faith. Among these were many books, not a few of which were written by welfare capitalists who had acquired an almost missionary zeal—"Golden Rule" Jones, the reform mayor of Toledo, and Boston merchant Edward Filene, to name only two. Dozens of articles rolled out, and traveling exhibits carried the word to state and world's fairs, among other places.[1]

All these, along with the inevitable news accounts of welfare programs, helped to bring a steady stream of visitors and a constant flow of inquiries to program sponsors. Prominent among the curious were those already engaged in, or embarking on, programs of their own. For instance, many welfare secretaries made annual tours of welfare companies in order to keep abreast of developments, and one company, Weston Electrical Instrument, sent an employee on a year-long inspection survey of welfare facilities prior to building their new plant.[2]

The welfare network included other forms of cross-fertilization. One was the fairly frequent exchange among companies of welfare professionals—Clarence Hicks, for example, worked at various times for International Harvester, Colorado Fuel and Iron, Standard Oil of New Jersey, and in the welfare programs of a number of other companies. Even marriage could serve as a connecting link; John D. Rockefeller, Jr. and Harold Fowler McCormick of International Harvester were brothers-in-law, only two of the surprisingly many welfare capitalists who were—or became—related.[3]

By no means were encouragement and information restricted to these informal conduits; organized mechanisms for the dissemination of information and propaganda soon developed both inside and outside industry. Probably the first such organization was the American Association for the Promotion of Profit Sharing, a short-lived group which did not last out the nineties but whose burden was quickly taken up by the League for Social Service—later known as the American Institute of Social Service. The league—or institute—was organized in 1898 by Josiah Strong, a protestant minister with an evangelical bent and a social philosophy which was impressively comprehensive and equally simple-minded. He believed that "material civilization" had changed more in the nineteenth century than in all previous history, and that all the problems of industrial society—such as housing, hygiene, temperance, divorce, crime, municipal government, labor relations—were interrelated. These new conditions demanded a "readaptation," and Strong meant to bring that about by the single action of collecting information on "all manner of human experience, so that everyone may know and profit by what others have thought and done."[4]

Given such a leader, along with the fact that the organization lacked funds, it would not have been at all surprising had the institute gone the way of its predecessor, perhaps even more quickly. But in fact the New York based group became the first of the two most important organizations for welfare promotion. That it did not die a quick death was due in the main to the financial contributions of the business community—a fact which accounted for its heavy focus on industrial problems. That it became so successful was due to Strong's most important executive decision: he gave his Director of Industrial Betterment, William Howe Tolman, a free hand.

Tolman was, if anything, even more zealously missionary than Strong. Whatever the struggle and sacrifice, Tolman once declared, he intended to devote his life to the cause of welfare capitalism. More important, he was energetic and productive. After acquainting himself with welfare practices in Europe, he toured the United States, extolling the benefits of welfarism to all who would listen. Under Tolman's editorship, the institute published a quarterly journal entitled *Social Service,* as well as a "Weekly Letter Service to Industrial Subscribers," both of which went regularly to a list of business contributors which included most of the important welfare companies in the United States. In addition, Tolman produced for a more general audience pamphlets, a series of articles, and a book—all in a ten-year span. If the institute ultimately fell short of Strong's goal, it was not for lack of effort on the part of William Tolman, its leading light.[5]

The second of the two principal welfare organizations appeared in 1901, only two years after the formation of the League for Social

Service, and if the parentage of the elder was a bit of a curiosity, that was even more true of the younger. The National Civic Federation was the child of strange bedfellows: advisor to President McKinley, Marcus A. Hanna, the prominent and wealthy Cleveland businessman, and Samuel Gompers, president of the American Federation of Labor. The explanation for the partnership lay in Hanna's attitude: he believed that unionization of American industry was inevitable, and he hoped to avoid industrial violence by bridging the gap between unionists and anti-union businessmen.[6]

The stature and influence of these two figures alone guaranteed that the National Civic Federation would get more than a passing glance from the public and the business communities. But the federation was also headed by a man who was William Tolman's equal in energy and only a little less ambitious than the all-encompassing Josiah Strong. Former Chicago newspaper editor Ralph Easley had an empire-building temperament, and he soon established a permanent staff for the federation and sent them into a variety of endeavors. In January 1904, employers who had initiated some form of welfare work met under Civic Federation auspices and organized a committee on welfare work. The delegates to the first meeting were somewhat surprised to find that many others had adopted welfare practices and so decided to schedule a full-scale conference for the following March. Many of the prominent welfare companies sent representatives to the 1904 conference on welfare work, and from then on the Civic Federation was a leader in coaxing support for welfare capitalism. For its efforts, the Civic Federation earned a reward: because the committee on welfare work was open only to employers, it attracted anti-union employers to the organization. Perhaps they could then be persuaded to alter their views and recognize unions.[7]

The Employers' Welfare Department acted in several ways to promote welfarism. Like the American Institute of Social Service, the National Civic Federation published a quarterly journal, pamphlets, and articles. The Welfare Department's full-time secretary, Gertrude Beeks, formerly of International Harvester, acted as a clearinghouse for information and as a propagandist for the movement. (Easley subsequently married her.) But while the American Institute of Social Service tried to bring welfarism to the employer, under Gertrude Beeks the National Civic Federation's Welfare Department brought employers to specific conferences on welfare work.[8]

Hanna's prominence in the business and political communities enabled the National Civic Federation to attract a large following in the business world. By 1911, in fact, the committee on welfare work included in its membership more than five hundred leading employers and public officials. Although Gompers, as a labor leader, was ineligible for membership in the committee on welfare work, he continued to lend his support to welfarism until World War I. Organized labor was so weak in the early years of the century and working conditions were so poor that any improvement was welcome. John Mitchell, president of the United Mine Workers, remained a member of the NCF until 1911, and like Gompers, was a frequent target of criticism from the left wing of the labor movement for his support of welfare programs early in the century. With the support of Hanna, Easley, Gompers, Mitchell, and others, the NCF became somewhat more influential and forceful than the American Institute for Social Serice, though the two organizations complemented, rather than rivaled, each other.[9]

Forces outside the business community enlisted in the cause. Only a short time after major American corporations adopted welfarism, American universities began to train students in welfare practices. In 1906 the Chicago Institute of Social Science, an outgrowth of a social science school at the University of Chicago governed by seven midwestern universities, offered courses in several kinds of philanthropic and social work, including industrial welfare work. In the same year Professor Graham Taylor, one of the founders of the American Economic Association, taught a class for industrial welfare workers in conjunction with the Chicago Commons, a West Side settlement house. Two years later Yale University offered a class in "industrial service work," and by 1916 more than 150 engineering schools offered similar courses. Much of the class work involved training young engineering students to teach English, first aid, or civics to foreign-born employees.[10]

Both state and federal governments helped to encourage the spread of knowledge of welfare measures. In addition to its 1900 exploration, the Bureau of Labor Statistics made full-scale studies of employers' welfare practices in 1913, 1919, and 1926. Besides these specific studies, a great many others touched upon various aspects of welfarism.[11] Government officials also began increasingly to offer outright support.

President Theodore Roosevelt was the most active proponent. In 1906, when construction of the Panama Canal began, criticism developed of working conditions in the far-off jungle. As a consequence Congress appropriated funds for the construction of five clubhouses along the route to be operated by the YMCA. But the construction superintendent had different plans; he hoped to equip each building with a saloon which would remain open seven days a week. A YMCA delegation promptly descended on Roosevelt, horrified by the thought of a saloon dispensing liquor on Sunday under the joint auspices of the United States government and the YMCA. Roosevelt quickly decreed that canal clubhouses would remain dry. In addition, the government requested that Gertrude Beeks go to Panama to supervise welfare work on the canal.[12]

Roosevelt gave two other indications that he favored welfarism. In 1904 he suggested to a visitor that American industrialists would do better if they located their factories in the countryside where more beautiful surroundings could be provided. More importantly, Robert Ozanne has shown that one reason why International Harvester engaged in welfare programs was to impress the president that the company satisfied his criteria for a "good trust." This would help it elude prosecution. Roosevelt indicated his approval of Harvester welfare programs, and, significantly, Harvester succeeded in avoiding prosecution throughout the Roosevelt years.[13]

William Howard Taft, Roosevelt's successor, began cooperating with advocates of welfare capitalism while serving in Roosevelt's cabinet. The National Civic Federation, seeing no reason that the public sector of the economy should be deprived of the benefits of welfare practices, organized a national "Committee on Welfare Work for Government Employees." Taft chaired the committee, with the omnipresent Gertrude Beeks serving as secretary. Under Taft's chairmanship the committee succeeded in improving conditions at the Bureau of Engraving and Printing and at the Patent Office. Later, after Taft became President, it expanded its scope to include inspection of army arsenals, navy yards, post offices, and other government agencies, recommending such improvements as the installation of lockers, safety features, lunchrooms, and recreation programs. Taft continued to maintain his ties to the National Civic Federation throughout his presidency, attending its 1912 dinner in company with 300 congressmen.[14]

Although the Wilson administration expressed high indifference to welfare capitalism during its early years, subsequent events forced it to take more interest in the movement. The possibility that welfare work could be used to cut labor turnover and thus increase efficiency eventually attracted the attention of the administration particularly concerning the war effort. The White House at first believed that America's chief role in World War I would be as a supplier of war material to the Allies, and it fully appreciated that American industry was unprepared for that role. Massive coordination was necessary if equipment was to be produced and transported efficiently, and this demanded an important new role for the federal government—organizer of the economy. Welfare work was one of the techniques the government used in its attempts to stimulate production.

In 1916, even before the United States declared war, Congress established the Council of National Defense as the chief coordinator of the preparedness effort. The council included six cabinet members, but its Advisory Commission conducted day-to-day activity, and it was within the latter body that welfare work received encouragement. The Advisory Commission created a Committee on Labor, whose general purpose was to increase productivity and prevent labor disputes from interfering with the smooth flow of goods. The Committee on Labor created in turn a Committee on Welfare Work, whose objective, in the words of its chairman, was "to bring home to employers, in the most forceful way, the necessity of establishing correct standards, to the end that the Government will receive from the industries, the best possible results and at the same time conserve the health and efficiency of [the working population]."[15]

Most of the members of the Committee on Welfare Work of the Council of National Defense were industrialists whose companies were prominent in the field. In order to make the fullest use of the programs available, they created three subcommittees. The first concerned itself primarily with sanitary facilities in factories and company towns, but it also had an advisor on home nursing whose function was to improve sanitary practices in workers' homes. The duties of the other two committees were to improve housing and to encourage recreational activities for employees. An official of the YMCA chaired the latter one.[16]

As the war continued, other agencies contributed to the spread of welfare practices. One of the Wilson administration's chief techniques of mobilizing the economy was to form government bodies to supervise such critical goods and services as food, fuel, railroads, shipping, and housing. Two of these, the United States Shipping Board and the United States Housing Corporation, encouraged welfarism in industrial housing. The Housing Corporation was created by the War Department to build homes for workers. It included a town planning division, chaired by famed city-planner Frederick Law Olmsted, which planned numerous housing projects near arsenals, munitions factories, and shipyards. Several developments qualified as full-scale model towns designed to give pleasant accommodations at mass production prices. The Housing Corporation spent a total of $194 million to house about six thousand families. In effect, the United States government constructed a whole series of "company" towns during World War I.[17]

In 1918 the Department of Labor established a Working Conditions Service whose general purpose was to improve working conditions in American industry. The goal of its labor administration division, according to its director, the labor economist William M. Leiserson, was "to spread the idea and the practice among employers of administering their forces on the principle that wage earners are human beings with the same feelings, instincts, prejudices, ambitions, and ideas of their own worth that other people have." The strategy of Leiserson's group was simple. Leiserson and three "employment specialists" visited and mailed information to several hundred firms throughout the country in the hope of convincing employers that it was cheaper to prevent accidents, sickness, and "labor disturbances" than to suffer their consequences. By representing improved working conditions as a paying proposition rather than charity ("not a welfare proposition, but a business proposal"), the Working Conditions Service hoped "to reduce labor turnover and develop a spirit of industrial good will." Thus it operated in much the same way that private consultants on welfarism had before the war.[18]

Besides fostering a need for increased production, World War I stimulated the move toward welfare capitalism in several other ways. One simple yet important influence was the effect of war profits. Welfarism always waxed in prosperity and waned in depression, and the time of World War I was no exception. When their pockets bulged, businessmen readily subsidized quasi-productive activities. At the same time some business leaders expected workers to demand a greater share of the profits, and welfarism was in some cases a way to head them off.[19]

Perhaps World War I affected the rise of welfare capitalism most importantly by disrupting the stability of the American labor market. For example, David Brody has argued cogently that, in the steel industry, stability on a nonunion basis existed as a result of a delicate balance between the supply and demand for labor. This balance had derived principally from two sources—a reasonably stable demand for steel and a steady flow of immigrants back and forth across the Atlantic as the demand varied. But the outbreak of war disrupted both; demand for steel increased while at the same time the source of new steelworkers dried up. Feeling a new sense of power and importance, steelworkers joined unions at an accelerated pace. Employers responded to the new situation by increasing welfare expenditures.[20]

The changed labor market additionally expanded the variety of welfare programs. Even before American entry, businessmen began programs to "Americanize" their immigrant employees. Just what Americanization meant was highly tenuous, but in general it included teaching immigrants English, encouraging them to take out citizenship papers, and getting them to adopt American customs and institutions. However imprecise the definition of Americanization, its main purpose was clear; to bind workers to their jobs. At the same time Americanization began, employers took increased interest in medical care and pensions for employees—programs which kept them alive and working for the same company longer.[21]

The final effect of World War I on welfare capitalism was indirect but very important. War provided the occasion for violent revolution in Russia, and the nature of the Bolshevik coup brought severe repercussions in American industrial relations. Capitalists had dreaded a labor uprising for many years, and when it finally occurred in Russia in 1917, it justified their fears. They knew, moreover, that conversion to a peacetime economy was likely to be disruptive and posed at least a possibility of a duplication of the Russian experience elsewhere after hostilities ended. "It is well to be frank with ourselves about the prospect before us," noted one writer in 1919. "The future holds out a sort of inevitableness from which we cannot escape.... Even now the realm of choice is limited: we can choose democracy or war." The same attitude permeated a large section of American business, and some of it translated into support for welfarism. "With labor crying for democracy," wrote the leading advocate of welfarism at the Plymouth Cordage Company, "capital must go part way or face revolution."[22]

Neither the end of the war nor the years following bore out the deepest fears of American businessmen. But the immediate postwar years did witness an increased militancy in the labor movement. Membership in the American Federation of Labor grew during the war years from 2.37 to 3.26 million and increased to 4.078 million by 1920. The number of wage earners involved in strikes in 1919 more than tripled over the 1918 level. In politics, radicals continued to hold some strength. During 1917 the Socialist Party elected candidates in a dozen American cities. Government repression nearly destroyed the radical Industrial Workers of the World, but an incipient Bolshevist movement replaced it as businessmen's chief bugbear. From the businessmen's point of view, the struggle was far from over.[23]

With wartime disruption and labor militancy as a backdrop, welfare capitalism moved ahead in the next decade to enjoy its greatest acceptance. Architects of the New Era, as the business culture of the 1920s became known, hoped to modify and improve the old industrialism by emphasizing a committment to a moral awakening, to productivity, and to the recognition of a mutuality of interests between labor and management. The new industrialism, of which Herbert Hoover was the greatest exponent, emphasized the development of the humane, rationalized corporation as the chief instrument of social progress.[24] The methods and goals of welfare capitalism fitted neatly into this almost utopian plan.

Except for a brief interlude during the depression of 1921, then, welfare capitalism continued to grow until the mid-1920s when it reached the height of its popularity. Workers lived in company houses, were treated by company doctors, attended company schools, played on company teams, purchased company stock, and were represented by company unions. After surveying 1500 of the largest companies in the United States in 1926, a researcher reported that 80 percent had adopted at least one form of welfarism and about half had comprehensive programs. At a minimum more than four million people worked for companies which engaged in welfare practices. A survey by the Bureau of Labor Statistics of just 190 firms revealed expenditures of more than $14 million. Expenditures ranged from a low of $14 per employee in the clothing industry to a high of $67 in shoemaking. The average was $27 per year, or about 2 percent of an average industrial wage earner's annual income. Perhaps even more suggestive of the massive expenditures devoted to welfare capitalism was the record of United States Steel. Over a twelve-year period ending in 1924, the corporation spent more than $22 million on playgrounds, schools, clubs, gardens, and visiting nurses. It spent another $104 million on sanitation, accident prevention, relief for injured men, stock sales to employees, and pensions. Smaller firms did not approach this figure, but their expenditures were nevertheless substantial.[25]

The heyday of welfare programs, however, would prove to be brief indeed. Like so many other facets of American life, welfare capitalism failed to survive the great depression of the 1930s. For reasons to be discussed in the following chapters, three decades after the New Deal only vestiges of welfare capitalism remained. Those aspects of welfare capitalism which did survive, furthermore, were seldom used in the same fashion as they had been used in the 1920s. Although the prime of welfare capitalism was short, it left its mark on American national life at an important, even crucial hour.

Goals and Strategies

As a term of action, "welfare" suggests benevolence, a disinterested concern for the general good of the people being served. As such it presents a very attractive image, and in fact among the goals of some welfare capitalists was pure altruism—specifically, the alleviation of the bleakness of industrial life. While admitting that the employer who engages in company welfarism "is indeed indirectly benefited by raising the standard of living among his employees, hence their efficiency," Henry Bruére of International Harvester insisted that "there seems to be no evidence of an invariably resulting economic advantage." According to this young executive, "betterment work must be considered an end in itself"; it "must be prompted largely by humanitarian considerations." New England textile maker J. S. Stevens concurred, claiming that during the company's twenty-year experience with welfare work, "the expectation of profiting thereby was never in our minds, and is not today."[1] Bruére wrote in 1903 and Stevens spoke in 1904, a time when avowals of altruistic motives appeared far more commonly than after World War I.

Curiously enough, however, no matter how flattering, such a stance was discomforting to most of those who had paid long homage to tough-minded practicality. Businessmen were more often than not in strong agreement with Augustus P. Loring, president of Plymouth Cordage Company: "as we approach the purely philanthropic we get further away from usefulness." Perhaps International Harvester did not object to Bruére's high-mindedness, but Director George Perkins, probably the company's most influential executive, set the record straight on its welfare approach, asserting that Harvester "went into these enterprises in a purely business spirit."[2] Indeed, time after time, businessmen denied that there was even a particle of altruism in welfare practices. "We try to make the place attractive to men . . . for a very selfish reason," testified Charles J. Harrah, president of the Midvale Steel Company; "there is no philanthropic thing in it at all." Another businessman brought the point home in amused logic: "When I keep a horse and I find him a clean stable and good food I am not doing anything philanthropic for my horse."[3] Some businessmen were so anxious to avoid the stigma of benevolence that they even charged money for the services to prove that welfare work was a hard business proposition whose results were to be measured, as they emphasized and reemphasized, in "dollars and cents."[4]

Although not amenable to such precise cost accounting, one form of profit in welfarism was improved public relations. While the businessman was not eager to be seen as Santa Claus, he was well aware that the public was more often inclined to view him as Scrooge and he used welfare to help correct that image. For instance, a company housing area near Commonwealth Steel's mill in Granite City, Illinois, was dubbed by its neighbors "Hungary Hollow" because of its immigrant residents, or alternatively "Hungry Hollow" because of the poor living conditions. But shortly after Commonwealth initiated welfare work, its Home Fellowship Department rechristened the area "Lincoln Place" and built a settlement house there which it called the Lincoln Progressive Club. Another large employer admitted in an interview that his company's stock ownership plan was a failure as far as it affected employees, but rather than switch to different programs, he planned to advertise the present one more widely in order to win public approval. In order to cultivate the public, companies presented displays in highly publicized arenas which often attracted large crowds—world's fairs, for example. They encouraged frequent trips to plants; National Cash Register even sponsored a special all-expenses-paid train trip to its Dayton plant for interested faculty of the University of Chicago, to impress them with what NCR was doing to make factory work safer and more agreeable. So closely related were welfarism and public relations to some companies that they systematically referred inquiries about welfare work to their advertising departments.[5]

As the tough stance reflected above suggests, these experiments in image building were not intended simply to salve the businessman's ego; they could pay real dividends in defending the power and independence of business. For instance, a sympathetic public could help undermine political support for antitrust litigation or restrictive legislation. At least equally important, the outcome of a strike was often balanced on the crucial question of public sympathy, which meant of course that readings of the public sentiment could determine company and union strategy, including the question of whether there would be a strike at all. If the public, particularly its influential members, could be convinced that a company took a benevolent posture toward its employees rather than a crassly materialistic one, union support could be eroded.

Indeed, at its heart, welfare capitalism was a defensive strategy. Particularly after World War I, it was a protective device aimed largely at trade unionism, the common devil which brought American businessmen together as no other issue did. Perhaps the greatest threat to business hegemony, unionism was considered by businessmen to be intrinsically bad, and they sought to prevent its encroachment in a variety of ways, including welfare work and public relations efforts. Through welfarism, businessmen hoped to convince the public and their employees that the system which granted them such a large share of influence was legitimate and viable.

The anti-union overtones of welfare were clear and definite. An important indicator is the parallel expansion and contraction of welfare and union activities; welfarism rose and fell concordantly with unionism. The spurt in welfare programs during the 1920s was in part a response to the gains made by organized labor during World War I. Another indicator is the fact that welfare work was often directed at skilled employees—those who seemed most susceptible to the troublesome pleas of union organizers. The evidence is supported by confession; businessmen were not reluctant to state this focus explicitly, even publicly. Elbert H. Gary of U.S. Steel, for example, once remarked in an interview that "we must make it certain that the men in our employ are treated as well as, if not a little better than, those who are working for people who deal and contract with unions." Even more explicit was a Plymouth Cordage executive: "The greatest argument for [welfare work] is that the professional labor leader is opposed to it. He hates it." To prove his point, the businessman happily pointed out that AFL President Samuel Gompers "called it 'Hellfare Work' before a committee of Congress." Businessmen in fact frequently measured the effectiveness and value of welfare work in terms of its ability to prevent strikes.[6]

But if welfarism's central thrust was an attempt to ameliorate negatives—unsatisfactory working conditions, high employee turnover, the threats of government interference and labor militancy—its aims were not totally defensive. For in welfare work, some employers saw a tool that might do much more than defeat a strike or throw up a defense against the laborer's evil tendencies. In the view of many employers, these were ignorance, slovenliness, laziness, and insobriety (the causes of inefficiency), or extravagance (which lay behind demands for higher wages), or disloyalty (the root of turnover and the even more dangerous militancy and unionism). Why aim solely at defeating strikes if they could be prevented altogether? Why merely fight the union's expansion if an atmosphere could be created wherein unionism would not breed at all? And why only attempt to limit the losses due to the worker's vices when it might even be possible to increase production by creating a virtuous laborer? Thus the ultimate goal of welfare capitalism was no less than the propagation of an improved American working man: thrifty, clean, temperate, intelligent, and, especially, industrious, and loyal.

This goal was quite consciously and explicitly promoted. Sometimes, as in the case of Bruére, the motive, it was suggested, was unalloyed humanitarianism. A Cleveland company welfare superintendent, Mary B. Gilson, said that welfare practices existed "primarily for the purpose of developing men and women. More and more are we coming to realize that the justification of industry lies in the opportunity it offers men and women to attain not only material, but mental, moral, and spiritual advancement." The motto of "Golden Rule" Jones's company was more aphoristic, but the idea was similar: "The business of this shop is to make men; the making of money is an incidental detail." But others once again insisted on the profitability, even the necessity, of "making men": as the labor division of the Goodyear Tire and Rubber Company put it, "without inculcating the essential habits of thrift and economic foresight, liberal pay is no check on industrial discontent." Even more pithy than its motto was an inscription on the fence outside the Jones plant—and though somewhat enigmatic, perhaps closer to the true heart's desire: "Produce great persons, the rest follows."[7]

But how to produce "great persons"? Employers offered a wide array of answers which were developed into programs. One simple answer was to provide alternatives to the existing evils. Was there ignorance of American customs or of the English language? Then provide classrooms, bring in teachers, educate. Was there fatigue and languor? Provide varieties of recreation and amusement. Where there are unions, offer a different brand of collective action.

Company libraries, clubhouses, YMCAs, churches, and other programs were thus designed in part to provide an alternative to what was regarded as the dingy side of employees' lives. Nowhere, however, was this aspect so clearly shown as in the factory and home beautification movement. Hundreds of companies across the United States began to plant shrubs and flowers to beautify their factories. Many companies which owned houses sponsored annual garden contests to reward residents who dressed up their homes, and sometimes rewards were so lucrative that some company housing came to resemble botanical gardens. A profusion of flowers decorated the Georgia textile mill whose president was G. Gunby Jordan, a philosopher of the program who set out its principles in appropriately florid terms: "Clean, attractive and beautiful surroundings influence myself and all employees beneficially, because anything which tends to contentment, peace of mind and creates a love for the beautiful, has a salutary effect on mankind, and this effect is as valuable in business as in home life. . . . Create a love for the home beautiful, wreath it with flowers of happiness, then contentment and the highest forms of patriotism are developed."[8]

This focus on the home was not incidental. Welfare strategy derived in part from a theoretical estimation of the root cause of distress in industrial society. The source of unrest, business believed, was the disruption of family life. They found evidence which indicated that as women and children swarmed to the factories in the early twentieth century and began to contribute to family support, husbands lost some of their viability as masters of the household and family bonds weakened. The results were likely to be upsetting to all concerned, including the employers.

Though businessmen as a whole perceived this situation only dimly at best, some employers did consciously design their welfare programs to be a means of shoring up the weakening family structure. One Bethlehem Steel official described the home as "the shrine of contentment—the factor in life which is the greatest industrial stabilizer and greatest nursery of Americanism." Another exponent of welfarism argued that "the care of a family and the ownership of property are balance wheels which keep the individual normal and sane. Employers should encourage both to the limit." Improvement of home life, in fact, became almost a panacea for the ills of industrial society. "Comfortably housed, sane-thinking families," stated the White Motor Company, ". . . are not fertile soil for revolutionary propaganda."[9]

Home beautification was one of the simpler ways of using the family to make better workers; one of the more ingenious was the education of children. First of all, children were more pliable than adults, more "educable." Older persons were established in their ways, but children could be bent. A visiting nurse of the Colorado Fuel and Iron Company explained that unlike a parent's "fixed habits and ideas," a child had a "plastic mind eager for knowledge." Second, if the habits of children could be changed, perhaps parents would take the hint and change their ways as well. New ideas brought by one's child might well be less coolly received than when offered by a stranger in a strange tongue. Thus the Witherbee, Sherman Company, a mining firm of Mineville, New York, formed "little mothers" clubs where girls learned first aid, sanitation, hygiene, and infant care. "In this way," explained a Witherbee executive, "the mother learns from the 'little mother.' "[10]

There were, of course, programs of adult education as well as other attempts through welfare and other means to affect the worker. Nevertheless, in spite of the golden promises of benefits in building the good worker, businessmen often despaired of improving their present workmen. The Solvay Process Company characterized this attitude, averring that it was "very difficult to get at the workmen." But they did not thereby abandon their attempts to influence the family: on the contrary, for even if the children could not influence their parents into becoming "better people," the children themselves were the better people of the future. As the Solvay Company noted, "our experience has been than the boys of our workmen grow up and take positions of various kinds in our works, and the girls grow up and marry and become the wives, in many cases, of these boys." The conclusion was self-evident: "We, therefore, think that if we can train the children in the way that they should go, we will improve our workmen." President Harrison Robert "Harry" Fitzgerald of the Riverside and Dan River Cotton Mills agreed. His company first directed its welfare programs toward its present employees, but, as Fitzgerald explained, "we soon recognized that it was a question of business necessity to begin at the very bottom with day nurseries, kindergardens [*sic*], primary departments, as well as district nursing and medical departments, if we were ever to develop a nucleus of capable and efficient workers."[11]

Welfare capitalism, then, was an array of practices designed with specific purposes and carefully considered strategies in mind. To the extent that practitioners of welfare captialism sought to recast employees in a business mold—to build a New Capitalist Man—their goals were not only ambitious but almost utopian. It was that enthusiasm which brought them into conflict and accord with other visions of their time.

A competing philosophy of efficiency and uplift was scientific management, or "Taylorism," as it is sometimes known, after its founder, the engineer Frederick Winslow Taylor. Taylorites, like welfare capitalists, were sanguine about the benefits which factory-style production offered human society and hoped to maximize them. But there the similarity ended: Taylorites differed sharply with welfare capitalists on how to achieve efficiency. Taylor and his exponents sought to reduce the productive function to its elements through careful time studies (thus to apply the scientific method to production) and then to increase production by minute wage incentives. The Taylorites emphasized the immediate and the practical; they were often scornful of welfare capitalists who argued that basic changes in the outlook and attitudes of industrial workers were necessary if progress in the area of efficiency and contentment was to be made. Taylor himself called welfare capitalism "a joke." But as if to emphasize the impersonality of the corporation, Taylorism and welfare capitalism occasionally existed side by side within the same company. Following World War I, the antagonism between them moderated.[12]

Progressivism, that elusive set of reforms which gives historians so much difficulty, had a complex effect on the goals of welfare capitalism. Some of the programs advocated by welfare capitalists—the factory beautification movement, for example—were very much in tune with the moderate changes called for by progressives. Some welfare capitalists, moreover, made their mark elsewhere in the progressive movement. Samuel "Golden Rule" Jones became the reform mayor of Toledo, while George Perkins was a leader of the Progressive Party in 1912. Similarly, some progressives hoped to transfer the principles which had led to business efficiency to government operations.[13] But undeniably, some aspects of welfare capitalism were meant to ward off more drastic changes demanded by business critics. Except for a handful of aberrant exceptions, welfare capitalists uniformly opposed unions. Not all progressives favored unions, to be sure, but nearly all supported some weakening of business prerogatives, if not by unions then by government. But welfare capitalists, like other persons, were jealous of their prerogatives and resisted attempts by liberals to redistribute power. Welfare capitalism was affected by the progressive milieu, even to the extent of the ambitiousness of its aims, while managing to remain apart from it.

5 Housing

The dictionary of American industrial relations is filled with highly charged terms like "blacklist," "yellow-dog contract," or "scab," but few are so powerfully negative as "company town." It generally evokes visions of the misery, squalor, and filth that accompanied the industrial revolution. So pervasive is its imagery that attempts to moderate the portrait inevitably risk sharp reaction.[1]

But however colorful, the phrase is nevertheless very imprecise. Large cities, including New York, for example, contained company housing, but no one called them company towns. Although every industrial village included housing built by companies for employees, the degree of company ownership and control varied from place to place: in some places it was total, and in others it was nonexistent. The term "company town" adds little beyond invective to what contemporaries recognized as a central aspect of welfare capitalism.[2] A proper view requires that we see company housing as part of a system of industrial relations.

Company housing was nearly as old as American industry itself. By 1900 it had passed the experimental stage and was no longer a curiosity, and by 1916 at least a thousand American firms provided housing for at least 600,000 employees and their families, roughly three percent of the population of the United States.[3]

Very early in its history, company housing developed a distinctive architecture. Houses and entire towns constructed in the early twentieth century retained much of the appearance of Lowell, Massachusetts, built a century earlier. Designed by Kirk Boott, chief executive officer of the Merrimac Manufacturing Company and a former British Army officer, Lowell reflected in part Boott's autocratic, military temperament. Houses were built in several gradations, and these were directly related to the occupant's status in the company. The poorest houses were cottages built in long, barracks-like rows—thus, "row houses." Slightly higher in status were two-family dwellings, or semidetached houses. Only people at the pinnacle of Lowell society lived in single-family residences.

Lowell was not, however, simply a military barracks. Its red-brick construction, typical of the pleasant architecture of New England, was reminiscent of the handsome buildings of Harvard College. The town also borrowed from the utopian visions of Robert Owen, who constructed model villages in both England and the United States. But that idealistic forecast for the future of company towns in the United States proved, unfortunately, to be short-lived, for it was the least attractive of Lowell's designs which proved to be the most influential.[4]

Following Lowell's example, semidetached and row houses dominated industrial housing for half a century.[5] The latter were popular mainly because they were cheap to build. Semidetached houses had, however, several advantages. For one thing, semidetached units each had three outside exposures, making them less crowded and better ventilated and thus safer than row houses in case of fire or similar emergencies. At the same time, semidetached houses were more economical than single-family, or detached, dwellings. Two units could be built on one foundation, heating and plumbing systems could be shared, less land was needed, and with one less exposure, less heat escaped.

But after 1881, the popularity of individual dwellings grew sharply, and by 1916 they comprised half of all company houses, with semidetached accounting for a third and row houses only a tenth. The shift occurred chiefly as a result of expansion of company housing into the southern cotton textile industry. Individual units were popular in the South because of climate and cost: the weather made maximum ventilation important and expensive cellars unnecessary, and land was cheap. Where land was expensive, as in northern cities, row houses continued to be popular; some were still being constructed as late as 1917.[6]

Most company houses (almost 90 percent in 1916) were of wood-frame construction; the rest were built largely of brick, stucco, concrete, and hollow tile. Again, cost was the usual determinant but not the only one. For instance, in the case of the Delaware, Lackawanna and Western Railroad, a prime factor was the company's estimate of the sort of people who worked for them: for the houses built near Nanticoke, Pennsylvania, the company chose concrete so that even a bonfire could be built in the living room with no greater destruction than smoke damage, and so that the building could be cleaned with a hose.[7]

Architecturally, company houses were generally very simple. Most were cubelike structures of four to six rooms, with hip roofs, clapboard walls, and a single chimney. When a cellar was omitted, the whole structure rested on brick piers. The prevalence of four-room houses may have been an importation of British tradition: English coal mine owners believed that four rooms were enough for a miner and his family, regardless of its size. In American company housing, a group of southern families averaged 8.5 members per house and a group of northern families, about six members, while the cubes typically measured thirty-two feet square and contained two bedrooms. The other two rooms were a kitchen and a dining/living room. The resulting conditions frequently led to the obvious remedy of turning the living room into a third bedroom.[8]

As a symbol of status, the proverbial key to the executive washroom might well have had its roots in the indoor toilet of the company house. One study found that only one-tenth of company houses had inside toilets and that these houses were occupied chiefly by company executives and their families. Most companies provided outdoor toilets of varying degrees of uncleanliness, some requiring occupants to share privies. The very worst houses had no facilities at all.[9]

Indeed, modern conveniences of any sort were hardly the stock-in-trade of company houses. Half had no lighting. One-third had no running water. Heating arrangements were similarly primitive. Typical four-room cottages had only a chimney in the center, with fireplace grates to heat each room. Flooring was usually of cheap wood full of knotholes, and when dried out, the floorboards developed cracks as much as an inch wide. Where no cellar existed, cold winds blew under the houses and were sucked into the living areas through the natural vacuum caused by the fireplace.[10]

Besides the discomfort, the poor heating arrangements contributed to what was apparently a general bleakness in the interior of company houses. While the inside walls were customarily plastered and painted, this was more for protective than for aesthetic reasons. But if it helped to ward off fire, it was not sufficient against the cold, for often old newspapers, scraps of wallpaper, or brown wrapping paper was stuffed in cracks or nailed to walls to keep out the cold drafts.[11] The houses were seldom wallpapered, for wallpaper added nothing to the value of the houses and was a potential harbor for vermin.

Little else is known about the interior of company houses, though one visitor offered some telling details, describing them as having "bare, often unswept floors, their space dominated by two or three beds in each ill-ventilated room; walls covered with calendars, enlarged pictures and magazines suggesting the sensationalism which the lives of the occupants lack; the family shelf lurid with varieties of patent medicines whose appeal has been effective for the credulous, careless and vacillating; mantels berowed with the perennial and work-easing snuff boxes. Sometimes a few books litter a table in a corner; and again a talking machine or an installment piano enlightens the gloom considerably."[12]

Outwardly, company houses presented an appearance of unrelieved monotony. It is perhaps impossible to arrange a large number of identical buildings in a pleasing manner, but ironically, rather than attempt to mitigate the endless uniformity, employers in fact accentuated it. After row houses went out of style, businessmen persisted in laying out semidetached and detached houses in long, equally spaced rows. Though freed from the necessity of retaining one of the ugliest features of company houses, they retained it. If this were not enough, company houses in a community were usually all painted the same color, and this more often drab than otherwise. Frame construction suggests a white house to most Americans but company houses were seldom painted white. The preference was for dark gray, brown, slate, or most often drab red (red paint was cheaper than white). Given such an exposure—a repetitive simple geometry of similar or identical structures, all the same dull color—visitors responded predictably: they found in such company housing a monotonous and wearisome sameness. Unfortunately, while this passion for repetition and exaggerated orderliness clearly indicated a kind of planning, it was only an amateurish one. The Bureau of Labor Statistics found that town planning experts helped plan only 15 percent of company towns.[13]

Perhaps a certain conservative desire for neatness and order was in part responsible for the monotonous appearance of such arrangements, but the basic motive seems to have been the same as that which lay behind the choice of materials and the architecture: the never-ending drive for economy in construction. It may be ironic that in certain ways this drive led to forms of disorder and disarray. For instance, storage space in company houses was at a premium; they lacked basements and were short on closets. Families found that there was simply no place to put things so they put whatever overflow there was in the back yards, not always meticulously. Thus while the untidiness which bothered middle-class eyes was doubtless a cultural matter in part, it was also in part a physical necessity.[14]

Contemporary descriptions suggest that community services provided in company towns varied greatly. Visitors referred to some towns as filthy hovels; others they called picturesque. Objective data are hard to find, but the most reliable information states that, in 1917, 17 percent of the towns had no electricity, 19 percent no sidewalks or gutters, 45 percent no paved streets, and 40 percent no sanitary sewers.[15]

Mining towns were notoriously unsanitary. These were often built in a valley with houses on either hillside and a stream running between. As a rule, employers installed sanitation systems only after the creek became clogged with filth. General healthfulness and cleanliness also depended on fences. Without fences, domestic animals ran unchecked, the result being a sustantial lowering of the general sanitation level as well as a substantial increase in stench. One who visited many company towns remarked that often a "stagnant miasma" hung over them as a result of "animal offal, pigsty, privy, steaming manure heaps, chicken coops, kitchen slops, goose puddles, and soggy ground." Some companies recognized the desirability of fences and built them around each house or provided fencing materials free of charge. They may have had in mind other values beside sanitation; fences fixed responsibility for care of a specific tract, they protected privacy, encouraged gardening, and in general stimulated a feeling of proprietorship.[16]

While the foregoing descriptions may suggest that company towns in general were uniquely unsanitary communities in their time, and indeed many charges have been made to that effect, the most careful studies to date will not support that view. Between 1914 and 1917, United States Public Health Service physicians surveyed 123 industrial communities, large and small, in various industries, company owned and independent, in twelve states. Conditions varied widely but there was no pattern to indicate that company ownership resulted in poorer conditions than did other types of ownership, nor did anything indicate that company towns were substantially better.

In 1923 the Public Health Service made a similar study of 123 mining towns and once again found that, though the general sanitation level was "low" in both independent and company towns, neither kind of town had consistently lower levels than the other.[17]

A similar appraisal can be made of the general living conditions in company towns. While only the most disparaging terms adequately described some of them, others seemed to be models for the times. On the one hand, there were the homes of the Fulton Bag and Cotton Mills of Atlanta which a government inspector found "simply terrible" and a local civic leader "unspeakable," and even the mill manager himself "agreed . . . absolutely" that conditions were despicable. Perhaps there was even some truth to the allegations of a textile union leader who claimed that the walls of some southern textile houses were so thin that one could throw a baseball through them. At the same time, there was justification for the testimony of a coal executive who argued that "the sun shines in our mining towns. The children play there in well-equipped playgrounds and run about the streets of crushed limestone and clean, yellow granulated slag. The houses, painted in most of our towns in four or five attractive colors, are electrically lighted. The yards are neat and free from dirt and rubbish, for each village is under strict sanitary supervision." Living standards were low in company towns, as in other industrial communities, but wide variation was the most striking characteristic.[18]

Wide variation in the quality of company housing was indicative of wide diversity of its purposes. The quality of company housing was a matter of great controversy, and the reasons behind it were controversial. Foes of businessmen thought of company housing as an avaricious form of exploitation; businessmen usually replied that company housing was simply a matter of necessity, that the failure of private developers to provide the needed housing forced companies to step in.

There was, indeed, much truth to the argument that housing workers was a necessary part of business enterprise in the early twentieth century. Housing was necessary in newly developed mining areas, but a miner could not be expected to build a house near a mine whose longevity was unknown and where working conditions were uncertain. Even if they wanted to build their own homes, American coal miners could seldom get the necessary money together. Nor, perhaps surprisingly, was this situation restricted to the mining industry. Managers of manufacturing plants also cited the failure of private interests to supply housing as the most important factor in their decisions to construct housing themselves.[19]

Simple necessity was nevertheless not the only factor. The Bureau of Labor Statistics found that of 236 developments on which it had data, only 157, or two-thirds, were located on undeveloped land which required laying out a new town.[20] Presumably, independent developers could have built the housing on the other third. Not all company towns in the United States *had* to be located away from already developed areas; on the contrary, many factories could have been built in established communities. The argument of necessity was, therefore, not always or entirely valid. But it was almost always attractive, and while businessmen frequently emphasized the necessity of company housing, they did so most often when defending their housing against critics.[21]

Another important reason for company housing was its function in controlling the labor supply. The reasoning was simple: by providing good housing at low cost, one could attract superior employees or at least induce able employees to stay. As one Pennsylvania coal company put it, the company supplied housing in order to "regulate the prices so as to choose the best class of miners or mechanics as . . . tenants." Where there was relatively intense competition for labor, as in cities, housing was an inducement of real importance.[22]

The central factor of this inducement was of course low rents. Favorable rents were, in effect, partial subsidies. Yet some businessmen cited direct profit as a reason for providing housing. The profitability of company housing, then, tells much about its purpose: it could either bring a direct return to the company or an indirect return through decreased labor turnover. It is impossible, unfortunately, to measure the profitability of company housing precisely; there were simply too many companies involved and too many variations in the cost and quality of housing. One can, nevertheless, determine whether or not rents were exorbitant.

In 1916 the Bureau of Labor Statistics surveyed sixty companies in a variety of industries which had built houses costing a total of more than $15 million. These companies reported that over a five-year period rent receipts brought a gross annual return of 8.3 percent of the original cost.[23] This amounted to slightly more than the break-even point. In order to realize a net return on his investment, an employer would have to cover such costs as land, repairs, taxes, street cleaning, garbage collection, insurance, bookkeeping, and incidentals. This amounted to 3-5 percent of the original cost per year, while depreciation added another 3 percent per year.[24] If one includes an "opportunity cost" (the gain that might have been realized had the capital been invested elsewhere), a net loss resulted. Thus in most cases the direct return from company housing was scant, and even when companies succeeded in grossing as much as 12 percent annually, as some did, the return was not outlandish.[25]

Among other means than rents for making company housing financially profitable, one was the most controversial element of all, the infamous company store. Labor maintained an outspoken dislike for company stores throughout their existence, and the various nicknames reflected this view: they were known as "gip-me stores," "pluck-me stores," "gip-joints," "robber-saries." Sometimes antipathy did not end with name calling; as early as 1849 complaints against company stores helped trigger a strike in the anthracite coal region of Pennsylvania, and they remained a grievance in countless strikes afterward.[26]

There were four chief complaints against company stores. Prices were supposedly higher than in independent stores. Companies allegedly exerted explicit or implicit pressure on employees to get them to shop in company stores. Company stores were felt to lack variety in the kinds of goods carried. Companies were accused of preventing competitors from starting stores nearby.

For overpricing, the company store was guilty as charged according to several reliable studies. The most elaborate investigation, made in 1934 by the National Recovery Administration, found that food prices in company stores averaged 2.1-10.4 percent higher than in nearby independent stores. An eleven-state study conducted by coal mine operators themselves compared prices in 388 independent stores and 146 company stores. They found that in eight of nine localities prices were higher in company stores, and in the largest number of areas the difference ran from 3 to 4 percent.[27]

Of the charge that companies pressured their employees to buy at company stores, there were more allegations than hard evidence, but enough evidence exists to make the presence of coercion undeniable. Among the most irresistible forms of influence was their easy credit, whose lure was enhanced by low wages and infrequent pay days. A National Recovery Administration study found workers who had received no cash payments for fifteen years.[28]

The companies did indeed attempt to discourage competition for the worker's dollar by using several techniques to rid themselves of itinerant merchants attracted to towns with high-priced company stores. Company detectives were often directed to keep peddlers from plying their trade, and whole company towns were often surrounded by fences partly to keep the peddlers away. Detectives and fences were usually effective, but the peddlers did not always leave quietly. In one lumbering area of Louisiana, for instance, a pugnacious group of mixed-breeds (of white, Negro, and Indian lineage), known as "Red Bones," retaliated. They secretly drove spikes into company timber which went undetected until the timber reached the mill and ripped expensive saws to pieces.[29]

The lack of competition was partly responsible for the lack of variety in company stores, for store managers had little incentive to stock a large inventory of goods, and apparently few did. A government investigator found in company stores "an appreciable sameness in the kind of food, the quality and character of dress of the employees, and in the many other commodities that enter into the comfort and the details of the home." While admitting that residents seemed satisfied by the goods obtainable, he pointed out that company stores offered "no stimulant to variety or originality." But some customers were unenamored. "Butcher meat comes only once a week to lots of camps," one miner complained, "and sometimes it's from the identical cow that Noah took into the ark of safety, or not far descended from it." If company housing began the monotonous grayness of company towns, company stores extended it into such aspects of everyday life as food and clothing.[30]

If the crowded living conditions of company towns were partly a result of the physical size of the houses, they were also partly a result of the mere fact that companies owned the houses and stores and pursued the opportunity to maximize their returns. Full houses meant full rents, sales in the stores, and workers for the companies, and fuller houses could at least mean larger store sales. Workers often charged companies with giving preference in assigning houses to families with many children, and a North Carolina textile company sent this notice to one worker: "This is to notify you that we wish you to vacate our house immediately. There is but one of your family working in the mill, and we need your house for larger families."[31]

Even in slack times (and fluctuating economic conditions were characteristic of early twentieth-century American industries, particularly many which maintained company houses and stores, like bituminous coal mining), employers had an incentive to maintain full occupancy of company houses. For it was more desirable to have thirty men working short weeks with full occupancy than to have twenty men working full time with ten vacancies; rent receipts and store sales would both be higher.[32]

Similarly, stores and houses cushioned the effects of outright depression and added to the prosperity of boom periods. When a company could provide no work, its store became the chief source of credit for unemployed workers, and when prosperity returned, outstanding bills as well as back rents had to be paid. The system could be made even more profitable for the company, if less for the worker, for if conditions became prosperous enough so that employees had money in their pockets, a company could encourage them to make larger purchases at the store by extending their credit; nor was there an incentive for employers to increase wages beyond the subsistence level: money saved by an employee could be taken out of town and spent elsewhere.[33]

In at least some instances, and possibly as a general practice, companies recovered in company stores what they lost through low returns on company houses. In fact, although no broad, reliable survey of their profitability has ever been made, it can be reasonably assumed that company stores were often very profitable. High profits were likely not only because of the higher prices and the "captive" consumer, but because they needed no advertising and the joint relationship with the parent company made it possible to cut bad-debt losses to the minimum.[34] No doubt few of them were able to match the company store in Harlan County, Kentucky, which returned a profit of 170 percent on its investment in its first year, but many of them returned a steady 10 percent. This was an important and sometimes critical supplement to the primary business of many American companies, as a West Virginia coal mine operator affirmed; "half the operators [in his district] would have to cut wages or go out of business without this assistance." Further evidence of the profitability of company stores appeared in 1933: the National Recovery Administration proposal to outlaw the scrip system in company stores was opposed by no fewer than nine trade associations.[35]

The company store added no small portion to the frustration and emptiness of life in company towns and earned its position in labor's hall of demons, but like the company town itself, the store had its defenders. Businessmen asserted that those who developed a town should have first priority in receiving whatever gain was to be made from it. They also contended that though prices were higher in company stores, employees were generally better off than if they had remained living on farms. "Prices are high, 'tis said: but contrast the weary woman bent over her tub of clothes, scrubbing, moiling, late into the evening, with the same woman today who has purchased from the Company Store an electric washer and who now sits calmly reading or sewing while the washer does the work."[36]

However unpleasant might be the living conditions in company towns, other aspects of company housing were perhaps even more damaging to employees' well-being. Company housing became a superb method of social control, serving on occasion to keep unions out, to break strikes, to keep wages low, to enforce social segregation, and to control local government.

As an anti-union weapon, company housing operated in several ways. First, low rents could be used as an inducement to keep employees from engaging in any union activities whatsoever. At the Amoskeag Manufacturing Company of Manchester, New Hampshire, company policy treated housing "as a premium to be allotted only to cooperative, loyal and peaceful workers," and a survey of housing lumped together Amoskeag residents who were "undesirable as to character, not in harmony with the Company, active in textile labor organization." A man would not have to be especially timid to be reluctant to join a union in Amoskeag.[37]

Most occupants were made to sign leases that were effective weapons against unions. Most leases stipulated that if for any reason an employee left the service of his company, he had to vacate the premises on short notice. This was of crucial importance in a strike situation. If an employee joined a strike, he had to be prepared to move his family and belongings elsewhere within two weeks or more usually within five days. The leases of three Pennsylvania coal companies specifically bound the occupants "to leave peaceably within 10 days after work has been suspended at said works in connection with a strike." Other leases commonly contained clauses granting employers the right to use "such and so much force as may be necessary" to remove the family and their effects. Employees of the Latrobe-Connellsville Coal and Coke Company had to grant not only such a right of eviction ("without legal process") but also had to absolve the officials from prosecution or claims for damages that ensued. Nor were these documents purely weapons of psychological warfare; evictions were not rarities. According to United Mine Workers records (which should be accurate, since the UMW provided alternate housing), between 1922 and 1925 in West Virginia alone employers evicted more than ten thousand miners and their families, about fifty thousand people.[38] Eviction was particularly serious in the coal industry: the best time to strike was during the peak demand for coal—in winter.[39]

As a strikebreaking weapon, eviction could be double-bladed, for vacant company houses were ideal places for housing strikebreakers. Leases could be used in even more radical ways as a means of smothering union activity altogether. Some leases contained clauses worded so that union organizers could not even enter a company house, nor could a union meeting be held there. The house leases of several companies, for example, limited "ingress and egress" to the occupant and his family. The lease of the Keystone Coal and Coke Company contained this thinly veiled attempt to exclude union organizers: the company reserved the right "to keep out and away from said premises any person or persons it may deem necessary or expedient."[40]

Unionists too could take advantage of company houses. For instance, if strikers could squat in company houses, they could materially increase an employer's difficulties by adding the physical and economic burden of housing strikebreakers. George Anderson, executive vice-president of the Consolidation Coal Company, explained that "[the unions] know . . . that if you can hold the enemy's trenches of course the enemy can not advance, and if you can keep your men idle in these company houses not a man can work no matter what he wants." If conditions were suitable, strikers were able to intimidate strikebreakers living in the vacated houses. From the hillsides above mining camps, for example, strikers rained riflefire on thin-walled company houses occupied by strikebreakers. (It was also claimed, but never proved, that strikers sometimes rolled barrels of blasting powder down on the hapless scabs.) At the very least, a strikebreaker hardy enough to brave ugly epithets or even a hail of rocks or bullets was not likely to work effectively under these conditions.[41]

Businessmen were well aware of the critical necessity to control housing, and they took steps to maintain their control. They frequently employed private detectives and company policemen to evict striking employees bodily, or they forced eviction by such harassments as were used by the Pittsburgh Terminal Coal Company. In 1927 during a strike in Coverdale, Pennsylvania, the company allowed an inefficient sewage system to go uncleaned and refused to repair or let the tenants repair the resulting breakdown in the toilets. A visiting journalist described the consequences: "As we approached the homes of several strikers . . . we were very keenly aware of an overpowering stench, a terrible odor." In other towns the same company turned off the flow of water and electricity to company houses occupied by squatting strikers. Several times the company ripped roofs from houses, and in one case it barred milkmen from the camp for refusing to sell milk to strikebreakers.[42]

Anti-union motives gave rise to what was often called the "closed town," one where the owning company constructed a fence around the periphery. Mine guards or deputy sheriffs guarded the confines, preventing union organizers from entering and preventing union workers from intimidating nonunion workers. There were many such closed towns in mining areas and near lumber and textile mills. The success of this arrangement in each case depended on cooperation of local authorities, who granted police jurisdiction to the companies. This was usually made possible by county residents who wished to avoid paying for police in company towns, preferring instead to allow companies to pay the wages. In one Pennsylvania case a sheriff contracted with a mining company to provide seven deputies at $7.50 per day each. The deputies, however, received only $5.00 because the sheriff kept the rest.[43]

Local authorities and company policemen occasionally engaged in jurisdictional disputes. One day in 1927, for example, a company policeman at Coverdale, Pennsylvania, jumped his horse over a child playing in the street. The child's father immediately swore out a complaint before the nearest justice of the peace, but when the justice and a constable set foot on company property, three company policemen attempted to arrest them for trespassing. Possessing a faster automobile, the justice and the constable managed to escape. Quickly returning with reinforcements, they took on the company police in a donnybrook.[44]

Businessmen had a ready reply to charges that evictions, company policemen, and closed towns violated workers' civil liberties. Deputy sheriffs were perfectly legitimate, explained a spokesman for coal operators, because railroads employed policemen, banks employed guards, and hotels employed detectives. There was "no difference" between these situations and mining towns. Regarding the closing of towns to union organizers, the same spokesman claimed that this was what nonunion employees wanted—unions meant only violence. "Of course [the closed town] violates certain civil liberties," he admitted, "but at least it protects other and more fundamental civil rights. It is not to avoid unionization that the closed town primarily exists. It is to prevent the violence and murder that invariably accompany attempts to force unionization; to preserve to the non-union miners the right to work as they wish to work." Another spokesman for coal operators explained that the worker who lived in a closed town "infinitely prefers to sacrifice the academic civil liberty of harboring agitators for the very practical civil liberty of not having his home dynamited."[45]

For some, however, this sort of defense was not satisfactory. In 1915 an investigator for the United States Commission on Industrial Relations interviewed F. R. Wood, the president of a Colorado coal mining company, suggesting that "it might prove beneficial" if the closed town was eliminated. "I don't agree with you," replied Wood. "The closed camp is better." "Suppose then," the investigator asked, "that every business in America should establish closed towns, would this be an improvement?" "Yes," he answered. To this the investigator objected that "that would be feudalism, not democracy." Wood replied, "To hell, with democracy!"

Later, recalling these words, the investigator wrote: "A man who in the struggle of life has no home to retire to; whose rug lies upon another's floor; whose fire is in another's grate, can neither become great himself nor inspire greatness in his own family. No great thoughts have been inspired by an incorporated landlord. God gave to the songbirds the right to build their own nest; to the foxes the right to dig a hole; and to man the right to own his own habitation."[46] Company housing, which shared the goals of other forms of welfarism, also shared the central difficulty which would plague most of them.

Education

In 1815 a Pennsylvania physician named Thomas W. Dyott constructed a glassworks. "I soon discovered that the workmen were *more immoral* and *intemperate* in their habits than most classes of artisans," he recalled. "Finding it impossible to reform the old workmen, I conceived the idea of producing a new set with entirely different habits."[1] To carry out his plan, Dyott provided his glassmakers with a dairy, a chapel, a shop committee, and a school. The latter was probably the first company-owned school in the United States. Within a century American employers would sponsor, in one instance or another, every level of education from kindergarten through high school and continuing education. By 1881, teachers employed by the Cambria Steel Company taught classes in industrial arts, mathematics, chemistry, geology, and political economy. Five years later a school operated by P. Lorillard and Company in Jersey City, New Jersey, had 350 students, a 10,000-volume library, and educated children and adults of both sexes. By 1913 a group of interested companies had established the National Association of Corporation Schools. Yet the fundamental philosophy—that of producing an improved workman—remained unchanged.[2]

On the simplest level, businessmen believed that education could uplift employees. One spokesman for nonunion coal operators explained that when capital developed a coal field, it brought with it schools and "upon the heels of education the desire to live well"; this fought the "pernicious heredity and environment" of the miners, improved their "mental calibre," and helped them "acquire habits of industry." Unlike many of the other welfare programs businessmen supported, education, explained an International Harvester executive, was the "sole thing to give . . . a lasting value to the workingmen."[3]

Education, in other words, had persistency. It lasted so well, in fact, that a committee of the National Association of Manufacturers regarded education as the "solution of the majority of our industrial troubles." Training citizens was so important, the NAM believed, that it was dangerous to leave it to boards of education. What the country needed was "education along the lines of what constitutes the foundation of good, clear, sound-thinking citizens." Most businessmen, the historian Edward Chase Kirkland has argued, believed that education was the likeliest source of contentment and stability in their labor forces. It was these beliefs—that educated, uplifted workers would last and that education could be the solution to the problems of an industrial society—that marked every aspect of businessmen's involvement in their employees' education.[4]

Company education began almost at the cradle. In southern cotton mill towns children only six to eight weeks old were admitted to company nursery schools—a convenience to mothers, as it freed them to work in the mill. Company kindergartens served the same purpose, although there were other purposes, as evidenced by the popularity of kindergartens in mining fields, where no mothers toiled. Dr. Richard W. Corwin, who headed the Sociological Department of the Colorado Fuel and Iron Company, termed kindergartens the "master key to the whole social betterment situation." Kindergartens, Corwin explained, offered the opportunity to "begin the all around development of the child at the most impressionable period of [his] life." In a kindergarten "every class and nationality is on an equal standing, and while recognizing differences . . . it attempts to inculcate the true democratic spirit."[5]

A subsidiary of Lackawanna Steel, the Ellsworth Colleries Company conducted a kindergarten for precisely this reason. Its idea was to have children of foreign immigrants grouped together for two years before beginning grammar school. This would give them greater exposure to the English language and they would later find it easier to write English if they spoke it first. Offspring of New Jersey Zinc workers learned thriftiness in the company kindergarten by organizing a "penny provident bank." A final purpose of company kindergartens was to get at the parents through the children. Kindergartens enabled Colorado Fuel and Iron teachers, as Corwin put it, "to get into the house and win the confidence of the mother." Once admitted the teachers formed weekly mothers' clubs, listened to a short literary and musical program, conducted a brief business meeting, and spent a social hour. Not only were toddlers uplifted and Americanized by company kindergartens, but their parents were as well.[6]

American companies supported grammar schools with much

enthusiasm. As company houses sprang up, a company school typically appeared nearby, though often lagging by a few years. A 1929 survey of educational activities of North Carolina textile mills indicated the extent of interest there. Of 147 mills not located where children could attend an established school, fully 129 voluntarily subsidized education to some degree. Only eighteen, or one-eighth, contributed nothing whatsoever. Interest in education in southern textile towns was easily explicable; at the outset southern mills mainly produced coarse cotton goods, leaving high quality production to the skilled labor of nothern mills. Education could produce the skilled labor necessary to compete with the North.[7]

Typical practice was to construct a school building or partially to subsidize a teacher's salary. Not surprisingly, local governments were often cool to the possibility of supporting a teacher and building a school in a company town. John R. Buchtel, who as general manager of the Akron Iron Company built and lent his name to the town of Buchtel, Ohio, appropriated $3000 for a school building, but only after some wheedling managed to get a $1000 contribution from the local school board. In some cases, companies built a school, hired a teacher, paid the salary, and supervised the education of the children entirely.[8]

Companies which made substantial contributions often encouraged or outright forced employees to send their children to school. The Pelzer Manufacturing Company, which owned the textile town of Pelzer, South Carolina, subsidized its schools to the extent that they remained open ten months a year though neighboring schools operated only four months. As a prelude to employment the Pelzer Company required that new employees pledge that all members of a family between the ages of five and twelve would attend school every day during the school term. More commonly, companies used subtle pressure. The president of the Piedmont Manufacturing Company, a Greenville, South Carolina, textile firm, denied that he forced attendance but admitted that he used "moral suasion" and "my influence," explaining: "I make teachers go out every Friday afternoon—go over town after the children who ought to be in school."[9]

Another means businessmen used to secure a return on their investment was by making their schools as efficient as possible. The kindergartens and nursery schools were an example of this effort; if children could be educated earlier they would likewise be ready to work earlier. Businessmen also attempted to maximize the amount children learned during their school years. In so doing, they anticipated many of the innovations later made by public school pedagogues.

Colorado Fuel and Iron, which owned thirty company towns, was a model of educational efficiency. Although each town elected a school board, Colorado Fuel and Iron's Sociological Department was more influential. Each town had a standard school building, carefully designed to provide each student with 200-220 cubic feet of air. Folding partitions formed the schoolrooms in order to permit multiple use of the structure. The company adopted a uniform course of studies for all districts and provided free, standard textbooks to accompany it. Bulk purchase of textbooks, school furniture, and other equipment saved money. The company loaned money to local boards for buildings, teacher salaries, and furniture, and gave them free legal advice. The Sociological Department even recruited "good" teachers, very likely from the Pueblo Normal and Industrial School, which it subsidized. Integrated educational control, finally, allowed the company to establish circulating libraries and art collections. In the latter case, a set of twelve pictures accompanied by a short description hung in each school periodically.[10]

But the quality of company schools was at least questionable. Evidence suggests that they improved rates of literacy in some company towns. In Pelzer, South Carolina, the rate increased from 25 percent to between 80 and 85 percent in eighteen years. In 1900 two other South Carolina mill owners testified that their only illiterate workers were those who had recently left the farm. Considering that the literacy rate in South Carolina was about 55 percent in 1890, textile towns came out well. President Simpson Bobo Tanner of the Henrietta Mills was satisfied also that employees were being uplifted. Asked if he found "the moral character of the children improving as their education advances," Tanner replied that he noticed "very plainly" that there had been "considerable improvement in that direction."[11]

An early student of company education, however, criticized the teachers selected, claiming that they were often needy relatives or friends of mill officers. Some evidence suggests that teachers in company schools were less than effective, though educational "quality," admittedly, was and is an elusive thing. One investigator administered I.Q. tests to students taken from grades two to seven in two North Carolina textile towns. In the first case, 591 students averaged 86.5 (as opposed to the norm of 100); in the second, 418 students averaged 82.5. In order to check his accuracy, he administered a second type of test to 310 students in the second school; they averaged 88.0.[12]

Whatever was the effectiveness of teaching in company schools, they did have an adverse effect on some citizens by enforcing racial segregation. In southern textile towns, racial segregation was largely the result of job discrimination. Mill owners did not grant employment to black men except occasionally in very menial positions. Denied access to employment, blacks were also denied access to company schools, which in many cases were the best and in some cases the only ones available.[13]

It was not only in southern textile towns that company schools were segregated. Segregation prevailed in mining towns as well. In 1923 investigators employed by coal mine operators visited twelve "representative company-owned communities" in southern West Virginia. All twelve provided schools for white children; five had separate schools for black children. At Holden, the Island Creek Coal Company operated what the owners considered a model mining town. It had a ten-grade school for white children and an eight-grade school for blacks. The Red Jacket Consolidated Coal and Coke Company operated similar facilities at Red Jacket, West Virginia. The white school had 240 pupils, six classrooms, seven teachers, steam heat, and playground equipment. The black school had fifty-seven pupils, two classrooms, and two teachers. White students could pursue a junior high school education under a teacher with an A.B. degree; blacks could get only grammar school classes taught by teachers with normal school certificates. Conditions were worse for blacks in southern mining towns. A white miner from the town of Searles, Alabama, reported that his employer taxed his employees, both whites and blacks, for school costs because the county failed to supply sufficient funds. Whites elected their own teachers but blacks had no voice in the matter. Black teachers, accordingly, were not qualified, the white miner said, "to teach monkeys to climb trees." Company cooking schools were sometimes segregated, and one company magazine placed news of black and white families in separate sections.[14]

The dual role of instructor and employee played by company teachers both directly and indirectly affected the quality of company education. Critics charged that all too frequently company schoolteachers turned out to be company propagandists. A group of coal mine owners dismissed this charge as "absurd." They reasoned that, since company schools emphasized the three R's, it would be very difficult for teachers to impart bias—so difficult, in fact, that it would even be counterproductive for an employer to fire an effective teacher who happened to harbor disagreeable viewpoints. But though the mine owners thought it "fantastic" to suppose that anyone had ever been fired for this reason, they admitted that it was "probably true" that companies exerted "a certain control" over teacher selection. They argued, however, that their counsel helped secure "more competent" teachers. International Harvester selected only employees to become teachers. The first prerequisite of all Harvester teachers was that they be "plain, democratic men and women, the sort of people the average man respects, and likes"; only secondly was it important that they have a "first hand knowledge of their subjects."[15]

Teacher selection was only one of the educational areas affected by company subsidization. In everyday administration, company officials constantly influenced decisions. One student who interviewed teachers in Appalachian coal towns found them "usually very guarded in their statements and hesitant about making a decision on school matters until the operators are consulted." No one, he added, bothered to question the arrangement—"It is just the customary method of procedure." An investigator employed by the United States Commission on Industrial Relations interviewed a school principal whose building was owned by the company. Although the county contributed to his salary, the principal thought of himself as an employee of the company and took orders from its executives. Even in cases where employees contributed to schools through payroll deductions, company officials had the final say in school matters.[16]

Some companies were not averse to applying direct pressure. One company asked its county superintendent of schools to dismiss two teachers known to be union sympathizers. When the superintendent refused, the company got the school board to remove not only the teachers but also the superintendent himself. One leading West Virginia coal operator, Board Chairman William H. Coolidge of the Island Creek Coal Company, belied the noninterference claims of his colleagues. Asked before a Senate committee what he would do if a teacher taught that the United Mine Workers "was a very beneficial and altruistic organization" and that pupils' "future welfare" depended on their joining, Coolidge denied that he would do anything to stop it. He pointed out, however, that this was an unlikely situation, as county authorities would dismiss such a person first. Asked if he would be in favor of such a dismissal, Coolidge replied: "I certainly would be."[17]

With the eighth grade, business interest in education of a traditional kind came to a halt. Examples of company sponsorship of high schools are hard to find. One student of southern textile towns, indeed, reported that high school facilities were "practically unknown." Many businessmen feared that a high school education would induce youngsters to seek employment elsewhere. Industrial education, on the other hand, would serve to bind them to manual employment and very likely to employment with the particular company that provided it. "High school development tends to educate the young away from our industries rather than for them," argued John E. Warren, agent for a Maine textile mill. His company inaugurated manual training, Warren explained, "in order to somewhat offset this tendency . . . and to dignify in the minds of the young the work that is going on in their own community." Many businesses, accordingly, offered only manual training after grammar school—a kind of education hard to classify as welfare capitalism.[18]

Though employer interest in industrial education was easily explicable, for less obvious reasons businessmen expended substantial sums on cooking and sewing schools for girls. Companies as diverse as West Virginia coal mining companies and New York department stores offered this kind of training. The most frequently cited reason for doing so was to indoctrinate habits of thrift, simplicity, and economy. The women and girls studying cooking at one school learned, for example, about "making the most of inferior cuts; . . . soupmaking; . . . steaming stale bread; cooking homely and inexpensive dishes." Other companies emphasized "plain cooking," "cheap cuts of meat," or "wholesome and economic foods." One school emphasized canning—a form of thrift. Another company hoped to develop "the tissues of the body and brain" through improved dietary habits. Cooking schools were even a tool for assimilating immigrants. The Ludlow Associates had a special class to teach Polish girls to prepare American dishes. U.S. Steel used homemaking classes "to inculcate American Ideals in the minds of the boys and girls, and through them to reach the parents." At

Plymouth Cordage both immigrant girls and boys learned to make such traditional New England dishes as fish chowder, Washington pie, and American chop suey (hamburger and macaroni).[19]

Sewing schools had much the same objects. The Wm. Wrigley, Jr., Company, a Chicago gum manufacturer, sponsored a series of talks so that its girls would learn to plan a clothes budget of $200 a year. Other companies taught girls to make their own clothes. Plymouth Cordage carried the theme to its sewing classes as well; it taught Italian girls to make "middie" blouses.[20]

Dr. R. W. Corwin of Colorado Fuel and Iron believed that his company's cooking classes would bolster and preserve the family unit against its direst enemy. "A poorly cooked meal may ruin a man and his family," Corwin said. "To a hungry man a home's attractiveness begins at the table. But if he comes home to a supper of tasteless, indigestible food, served without any attempt at making it inviting or the table attractive, is there any wonder that he seeks the saloon for stimulants?" Cooking and sewing schools were even used in one case as an argument against unions. A spokesman for coal mine operators suggested that the "dainty little frocks" and "savory concoctions" made by twelve- and thirteen-year-old girls in company schools were solid evidence that "these charming little misses will know how to organize homes even though reared in an unorganized field."[21]

Assimilation of immigrants was the main purpose behind company sponsorship of adult education. Probably the first factory classes with this purpose in mind were conducted in 1906 at the Boston Woven Hose and Rubber Company by students from neighboring Harvard College. Other companies followed soon afterward, and largely as a result of World War I, factory classes for immigrants gained wide acceptance between 1915 and 1918. Some classes simply taught English, but more commonly they went under the general title of "Americanization." What it meant to be Americanized was imprecise, but generally it included knowledge of the English language, cleanliness, wearing of American clothes, and eating American cooking. The curriculum of company-sponsored nontechnical adult education, accordingly, centered around language classes but included the other themes of "Americanism" as well. Classes at the Ford English School, sponsored by the Ford Motor Company, included instruction in "care of the body and teeth, matters of state and national government, and instruction in the routine of naturalization." More than 16,000 men graduated from the seventy-two-lesson course. Other companies taught employees how to use the telephone, how to make partial payments, and how to calculate a percentage of interest. (Credit was by then, evidently, already part of the American way of life.) One method of teaching English was the "pictorial lesson," in which a cartoon illustrated the action of a simple English sentence. Next to the English sentence were translations into various foreign languages. One pictorial lesson, translated into Polish, Hungarian, Italian, and Yiddish, promoted the American fetish for cleanliness by translating and describing the following action: "I fill the tub with water. I take off my clothes. I get into the bathtub. I wash myself with soap."[22]

Americanization classes could also be tools of undercutting unions. At the Plymouth Cordage Company, Charles P. Marshall, an executive known for his anti-union opinions, lectured Portuguese and Italian immigrants in American history. English language classes, in fact, were in themselves an implicit means of undercutting unions. Some employers felt that unions arose from a lack of understanding, and a common language could certainly combat that. In any case, if non-English speaking employees had a grievance, they needed an interpreter to voice their complaints. If they could speak English, they had one less reason to organize.[23]

At least as popular with businessmen as the adult education classes was another characteristic institution of welfare capitalism, the company library. The earliest company library was probably that of the Cambria Steel Company of Johnstown, Pennsylvania, constructed in 1881 at a cost of $30,000 (not including books). By 1916 at least 155 companies had either a library of their own or a branch of a public library located on company property. Company libraries usually had between one and ten thousand books, but the largest numbered 45,000 volumes.[24]

Reading, businessmen thought, would improve the mind and thus contribute to efficiency. The National Cash Register Company claimed that it was "possible to trace an almost direct line from the library to the suggestion box." Libraries could also combat the pernicious influences of the saloon and the city streets. In effect, libraries were a surrogate for the saloon. Hours spent in a company library were hours not spent in a saloon, or, in the case of working-class children, hours not spent roaming city streets. A librarian employed by Plymouth Cordage directed activities for the "American-born foreigners . . . for they represent the citizens of the future."[25]

Businessmen also hoped that company libraries would ease the strains of industrial conflict. Jane C. Williams, the employment manager of a Norwood, Massachusetts, firm, hoped to open up "avenues" so as to get into "close touch" with employees. She called the company library an "important channel" that helped the employment department get "to know each worker individually." Books were also important, several companies argued, for their liberalizing influences. One advocate of company libraries argued that reading would "open the vision of the people and widen the horizon so that they can see that both laborer and employer are working for the same end, and that industrialists through the accumulation of wealth have pulled all levels of society to a more comfortable and broader life." He admitted that a library could not "eliminate every possible source of conflict between laborer and employer" but felt that it could "produce a change in the state of mind."[26]

The objectives of company libraries flavored the holdings. The largest number both of books held and books read were fiction. Reports on the quality of the fiction varied: the J. H. Williams Company of Brooklyn claimed that its employees' tastes ran to Dickens, Hugo, Twain, and Howells; but Charles J. Harrah of Midvale Steel testified somewhat ruefully that his employees eschewed the classics in favor of *Squint-Eyed Bob, the Bully of the Woods*. Company libraries also emphasized biography, history, technical matter, and popular magazines. The popularity of biography represented a belief in Horatio Algerism. One donor to the Cleveland Hardware Company's library remarked that he thought it important that employees read of a man who had "worked his way up from small or very moderate beginnings to positions and prosperous conditions, . . . which are certainly attainable under our beneficent form of government by every American citizen." International Harvester gave its employees subscriptions to popular magazines at Christmas, including with each gift a booklet titled either "Letters from a Self-Made Merchant to His Son" or "Makers of Millions and Their Methods."[27]

As in the case of company schools, company management colored the administration of company libraries. In 1902 Elizabeth C. Wheeler, the social secretary of a Providence, Rhode Island, firm, mentioned that one of her duties was to guard the reading room and its periodicals to see that "no discordant element[s] creep in to annoy the occupants."[28] But it was at Colorado Fuel and Iron, a leading welfare firm in many ways, that the most flagrant censorship of libraries came to light. In 1914 an investigator from the U.S. Commission on Industrial Relations asked several pressing questions of the Reverend E. S. Gaddis, then general manager of the Sociological Department. Gaddis explained that he had a "certain amount of freedom" regarding book selection but that a vice-president had the final say. When the investigator asked if Darwin's *Origin of Species* could be purchased, Gaddis, a good Methodist, replied that "anything contrary to the older conception of Christianity and morality would be barred." The *Rubaiyat of Omar Khayyam*, he added, would be acceptable only if it was expurgated. The investigator then asked about socialist literature and nonsocialist literature critical of the company. All socialist literature would be excluded, Gaddis replied, because "socialism . . . is a delusion and a dream." "But supposing your employees should not think so?" the investigator continued. "We would not let anything go in that we considered detrimental to them," was the answer. "But supposing the men should want to read something that was detrimental to the company?" "Anything that was detrimental to the company would be detrimental to the men," Gaddis said. Even nonsocialist material like *Harper's Weekly* (which had criticized conditions in southern Colorado) could not be accepted without permission from "a higher authority."[29]

From company libraries it was only a short step to production and distribution of written material by the companies themselves. As early as 1847 a "house organ" was published as a sales tool to be distributed to salesmen and customers, but it was not until 1890 that National Cash Register published the first company publication directed primarily at employees. By 1907 fifteen more "employee magazines" (as distinguished from "house organs") had appeared, but a substantial number did not exist until the period 1915-20. As a result of wartime prosperity and the threat of labor disruptions, at least 428 company magazines were published.[30]

Employee magazines developed a genre of their own. They typically appeared monthly and averaged about twenty pages. News of events in employees' private lives occupied about a quarter of the magazine, while the rest was a potpourri of editorials, descriptions of company processes, inspirational articles, announcements, and humor. From this format there was very little variation, partly because editors often borrowed from each other. One company poet was so frequently plagiarized, in fact, that he found it necessary to express his outrage by means of form letter.[31]

The purpose of the employee magazine was to bind the organization together. It was designed, first of all, to convince employees that the company cared about their personal goals and aspirations. For this reason, as well as to build interest, the magazine continually reported milestones in the lives of employees—births of children, marriages, vacations, promotions, and so forth. One editor asserted that an ideal magazine should publish two thousand names a month so that each employee would see his name in print at least once a year. When employees saw their own goals and the goals of their friends materializing, they would develop a consciousness of their stake in the company's success. The feeling that personal goals could be achieved by association with a company would manifest itself in an enhanced spirit of cooperation, mutual respect, and esprit de corps. An International Harvester executive recommended publication of a magazine that would be a "journal of the sayings, doings, and *aspirations* of the employees," which he hoped would lead to "broader life and better citizenship." Translated, "broader life" meant a kind of enlightened self-interest in which one saw one's personal goals as inextricably a part of a company's goals. The purpose of the Commonwealth Steel magazine, likewise, was to air "the men's ideals" to bring about "great cooperative effort."[32]

A second way that employee magazines operated to cement business organizations together was by building trust in management. Company magazines, accordingly, worked constantly to impress employees with their management's wisdom. This was accomplished by depicting the chief executive as knowledgeable in economics. Often the executive wrote a column for the magazine, an editorial, or a series of articles having economics as their theme. One editor explained that such articles emphasizing economics were "very impressive" and would "influence the thinking of large numbers of workers" if signed by the company president. "Capitalize his personality. He has a following: cash in on it. That sounds harsh and materialistic, but it is good common sense, and likewise good business sense, if into every word he pours his own sincerity, honesty, sense of fairness, tact, and recognized business judgment. Make use of his prestige. Such a series will increase it." And, the editor added, if the company president had not the time to compose a series on economics, he suggested that someone "steeped" in the subject should ghostwrite it.[33]

Similarly, magazine editors sought to build trust by personalizing management. This usually meant portraying executives not as impersonal bureaucrats who manipulated lives from afar, but rather as flesh-and-blood individuals. Such men resided not in distant offices but rather had photographs, biographies, and human concern for the plight of even the most lowly employee.[34] Other companies increased confidence by emphasizing a president's long experience—how he had worked his way up the ladder like a Horatio Alger character. Supposedly, he would then have intimate knowledge of every aspect of the business. This sort of biography of the leader's business career simultaneously contributed to the employees' contentment with their own lot, for if one could work up so could another. A Boston department store told its employees in the first issue of its journal that the publication "will show you from the start that no position is hopeless, no matter how insignificant or unimportant it may seem to you now." Another was careful to note the low wage at which the president started and how his mother originally had deplored her son's employment in a position not considered "genteel." A third company carefully placed photographs of high officials on the same page with photographs of common workmen in order to draw management and labor together by implying—and thus creating the impression—that every individual was equally valuable.[35]

Once the employee accepted management's expertise, it was fairly easy to keep him contented with his lot, so the assumption went. Contentment was a prime goal. The same Boston department store quoted above added of its publication, "if it helps you to think clearer and makes you more hopeful and more contented, that is something. If it succeeds in making you laugh, that is something more." Another editor, whose magazine had a readership of 15,000, said his journal was "a means of keeping the workingman at peace with himself and with the company for which he works." What contentment really translated into, however, was a willingness to accept a business view of industrial conditions. A properly contented employee would willingly accept President Clarence Howard's statement in Commonwealth Steel's magazine *Commonwealther*: "No one regrets more deeply than I the necessity for this present lay off. . . . As soon as we can all settle down to a big family basis, willing to give and take and help each other, then we will get a great business."[36]

Another means of building contentment was by creating the impression that one belonged to what was really "one big happy family." This conception of industrial relations constantly appeared in the names of company magazines. Cognomens emphasizing a family relationship included: *The American Sugar Family, The Minute Family News, Partners, The Stanoclan, The Geometric Comrade, We, Us, Ourselves, Monitor Family Circle,* and many others. Others sought, perhaps, to dispel the bleakness of industrialization by injecting—with varying success—a touch of humor. A bank's publication, accordingly, was named *The Teller,* a saw company's was *The Buzz,* and a steamshovel company's was the *Bucyrus Scoop.* A meat-packing company christened its journal *The Squeal,* and in the lumber industry one could find *The Log* and *The Hardwood Bark.* One soap company attempted to combine both worlds by titling its magazine *The Family Wash.*[37]

Some company magazines rejected the subtle approach in order to promote more specific goals than just vaguely building contentment. One such goal was efficiency, and editors occasionally reminded employees of the value of eliminating waste and tardiness. Halcomb Steel Company's magazine cheered assiduously for more attention to safety in the mill. Others exhorted employees to sleep long hours, to spend little on amusement, to avoid unscrupulous moneylenders, or to buy company products. Sears, Roebuck advised readers to substitute the twin virtues of diligence and thrift for the twin evils of drinking and smoking.[38]

But most company editors preferred the indirect method of conveying their social message. A 1922 report by the National Personnel Association, in fact, showed that editors treated frank discussion of controversial topics much like a cat treats water. A survey of 300 employee magazines found only three that even mentioned the wage disputes arising during the depression year of 1921. The soft sell, however, in no way nullified the social content of employee magazines. "Call it education or propaganda or what not," a former Eastman Kodak editor told his colleagues, "a continuous campaign of thought direction is necessary . . . in order to produce the greatest degree of loyalty and efficiency." Though he believed that "internal industrial propaganda" could be "exceedingly worthwhile," he criticized his fellow "industrial propagandists" (as he called them) for straying from the subtle approach and becoming too earnest in "combating radical agitators." Behind the trivia and folksy humor of employee magazines, a design existed which belied their light-hearted nature.[39]

7 Religion

Had Marx lived to witness the fruition of American welfare capitalism, he might have found a sour satisfaction in at least one of its aspects. When he wrote that religion was the opiate of the people, Marx meant that, like a drug, religion soothed the hardships of life; but in part he meant that rulers used religion to pacify the ruled. And surely enough, though their motives did not always conform to the Marxian view, the welfare capitalists made encouragement of religion one of their most popular concerns.

This interest was first concretely manifested in Samuel Slater's Sunday school, and in 1826, when the Merrimack Manufacturing Company built its famous textile mill at Lowell, Massachusetts, it followed Slater's example by building a stone church costing nine thousand dollars. But this early enterprise in religious management was subverted by the ineptitude of the mill supervisor, Kirk Boott. This ex-British Army officer determined that the church would be Episcopalian for the excellent reason that he was of that faith, and he decreed that each worker must attend services and pay 37.5 cents a month toward church support. Unfortunately, most of them were not Episcopalian, and though Boott apparently felt that this mattered little, the arrangement was terminated.[1]

George Pullman was no Kirk Boott; he cared little about doctrinal matters and attended the services of several different Protestant denominations. As a good businessman, he recognized the waste and loss of having a separate building for each sect, so in 1882 he constructed in his model town the Greenstone church, meant to house all the community's denominations. It was a symbol of efficiency, but not in a mean sense, for it was large and ornate, more elaborate and beautiful than any of the separate sects could afford, befitting the importance Pullman placed on religion. But if Boott's workers refused to be parochial, Pullman's refused to be ecumenical, especially when the rent called for 6 percent interest on the initial investment. Pullman's attempt, too, was a failure.[2]

But these failures did not dissuade other American businessmen who enthusiastically boosted religion in several ways. The most modest were shop Bible classes, often conducted by the Young Men's Christian Association. In 1904, according to the YMCA, 175 factories in 115 cities held Bible classes, with noon and midnight meetings drawing an average attendance of 25,000.[3] But many a businessman went much further, donating or leasing land for churches, sometimes building one or more church buildings, paying part or all of one or more clergymen, even building parsonages.

Sincere Christian benevolence notwithstanding, such acts were not without potential earthly reward. On the one hand, involvement in the worker's religion offered a new means of appraising his thoughts—either directly, as in teaching Sunday school, which many company presidents did, or through the clergy, the company could take the employees' pulse. "It is a great thing to keep in touch with the priests and clergy," Judge Elbert H. Gary advised presidents of U.S. Steel subsidiaries. "The pastors are in contact with the families and the workmen themselves."[4]

Simple alliance could be a force in itself, the opposite of guilt by association. After all, a company which supported Christianity could not be all bad, and when the company had built the church and the rectory and paid the pastor, it could become difficult to tell where the company left off and Christianity began. And how could a line be drawn between the domineering employer of the weekdays and the man who on Sundays worshipped with his employees as an equal in the eyes of God? Surely an important man who sacrificed his own leisure time to teach Sunday school for his workers must be concerned for them. And surely such a godly, Christian man would do right by his employees as far as wages, promotions, and dismissals were concerned. Why, then, would anyone need to seek protection against him, such as in unions?

Sometimes association became identification; the company became the church, as when faith and obedience to God were translated into loyalty to the company. Prayerful slogans tacked to the walls of a New York company beseeched the Lord to "keep this man such as he was by nature, Reverent, Faithful, High, Unterrified, Unshaken of Passion, Untroubled," and to "teach us to be kind before we are critical, and sympathetic before we condemn."[5] Thus not only joining a union but also a grudging acceptance of orders, a frequent changing of jobs, a demand for wage increases could be translated as forms of disloyalty—and not simply to the company, but to a higher power.

American religion was not simply a passive instrument, however, and business found little to oppose and much to encourage in its teachings. Churches could, for instance, be a tangential aid in "Americanizing" foreign-born workmen. A high-level executive of United States Steel made the point succinctly: immigrants, he said, arrived with such "undesirable" customs as doing their laundry in rivers and streams, sleeping on porches, poorly furnishing and overcrowding their houses, eating from a common dish—but churches, schools, and company policy taught them to beautify their homes with carpets and better furniture, to avoid overcrowding, to prepare "better" meals, thus making them better people, more American. Like the company library, the company church offered an alternative to the saloon, but again there was no need to be passive about it, as one Indiana businessman recognized. Concerned with excessive drinking among his men, he hired a minister to preach temperance at weekly meetings in the plant (with little success).[6]

The churches did not need such special invitations to be articulated with business, however; even left to themselves, they constituted a force of general support for the owners and managers. Almost all emphasized the virtues of faith and obedience, for instance, and most preached that one must be grateful for what one had, rather than complain and ask for more. They demanded patience with maladjustment, whether social or economic. Most of them promised a better life to come and helped to take men's minds off the present moment. At the very least, American churches of the time seldom produced, and commonly undermined, the psychological posture necessary to be contentious, to make demands, to unionize.[7]

If the businessman considered almost all Christian denominations his friends, his darlings were certain "fundamentalist" sects, particularly in the South. Most Protestant groups there, rooted in the poverty of the area, were well equipped to help mitigate the hardships of industrialization. Moreover, the special emphases of some of the largest churches and the tiniest Bible-reading groups spoke powerfully in favor of the employer and against the union.

For example, some groups distrusted many modern recreational activities such as dancing, cardplaying, motion pictures, and, of course, liquor. In fact they were suspicious of leisure itself; the more time spent on working, they felt, the less time was available to do the devil's business: "Idleness is the devil's workshop." This was particularly useful for business in the case of child labor, for parents could be led to believe that children running loose were easy targets for such engines of the devil as jukeboxes.[8]

According to Christian doctrine, faith is the center of man's purpose on earth; evangelical sects in particular demanded single-minded devotion and were jealous of other suitors, such as unions. The jealousy was not simply of the spirit: a worker could hardly attend a prayer meeting when he was off somewhere listening to union organizers. If the Christian religion was otherworldly in its concerns, evangelicalism was so with a vengeance. Some evangelists, for instance, strove to free themselves from the lusts of the flesh and the love of luxury, denying the value of earthly goods and riding toward an ideal future on such hymns as "Cabin in the Sky," "Beulah Land," "A Land that is Fairer than Day," "Beautiful Isle of Somewhere," and "Where Sickness and Death Never Come." Others, sometimes labeled "pessimistic sects," even taught that social progress was impossible in the temporal world, thus making unions irrelevant. A CIO organizer bitterly pointed out that, in denouncing material values, such sects implicitly made suffering a positive virtue.[9]

Even psychologically, evangelicalism could be an ally to business since it was invariably associated with emotionalism and so tended to drain off enthusiasm which might otherwise have been directed to labor's cause. Of course too much of a good thing can be bad: southern businessmen sometimes condemned the charismatics (who spoke in "tongues" and believed in visions and trances) and the adventists (who insisted on the immediate preparation for the imminent return of Christ). Businessmen lumped these groups together calling them "holy rollers" and complaining that their meetings became so fervent and boisterous that worshippers "stay up half the night and go to sleep on the job the next day."[10] These were the only such groups opposed by business, and it is not surprising that American business support of religion was strongest in the South.

Even left to its own devices, Christianity encouraged those qualities in employees which businessmen found desirable: temperance, frugality, honesty, discipline, industriousness, loyalty (to the company), and independence (from unions). That is why one southern textile mill owner said that he preferred his workers uneducated but very religious. Dr. Richard W. Corwin, of Colorado Fuel and Iron, had these qualities in mind when he tried to make certain that his company's towns avoided "the cheap missionary who is going off on a tangent," and tried to get only "the best men" so that services would "appeal to the best element in the mining camps." These qualities were summed up by businessmen in one of their favorite words: "character." Religion built character, and, as the head of welfare work for a New York firm put it, "from the president of the Company to the most humble 'sweeper-up', *character largely determines efficiency*." A man at the top could see the matter in larger perspective and could afford to put it in homelier, more charming terms: "Christian brotherhood," said William Cooper Procter, of Procter and Gamble, "helps a man to fill up his obligations."[11]

As already noted, business was not about to leave religion to its own devices. Although it was a ready-made influence for building the kind of character businessmen wanted, it could be made more effective with the right kind of support and direction. Nor were all its forms beneficial; so powerful a social organism had to be carefully managed so that its undesirable tendrils might be controlled and cropped as necessary. Many companies, then, made money available for churches and meeting houses. For instance, one study of North Carolina textile mills found that 258 of 322 mills aided churches financially on one or more occasions, and an investigation of twelve representative coal companies in West Virginia noted that in every single company town, the company had either built a church or offered use of the schoolhouse for religious meetings. In some cases, the ready availability of company funds for building meeting houses caused them to proliferate, leading one visitor to assert that many company towns were "overchurched." Perhaps so. The Pelzer Manufacturing Company built five churches for the six thousand citizens of Pelzer, South Carolina, its wholly-owned company town. Then there was the Delta and Pine Land Company, quite possibly the largest provider of sustenance for the laborer's soul, which put up no fewer than thirty-one churches on its sixty thousand acres of rich alluvial soil between Vicksburg and Memphis.[12] But most business leaders shared in Pullman's view and looked askance at the idea of providing a separate structure for each doctrinal splinter; one building seemed perfectly sufficient and, the failure of the Greenstone church notwithstanding, a single structure most often served all denominations and in some cases did double duty as community hall or school.

Wall signs could help build character, of course, but they were hardly a substitute for services, and services attended were more useful than services unattended, so company control was sometimes put to work to assure punctual attendance. One textile worker testified before a congressional committee that in several mills a worker who did not show up for services on Sunday was fired on Monday. In some cases, the pressure on attendance bore a closer resemblance to the carrot than to the stick. Consider the miners of Knightsville, Utah, Mormons all, who were actually paid to attend services. "Uncle Jesse" Knight, ruler of the Juab County town, closed his mine on Sunday and paid his workers an extra twenty-five cents a day to make up for the lost salary. Though apparently benevolent, however, Uncle Jesse was not likely to smile at an absence from church service. Jesse Knight was also a reflection of the fact that for some businessmen, such involvement sprang from deeply personal religious conviction.[13]

The "holy rollers" were not the only disrupters of character building. Factional rivalries between otherwise "acceptable" sects caused divisiveness in communities and undermined the stability so valued by business leaders. Protestant denominations in small towns especially had been noted for the heat generated by their conflicts. One means of lessening jealousies was the provision of a single church for all groups, but businessmen were not above direct intercession. One manager went so far as to order a clergyman to cooperate with a denomination whose practices the minister opposed, and when the man refused, the company demanded that he vacate his house, stating that it was needed for a company official. In fact the evicted minister's replacement was not given that house—the company gave him a better one.[14]

Company control of the pastorate was not often so ostentatiously muscular; it did not have to be. The company superintendent who taught Sunday school or attended services could, by his very presence, be a formidable symbol of the limits of the pastor's temptations. Moreover, company officials often held important positions in the lay structure of the church and could thus undermine the position of the pastor by creating dissension within the congregation.

But the sole fact that a clergyman's church received a subsidy either of land, building, or expenses placed him in the company's debt and weakened his independence, sometimes quite sufficient unto the purpose. In his careful study of the steel industry, David Brody argues that subsidization created a sense of dependence that was enough to align clergymen and YMCA men with company interests. Other industries were similar. One clergyman who had served a congregation in a company town during a strike told an investigator from the U.S. Commission on Industrial Relations that the subsidy "served as a strong bribe to keep the churches in line. . . . My own treasurer always kept his keen eye on this two hundred dollars in trying to guide the church affairs."[15]

The velvet glove could come off, if need be, in cases of emergency; the most frequent warning signal of need was unionism, and the most provocative sign of emergency, the strike. After the Roman Catholic priest of a Pennsylvania coal town began to attend union meetings, the town's owners, a Bethlehem Steel subsidiary, cut off both the water and electricity in his parochial school. In another Pennsylvania town, in 1911, a sympathetic pastor had his hands full trying to bury a striker killed by a company-paid deputy sheriff. He finally managed to lay the body in church ground donated by the company, but only after a two-day delay forced by the company's insistence that the deed forbade the use of the churchyard for a cemetery and its dispatch of deputies to prevent the burial.[16]

When company subsidies extended to a clergyman's salary, control was even more effective. One North Carolina textile mill, for example, paid the salary of its minister only so long as he held services in the company chapel. The businessman's confidence in the scope such control gave him is reflected in a letter to a company attorney from J. F. Welborn, president of Colorado Fuel and Iron. About the company's minister in Sunrise, Wyoming, Welborn wrote, "he has socialistic tendencies, . . . and I have been informed that his wife is a Greek. . . . We have thought some of changing [him]." The minister's real crime had been to speak out against the company after the bloody strike at Ludlow, Colorado, in 1914. The sentence was not carried out, however, for Welborn admitted that in spite of their un-American tendencies, the couple "may both be perfectly honest"; more tellingly, the minister "seemed to regret his action when informed of the facts concerning the disturbance."[17]

Neither so repentant nor so lucky was the Reverend W. Gilbert

Nowell, pastor of the Fawcett Methodist Episcopal Church at Hill Station, Pennsylvania, a town owned by the Pittsburgh Coal Company. When Nowell became pastor in 1926, he received the customary rent-free use of a company house and free coal with which to heat it. The following year a strike occurred, and while he did not speak out from the pulpit, Nowell sympathized with the strikers and openly conversed with members of his congregation on their picket line. Hearing of this, the local mine superintendent called Nowell into his office and demanded that he remain entirely neutral. The pastor refused, saying, "There is no neutrality in me, I am on either one side or the other, and I am on the side of organized labor." What followed was disputed—Nowell claimed that he was given ten days to vacate his house, and the company denied that such short notice was given—but the eviction itself was undisputed, and when Nowell made it public, the company threatened to fire any nonunion parishioner who attended his services.[18]

It might have been difficult for Reverend Nowell to remain neutral even had he wanted to be, for clergy and company did not always agree on the definition of "neutrality." Lead, South Dakota, was one of the largest company towns in the United States, owned by the Homestake Mining Company, which contributed annually to each of its churches. Roman Catholic Bishop Joseph Busch arrived there in 1905 to assume his first diocese, intending "to keep neutral as far as possible." For Busch, neutrality meant that while he would roundly denounce the radical Western Federation of Miners (which he equated with "socialism, anarchy, and irreligion"), he would also tell the miners that he thought they deserved a union. A month later, when a diptheria epidemic struck, the company closed all the churches but not the post office and railroad station. Asking the local health officer about the apparent inconsistency, Busch was referred to mine superintendent T. J. Grier (an Episcopalian), who warned him of his preaching and complained, as Busch recalled, that rather than remaining neutral, the Bishop was "trying to carry water on both shoulders."[19]

Busch's experiences in Lead constitute an enlightening illustration of what might happen when a powerful church and a powerful company collided in the company town. After the diptheria episode, Busch and Grier clashed again, this time over the closing of the mines on Sunday. Grier argued that the mines should remain open, thereby protecting the men's morals by keeping them out of the saloons; Bishop Busch countered that both the mines and saloons should be closed so that the men could attend mass. Grier refused to close the mines but ordered shift bosses to allow men to attend mass "without prejudice." This was unsatisfactory to Busch, however, as his parishioners distrusted the company's ability to prevent its foremen from discriminating against massgoers and were suspicious of the company's sincere desire in the matter. Busch organized a campaign to force Sunday closing but it failed for lack of support from the town newspaper, which, of course, was company dominated. Thoroughly beaten, Bishop Busch resigned and left town, but not before he struck a final jab by getting a Catholic member of the state legislature to introduce a bill requiring Sunday closing. It was a futile gesture, easily fended off by a Homestake lobbyist.[20] Though companies preferred to maintain small, easily managed religious groups and obviously did not relish battles against any sect, such was the power of a company when it owned a town that, in a showdown, it could defeat even the largest church.

One minister who was brave enough to criticize in subtle manner company dominance over the town became fearful when an investigator for the Commission on Industrial Relations asked to see a copy of the sermon. Afraid the government man might be a company spy, the clergyman declined to give him any information until the official displayed his credentials and travel account book. After several more assurances, he gave the investigator a copy of the sermon, but he was back in less than half an hour "very much frightened" and asked for the copy, explaining that there were only a limited number available.[21] The lessons of Bishop Busch and Reverend Nowell, of the lay organizations sprinkled with company officials, of the rent-free house, the salary, the two-hundred dollar subsidy, of the visage of the company executive in the first pew—these became a text in which the clergy could read of the power and the wrath of the company, much as they saw reflected in the Old Testament the power and wrath of God.

Recreation

It seems eminently logical that the American businessman, devoted as he was to the glorification of hard work, should be less than enthusiastic about the promotion of leisure-time activities. Men who loved to speak of "the dignity of labor" and "the value of honest toil" could well be expected to be indifferent about workers' recreation—or even hostile toward some types of it. In 1851 South Carolina textile manufacturer William Gregg forced the owner of the local dance hall to stop renting the hall for dances and threatened to fire any of his female employees who attended a dance. Dancing, said Gregg, had an "injurious tendency upon the morality and good order of the village."[1]

The apparent fitness of the attitude is what makes surprising the fact that businessmen of the early twentieth century devoted a good deal of money and effort encouraging their employees to participate in a wide variety of recreational activities: a 1916 Bureau of Labor survey of 431 firms in a variety of industries disclosed that more than half provided outdoor recreational activity on a regular basis, more than a third offered indoor facilities, and by 1926, at least 1.3 million workers had recreational facilities provided by their companies. Most of these were large companies (firms offering outdoor recreation facilities averaged 4,100 employees, according to one study), but many were small—they included about half of all the small coal companies in West Virginia, for example. In fact, perhaps more than any other welfare activity, recreation received support in both large and small companies in both large and small towns.[2]

The large companies in particular offered extensive programs and facilities—United States Steel, for instance, operated more than 125 children's playgrounds, while east of Pittsburgh alone, the Pennsylvania Railroad had thirty-two baseball fields, thirty-three tennis courts, seven athletic tracks, and a golf course. In its park site called "Hills and Dales," National Cash Register had children's play apparatus, croquet, quoits, a wading pool, refreshment stands, camping grounds, tennis courts, a golf course, pool tables, a basketball court, a dance hall (doubtless to the discomfiture of some), and an amphitheater. Indoor facilities alone could be quite extensive; in 1905, the Ludlow Manufacturing Associates, a textile firm, erected an employee clubhouse which included a theater, gymnasium and dance hall, poolroom, bowling alley, card and smoking rooms, baths and swimming pool, and locker rooms. This was more elaborate than the hundreds of other such facilities throughout the country, but it was not atypical.[3]

A transformation had taken place: the indifference or obstructionism of a Gregg at mid-nineteenth century gave way to the early experiments in recreation of the eighties, notably George Pullman's work, which included the Pullman Athletic Club, incorporated in 1881, as well as the company teams, the chess and whist club, the choral society, and the Pullman military band. Following on Pullman's heels came the Millville, New Jersey, company club, providing facilities for roller skating, baseball, bicycling, track and field, and choral singing, and the annual company picnics of the National Transit Company, beginning in 1886.[4] By the turn of the century, these seeds had flowered into an established feature of welfare capitalism.

Part of this change in attitude perhaps owed itself to a form of *noblesse oblige*, a sense of responsibility to meet the needs of the worker. The dislocation of the worker, particularly from country to city, left him without the more familiar forms of rural recreation: harvest gatherings, "raising" of new houses, or hunting. No doubt some employers felt the responsibility for replacing the loss. But necessity went far deeper than that, and one did not have to be ethically concerned to see the need. The laborer may have worked long and hard in the mine or the factory but he was not exhausted; on the contrary, for many, factory work compounded by the hectic pace of city life made existence positively nerve-racking and made release in leisure an inescapable drive. The worker had some free time; the question was not whether he was going to use it, but how, and some of the ways were considerably more threatening to the welfare of the company than dancing. Just sitting around grumbling about the company was bad enough, but there was also the possibility of drinking, along with all its usual accompaniments, including brawling, being less efficient on the job, thieving and general troublemaking in the town, or even union organizing. Even if one could effectively ban a certain activity, as Gregg tried to do, there were simply too many activities with potential danger—like the boy at the dike, one would not have enough fingers; water would pour through somewhere. The sensible thing was to find an acceptable alternative for the unacceptable. Thus, an executive of Ellsworth Collieries, objecting to the "immorality" of "rag-time" music, arranged matters so that local dances were furnished music by the company band, which played only classical works.[5]

The people at Ellsworth found that, to call the tune, you had to pay the piper; employers elsewhere discovered that they would have to pay the piper in any case. Especially in the cities, finding means of recreation was becoming more and more a public responsibility, but if the burden were assumed by local government, the required higher taxes would mean that the company would wind up financing recreation anyway—and subsidizing nonemployees as well. Moreover, they would not necessarily be calling the tune: public administration was likely to be slower and less efficient than desired, and recreational outlets might be other than those wished for.

Companies began to organize programs to rescue the worker from the evils of leisure. Baseball teams, like libraries and churches, were partly intended to substitute for the saloon. Children's playgrounds, similarly, functioned to "get the boys off the streets," where they were supposedly easy prey for such wickedness as vice and gambling. Many companies sponsored Boy Scout troops and other children's clubs for just this reason. Any of those evil "influences," as they were often called, was likely to ruin a productive worker.[6] As an antidote for grumbling and complaining, there were movies, whose hypnotic powers were soon recognized: "We have them every day at noon hour. They are remarkably successful. There is something about the movies that the employees can't resist. Even if they think that you are trying to put something over on them, they come in anyway. In this way, we fill up the employees' time during the noon hour and keep them from getting together in little groups and talking about their troubles."[7]

But all this does not account for the scope of company involvement or the enthusiasm with which employers dove into recreation. There was nothing the American businessman was more proud of than his resourcefulness and nothing he liked better than to turn a required expense into a smart profit. In the field of worker recreation, he quickly saw that he could do much more than simply substitute a baseball bat for a gin bottle. Necessity can also be the mother of opportunity.

For one thing, recreation could become a form of advertisement. It did no harm, for instance, to have the Pullman athletic teams perform throughout the Midwest, or to have Chicago parade watchers become familiar with the nattily attired Pullman military band. Nor was the appeal necessarily limited to the buying public; teams and bands could also be used as forms of recruitment. The recreation director of the Wagner Electric Manufacturing Company in Saint Louis likened the company athletic program to those in colleges: if athletic programs could make colleges famous and attract students, they could work similarly for businesses.[8]

In fact, such recruitment programs were like those in the universities: they were often designed not so much to attract and keep good workers as to get and hold good athletes and musicians. Athletes had no difficulty finding employment at Pullman, and in many companies baseball players received preference in hiring, greater job security, travel expenses, and time off for games. In some mining companies skilled musicians got soft jobs, and Bethlehem Steel treated its ninety-piece military band royally: the director's office in the luxurious "Band Home" had handpainted, imported wallpaper, and the bandsmen reclined in leather chairs. Several companies had paid music directors; a North Carolina textile firm even imported a full-time director from Italy. Nor was such professionalism limited to musicians; when athletic teams competed with opponents from other companies or other departments within a large company, there was often much discussion about whether players actually worked at a particular job and for how long.[9]

Such arrangements could work at cross-purposes with other company goals, of course. The well-treated mine musicians came to be known by their fellow workers as "gob-roosters," a term whose origin is blurred though its meaning is clearly disparaging, and favoritism toward athletes occasionally bred resentment among other employees, sometimes bringing quick action from company officials to end the preferential treatment.[10]

Just as the company could associate itself with Christianity in subsidizing religion, so could it associate itself with the nation and boost "Americanism" by supporting certain forms of recreational activity. The connection could be quite nominal and hazy—"Athletics mean competition, and competition is the very lifeblood of the American system," wrote one enthusiastic recreation director to a group of Flint, Michigan, businessmen—but it was frequently carried to much more substantial lengths. The most prevalent kinds of patriotic recreation were military drill classes, most of them involving the younger employees and children. National Cash Register organized three companies of the United Boys Brigade of America, a major boys' organization. The boys wore military-type uniforms and drilled regularly with wooden rifles. In summer they went on a kind of bivouac where they learned woodcraft, heard campfire stories, and marched. Similar organizations were called the Junior Army or the Cadet Regiment. Goodyear Rubber Company had "Companies X and Y" of the "Executive Drill Class," a group of company officials who met and drilled together; Company X was commanded by the factory manager, Company Y by the production superintendent. At least twenty firms had rifle clubs where employees could practice marksmanship and, presumably, prepare to defend the country.[11]

A quasi-patriotic kind of recreation was the company field day. Typically an annual summer event, often held on the Fourth of July to emphasize the patriotic flavor, the company-sponsored field day included such activities as sports and athletics, picnics, and, in particular, parades, sometimes very elaborate affairs. The line of marchers at the 1918 "Schoolfield Patriotic Pageant," sponsored by Dan River Mills, included the Red Cross, Garden Boys, Junior Army, Mothers' Club, Odd Fellows, Red Men, the mill employees by department, and finally, "loyal citizens." In 1900 National Cash Register devoted an entire week to a Fourth of July celebration which culminated in a procession to "Far Hills," the home of president John H. Patterson. It was a stars-and-stripes extravaganza, led off by the twenty-four-piece NCR Band, followed, in order, by the officers of the company, foreign delegates, district managers (each carrying an American flag), factory girls carrying red, white, and blue umbrellas, and, bringing up the rear, factory workers uniformed in gray suits and wearing broadbrimmed straw hats draped with the American flag.[12]

The obvious advantage of these activities was the patriotic public image of the company which they produced but that was not the only or even the most significant result. Far more important was the effect it had on the workers themselves. For one thing, of course, recruitment in such activities was relatively easy; quite aside from the intrinsic attraction of the particular events, reluctance to become involved could all too easily be interpreted as a lack of proper patriotism. More positively, association could become at times a form of identification; just as support of religion could lead to identification of company and church, so support of patriotism could result in identification of company and country, and as obedience to God could be transferred in part to obedience to employer, so might loyalty to the nation be partially transferable. If a company was helping to train militia in defense of the country, then the company could be seen as a complement to the U.S. Army or the National Guard and disloyalty to the company might become a kind of disloyalty to America. Indeed, even the titles of the various groups reflected the implication of national connection; the Dan River Mills band, for example, was officially named the "Riverside and Dan River Coast Artillery Band." Showing the colors was a favorite form of patriotic identification and some companies embraced the flag as closely as possible. Dwight Manufacturing, the Alabama textile firm, distributed a hundred American flags to employees. During World War I, a tanning company placed two American flags on each of its machines to remind workers of their patriotic duty to produce. It was also apparently their duty to limit toilet time, as the company placed nine American flags in the washroom. One of the most obvious signs of intended union was the joining or contiguous placement of the separate symbols, as in the common practice of flying flags side by side or on the same flagpole. The Sherwin-Williams Company, Cleveland paint manufacturer, elaborated on this idea; in its lunchroom was an American flag surrounded by four company flags.[13]

Attractive as the element of patriotism was, the fine thing about recreation was that it did not depend solely on that aspect to induce loyalty to the company. For instance, while the field day was more often than not related to nationalism in some way, company outings themselves, quite apart from that connection, could create a sense of unity in the company family. Everyone there could play baseball with the boss or march by his side, forgetting class and ethnic loyalties. At company outings, explained the Sherwin-Williams Company, "all differences of factory rank are for the time being forgotten, and members of the firm, managers, superintendents, foremen, and the ordinary employees, with their families, meet on terms of absolute equality." Goodyear billed its annual field day as "a real Labor Day bringing men and managers in close contact. They are all hard workers. Is it not better than a street parade, encouraging class distinctions?" Apparently it did not occur to these businessmen that assimilation might be counterproductive; in other words, if diverse nationalities learned to cooperate on the ball fields, they might also learn to cooperate in forming a union. Music, the only "common language" of diverse racial and ethnic groups, made a "great social cement."[14]

As in high schools and colleges, the successful athletic teams and well-known bands could create a sense of pride in connection even for those not directly involved. This is no doubt what the Wagner Electric recreation director meant when he spoke of bringing college spirit to his factory. The parallel was carried out in some rather remarkable ways. For instance, some companies awarded sweaters emblazoned with the factory letter to skilled athletes. The relationship of company song to school song is clearly indicated by Charles R. Hook, general superintendent of the American Rolling Mill Company, who explained that during his college days the school song had given "that indescribable something that makes men take a greater interest in their studies for the sake of 'the good old school.' " Hook felt that a company song could induce an equivalent spirit among his employees: "The something tells us, after all, that we are all brothers, no matter what our positions may be."[15] Even if one knew that Amoskeag was the name of a manufacturing company, one would find it hard to believe that the following (sung to the tune of "Maryland, My Maryland") could be anything other than a school song:

Through all the years thy name has stood
   Amoskeag, old Amoskeag.
For honest worth and nation's good
   Amoskeag, old Amoskeag.
When threatening storms and foes arise
To dim thy splendor, dwarf thy size,
Thy stalwarts will not yield the prize
   Amoskeag, old Amoskeag.
Thy breaking dawn reveals the way
   Amoskeag, our Amoskeag.
Co-operation wins the day
   Amoskeag, our Amoskeag.[16]

On the other hand, the words of the Dan River Mills song (to the same tune, which was quite popular in company songs) make rather more explicit both the object of adoration and the goals aimed at:

No more we'll toil by rule of might
  At Schoolfield and Riverside
We shall live the rule of right
  At Schoolfield and Riverside.

. . . .

Some day each brother's toil shall cease,
From work in rest shall find release,
Till then we'll have Industrial peace
  At Schoolfield and Riverside.[17]

A central function of company recreation, then, was indoctrination. Like company-supported education and religion, recreation could be used to imbue the worker with the right attitude, to help build and strengthen "character." A McCormick welfare executive stated the matter plainly: "An organization for purposes of recreation, loafing, physical comfort, merely, with no propaganda or serious purpose, would deteriorate in a very short time and would be, socially, quite as obnoxious and worthless as any other loafing-place."[18]

The values to be taught were of course those which led to loyalty to the company; in a broader sense, they were elements which composed in part what businessmen defined as Americanism, elements which, not incidentally, tended to make life easier and if possible more profitable for the employer, and harder, if not impossible, for the unions.

9 Profit Sharing and Stock Ownership Plans

Profit sharing was hardly a new idea in mid-nineteenth century America. One did not have to go back to the Roman Empire when slaveowners attempted to revitalize an inefficient economy by granting a share of profits to slaves as an incentive for increased production; sharecropping and the payment to hired fishermen according to a proportion of the catch were long-established forms in the country by the 1880s. Still, profit sharing in industry was practically nonexistent mainly because most businessmen wanted no part of it; in their view, profits belonged wholly to those who took the investment risks.[1] In fact, profit sharing was so rare in the United States in the 1880s that the usage of the term encompassed the entire spectrum of welfare activities from libraries to Thanksgiving turkeys. It was not until the first decade of the twentieth century that profit sharing came to mean a bonus in excess of wages paid at regular (usually annual) intervals. Even then, bonus payments and stock ownership programs for employees were often lumped together as "profit sharing."

Yet in terms of numbers of participants, profit sharing and stock ownership became the most popular of welfare activities. By the nineties two dozen companies were engaged in profit sharing programs, and in 1892 the Association for the Promotion of Profit Sharing was formed. After a lull caused in part by the depression of the period, Procter and Gamble, United States Steel, and International Harvester spearheaded a drive that saw some 250 companies involved in either profit sharing or stock ownership plans by the time of America's entrance into World War I, and that growth could only be called moderate in comparison with the explosion which followed. For of those 250, only 60 were involved in stock ownership plans; by 1921, the latter number had nearly doubled, and during the next six years, it grew to almost 400. Workers at Bethlehem Steel alone owned $40 million of company stock, while every one of the 14,000 people working for Firestone Tire and Rubber was a stockholder. A survey of 315 companies showed that about a third of their employees owned company stock, amounting to at least $1 billion. One educated estimate held that at the high point, 6.5 million manual workers owned stock worth approximately $5 billion.[2]

One obvious reason for the explosive growth of profit sharing and stock ownership plans was the psychology of the bandwagon. Important men and influential companies were early signers—N. O. Nelson and Procter and Gamble in the eighties, U.S. Steel, the first billion-dollar corporation, in 1902 (five companies copied the U.S. Steel plan verbatim),[3] and International Harvester in 1906. Not insignificantly, the designer of both the U.S. Steel and the Harvester plans, George Perkins, became head of the profit sharing division of the National Civic Federation. Businessmen were not likely to ignore the voices of Elbert Gary, Cyrus McCormick, Jr., or Andrew Carnegie.

There were, for the businessmen, other motives, spoken and unspoken, rationalized and real, selfish and unselfish, which led them away from the total opposition of the eighties to the almost total acceptance of the twenties. One of these—the one most commonly associated with the adoption of a profit sharing plan in preference to a stock ownership plan—was that of the Romans: increased efficiency. Tie the worker's compensation more closely to production—let him share in the profits—and, perceiving that his income could be increased by diligent effort, he would work harder.

The company which refined this technique to the highest degree was the Dan River Mills, the North Carolina textile firm. Each employee received an "efficiency dividend" based on the cost per pound of producing textiles. The system worked well when production and profits were normal; in fact, it may have worked according to theory, stimulating individual output. But the crippling flaw showed up in bad times when market demand fell off. Then, in spite of the employees' efforts, looms idled, production slackened, labor costs crept up, and workers lost their dividends through no fault of their own.[4] The simple fact was that in tying wages to profits, the system related the worker's income to the influence of the market, and its fluctuations had a much more significant impact than individual productivity could possibly have. The only way to avoid this result was to loosen the relationship between market and wages by keeping a large proportion of wages free of the profit tie. Thus profit sharing payments were seldom an important portion of an employee's wage and were seldom paid more than once a year. This of course undermined the incentive function. It is no wonder that very few companies claimed a measurable improvement in productivity after introducing a profit sharing plan.

But American businessmen confronted problems which Roman slaveowners seldom or never faced: labor unrest, labor turnover, and, particularly after 1917, the black cloud of Bolshevism. If profit sharing was not very good at increasing productivity, it might be refined and improved and put to use in dealing with these problems. Payment of an annual bonus was, in effect, a means of deferring compensation. Thus profit sharing was attractive as a disciplinary device, a carrot held out to encourage longevity. Profit sharing plans made it possible to distinguish between the good workers who were invited to participate and the poor workers who were not invited. Often automatically included in the latter category were strikers and unionists. It was only after N. O. Nelson's plumbing business had suffered heavy losses because of railroad strikes that Nelson introduced profit sharing in 1886, and Procter and Gamble's involvement followed hard on the heels of fourteen strikes against the company, all occurring the same year.[5]

There was another more provocative reason for profit sharing, one partially reflected in the plans which distinguished good workers from bad. Beyond the promise of increased profits or the avoidance of strikes, profit sharing was seen by some businessmen as one more possible means of human and social engineering. Strikes and unionism could be viewed as a threat not only to the individual factories or even the general economy but to the whole capitalist system, even to Christian humanism. The bad worker might not be simply an obstruction to productivity; he might be, seen in the proper light, a bad human being, a bar to all that was good. Thus N. O. Nelson noted that strikes "pitted one portion of the people against their neighbors, making us a community of enemies at home, hating each other when we should love and serve each other." Thus young William Cooper Procter of Procter and Gamble, who granted his employees Saturday afternoons off without reducing wages, took great satisfaction in the early success of his profit sharing plan, as evidenced in his employees' resolve that "we will not allow any *outside influence* to come between our employers and ourselves, but will work with them for the good of all."[6]

The results of profit sharing measures were not always satisfactory to businessmen. In spite of his initial optimism, for instance, years later William Procter expressed disappointment in the effect of Procter and Gamble's program. While the number of companies taking part in profit sharing had grown to 190 by 1916, some thirty-nine had abandoned plans or programs during the same period. George Perkins, the brilliant U.S. Steel executive, attributed the failures of early profit sharing plans to selfishness on the part of management. Rather than embodying what Perkins called "a true, an honest, and a fair spirit of cooperation," early programs seemed to have "a secret, perhaps an unconscious purpose"—that is, an attempt to get an extraordinary return from the employees. Perkins reasoned that this led inevitably to unfair demands on labor and eventually to the downfall of the profit sharing plan.[7]

Perkins believed that while profit sharing was attractive as an incentive to productivity and loyalty, it was nevertheless a crude tool. As its replacement, he advocated a far more subtle and imaginative plan—stock ownership for rank-and-file employees. The plan Perkins devised for U.S. Steel retained the advantages of profit sharing. In place of an annual bonus, a participant would receive a dividend so the incentive to produce remained. To retain the reward for longevity, Perkins borrowed an idea from the life insurance industry, the "tontine" concept, a type of insurance which gave buyers a special bonus if they kept up payments over a certain period of time (the tontine). Participating U.S. Steel employees were required to make installment payments on their stock purchases for a period of five years. If anyone failed to keep up payments, his dividends reverted to those who had paid regularly. The tontine system thus became a powerful force for stability and permanence of employment.[8]

As a refinement of the profit sharing idea, U.S. Steel's stock ownership venture attempted to break down the polarity between employer and worker. Consistent with its origin, whereby as a holding company it attempted to replace competition among steel companies with "cooperation," the year-old corporation introduced its stock ownership plan in order to put owner and wage earner on the same level, to break down the troublesome distinction between capitalist and laborer. Board Chairman Elbert H. Gary argued that stock ownership "makes the wage earner an actual partner . . . a real capitalist.... They have as keen a desire to see the institutions of this country protected as those who have greater riches, and they may be relied upon to lend their influence and their votes in favor of the protection of property and person." The range and strength of this view may be represented in the person of Clarence J. Hicks, who, speaking as a former executive of International Harvester, Standard Oil of New Jersey, and Industrial Relations Counselors, recalled that stock ownership was the result of "a strong desire to bridge the gap between capital and labor and to make employees part owners of the business."[9]

Implicit in this view was the fear that a worker without a special stake in the capitalist structure could become something worse than a slacker, a unionist, or even a striker; he could become a Communist. F. H. MacPherson, president of the Detroit Sulphite and Pulp Company, alluded to this point when he spoke of the benefits of stock sales to unnaturalized employees. This would give them a stake in America, MacPherson believed, and they would take out citizenship papers. In addition, "they will be the right kind [of American citizen] . . . —they are capitalists." Cyrus McCormick, Jr., was more blunt; he saw stock ownership as a "very practical step toward removing any possible danger of Bolshevism" because it transposed the have-nots "into the class of those who have." In an excess of optimism, the business journal *Commerce and Finance* translated this practical step into a capitalist dream; it declared that stock ownership would turn the country into "a nation of conservative Bourbons." Less euphorically, the *American Mining Congress Journal* stated the hope quite clearly: stock ownership was "a prophylactic against government ownership."[10]

For some employers, the difference between capitalist and non-capitalist went far deeper than simple financial involvement; the true capitalist man embodied a set of characteristics, and like so many other welfare activities, a prime purpose of profit sharing and stock ownership was character development. Instead of relating added pay increments to productivity, employers could relate them to some aspect of "character." For instance, the Thomas G. Plant Company, Boston shoe manufacturers, judged its employees on the bases of "Industry, Attendance, Quality of Work, Cleanliness and Deportment." Those ranking in the upper quartile received an annual bonus of as much as 100 percent, and those in the third and fourth 35 percent and 10 percent respectively. The Hammond Typewriter Company of New York City added to the above criteria such measures as punctuality, zeal and good will, courtesy, patience, and sobriety. By contrast, Procter and Gamble simply denied dividends "for cause." Deliberately vague, "cause" included such things as unreasonable waste and spoilage. One laborer lost his bonus for horseplay; he climbed aboard a locomotive, opened the throttle, and demolished a wall.[11]

Another key component of "character," as businessmen defined the term, was thriftiness. Business often despaired of how their employees spent their money and some hoped that employees who received a sizeable annual bonus or dividend would be more likely to save than would employees who received a slightly increased weekly wage. Not incidentally, workers who lived within their means, who had money in the bank, or who held stock certificates, might be less likely to see the need to strike for higher wages. Stock ownership thus might lead to thriftiness and thriftiness to "independence." Thomas G. Plant, of the Boston shoe company, believed that thriftiness was the highest virtue, and he distinguished some "independent" employees from "troublemakers."[12]

When it came to molding character, however, no businessman matched the ambitious plan of Henry Ford. In 1914 the famous automaker introduced a new wage system under which employees earned a basic hourly rate plus an added profit sharing increment, which in fact was not related at all to the rate of profit but was quite simply a form of increased wage. A worker at the bottom of the wage ladder received a basic rate of 34¢ an hour plus—if he qualified—a "profit sharing" rate of 28.5¢ an hour. (The $5-a-day total was so far above prevailing national rates that it became immediately famous.)

The disadvantage in the agreement was Ford's test for qualification. This included two basic criteria: home conditions and thrift. Regarding home conditions, the company told its employees:

> Employees should not sacrifice their family rights, pleasures and comforts by filling the house with roomers and boarders, nor endanger their children's morals or welfare by allowing them to associate with people about whom they know little or nothing.
>
> Employees should live in clean, well-conducted homes, in rooms that are well lighted and ventilated. Avoid the congested and slum parts of the city. The company will not approve, as profit sharers, men who herd themselves in overcrowded boarding houses which menace their health. . . .
>
> Do not occupy a room in which one other person sleeps, as

> the company is anxious to have its employees live comfortably and under conditions that make for cleanliness, good manhood, and good citizenship.

The requirements for thriftiness were equally stringent. Although varying conditions were taken into account, all employees were expected to save some portion of their wages, and for unmarried men this generally meant all of the "profit sharing" portion, or nearly half the total wage.[13]

Unlike other welfare capitalists who merely hoped wistfully that their programs would improve their employees' character, Ford sought to require that his charges toe the line. Every six months a corps of investigators (400 at first, later reduced to seventy-five) visited the homes of every employee to determine whether the requirements were being met. The visitors recorded such information as age, religion, nationality, language spoken, citizenship status, life insurance in force, and many other points on a lengthy questionnaire. They also observed the employee's habits and the state of his furniture. Among the impressions of habits were such entries as "Drinks and smokes," and "Good; smokes—does not drink"; those on furnishings included "Only bare necessities" and "Well." The investigators made a careful compilation of the employee's financial condition, indicating all savings account entries and debts. Finally, each investigator made remarks and a recommendation for acceptance or rejection as a profit sharer. One employee was rejected for having a houseful of boarders and keeping unsanitary, unkempt conditions (following recommendations, he remodeled his house, evicted his boarders and, incidentally, learned English, took out naturalization papers, and became a "profit sharer"). Others were disqualified for lying, having "domestic troubles," or failing to furnish proof of marriage. In addition, new employees with less than six months' service, men younger than twenty-two, and all women workers were automatically disqualified. For one reason or another, some 28 percent of Ford employees were disqualified during the first two years of the program.[14] Still, the three-quarter remainder could be interpreted as a clear success for "profit sharing" as a tool of human engineering.

Nevertheless, the programs of profit sharing were generally viewed as successful forms of welfare capitalism by businessmen, and for good reason. Aside from the rather questionable success story at Ford and the fact that the country had not gone Communist, there were clear gains. Profit sharing did tend, as employers had hoped, to divert employees' attention from wage questions. Particularly in the case of the programs similar to U.S. Steel's, they also tended to weaken employees' mobility and thus their bargaining power. Although George Perkins denied that unions had anything to do with the stock ownership programs he spoke for, he later praised their effectiveness in terms of "minimizing the strike menace to almost nothing." Finally, there was the public relations value of profit sharing, both generally and for specific purposes. There is evidence, for example, that when Perkins developed the program at International Harvester, one of his motives was to impress President Theodore Roosevelt of the magnanimity of the Harvester Trust and thereby lessen the pressures for prosecution of antitrust law violations.[15]

For some of these reasons and others, profit sharing and stock ownership were not so beneficial to the American worker. For instance, Perkins's tontine plan had other negative effects, aside from its impact on employees' bargaining power. Although an employee could buy fractions of a share in installments, the cost of an $80 share was still too high for those at the lowest wage stratum—unskilled workers making $600 a year. Only 10 percent of these workers joined the plan, and few even of those could afford to keep up the payments for the five-year period, so that many dropped out and their dividends reverted to the better paid members, who were able to stick it out. Thus the name "jackpot bonus," by which it came to be called, was fitting.[16] Since skilled employees tended to receive much larger sums than unskilled employees, either by means of the tontine or by being paid bonuses as percentages of their salaries, a divisive factor entered. Moreover, the advertising value of profit sharing and stock ownership plans had the effect of diverting public attention from questionable management practices. Too, workers could not but resent the intrusions into their lives which plans like Ford's promulgated.

Perhaps the most searching criticism, however, was levied by the philosopher Arthur O. Lovejoy, writing as a contemporary. Profit sharing, he wrote, failed to provide "any solvent formula of distributive justice." In spite of the fact that, according to the general theory of profit sharing, employees deserved their bonuses and were entitled to a share of the profits, the compensation levels were always determined quite arbitrarily by management. Most companies simply announced what portion of net profits would be returned to workers; some simply announced what percentage of annual wage would be paid as a bonus.[17]

There was an element of system in determining these percentages. For instance, the most common means for deciding the workmen's portion of the profits was first to skim off the going market rate for wages (which James M. Gamble of Procter and Gamble called a "reasonable salary"), then the "fair return" for the investors, and then divide the rest among investors and workers. The fair return ranged from the ubiquitous 6 percent which American schoolboys are taught is the definition of a just return, the "commercial rate of interest" used by N. O. Nelson and others, to what Charles A. Pillsbury called "a good round interest." "I shall not state," said the flourmiller, "precisely what rate of interest was adopted as a proper reward of capital but let me say that the percentage was a large enough one to cover safely the contingencies in years in which there might be a loss rather than a profit in business." After capital received its due, the remainder was divided according to different formulas. Some businesses, like Procter and Gamble, assumed that capital and labor had contributed equally to the profits and divided the remainder into two equal shares. Quite typical, on the other hand, was a division based on the ratio of total capital invested to total wages paid during the year. Thus if the total investment in a company was $90,000 and the wages paid in the year were $30,000, investors would receive three-fourths of the remainder and workers one-fourth. This technique nearly always had the effect of weighting the shares heavily on the side of the investors. In any case, however, whatever the system, as regards the fair return to capital or the division of the remainder, labor had no voice in the matter.[18]

Nor was stock ownership a particularly wise investment for the laborer. Workers who joined stock purchase plans placed their savings in the stock of a single company and thereby subjected themselves to too much risk. As the experience of the great stock market crash of 1929 proved, it was highly questionable whether unskilled employees should invest in risky ventures. As for making the shareholder a capitalist, an "actual partner" with his employer, that was almost all glittery talk. Except for the rarest instances, workers never gained more than the tiniest fraction of ownership—according to a 1922 survey by the Federal Trade Commission, employees owned only 1.5 percent of common and 1.9 percent of preferred stock in reporting companies.[19] Even "junior partner" is too lofty a term in such a case.

10 Medical Care

Mines, mills, and factories were exceedingly unsafe places during the early stages of the Industrial Revolution. Toxic chemicals, exposed belts and whirring machines, huge, powerful steam engines, along with the narcotic endless repetition imposed by the mass production process all took a heavy toll. Nevertheless, until about the middle of the nineteenth century, company involvement in employee health and accident care in the United States was a rare thing. For one thing, most Americans blithely entertained the notion that blame for nearly all industrial accidents could be attributed to individual workmen and that these blameworthy individuals ought rightfully to pay the cost of their carelessness. More important, the law was heavily on the side of the employer. He was under a duty to use "reasonable or ordinary care" in seeing to the safety of his employee, but that term was liberally interpreted according to the norms of the time, which were not, to say the least, models of safety. Beyond that, the burden was all on the worker: in most instances, in order to recover for injury, he had to prove that the injury was caused by the intentionally harmful act or negligence of the employer and often that he, the employee, was in *no way* guilty of negligence. (In many cases, "contributory negligence" was a complete defense, with some jurisdictions calling for the plaintiff to prove lack of such negligence.) Finally, the common law did not extend the rights of an injured employee beyond his death; his family could not recover or sue for damages after his death even when the employer was clearly at fault. David Brody has estimated that a steelworker's chance of recovering losses was less than two in a hundred.[1]

But times were changing. From the worker's point of view, by 1900 reform was long overdue, for he was clearly unable to bear the heavy brunt of increasing health hazards. Moreover, the increasing numbers of injuries were making the matter more and more a public concern. Besides the growing public pressures, management had other reasons for becoming interested: the lawsuits were naturally growing more frequent and the matter was patently a source of labor unrest. In terms of the law, the shifting sands were apparent: as early as 1838, Prussia enacted a law making railroads liable to their employees (as well as passengers) for accidents from all causes except acts of God and negligence of the plaintiff, and in 1854 that country further required employers in certain industries to contribute one-half to the sickness association funds formed under local statutes.[2] Even before the passage of the first modern compensation system in Germany in 1884, employers' noninvolvement was necessarily melting and various systems for meeting the problems were taking shape.

By the early 1860s Cornish miners in the copper fields of Michigan had established a system which later spread throughout much of American mining. Each month the mining companies deducted a fixed sum, in return for which a company physician treated the miner and his family. The amount deducted was arbitrarily chosen—a dollar a month for married men and fifty cents for bachelors—yet the technique and the sum nevertheless spread to the rest of the industry and became institutionalized: more than a half-century later, miners from the coal fields of West Virginia to the iron fields of Minnesota were paying the same fees. The plan, usually in much the same form, then spread to other industries, particularly railroading and steelmaking.[3]

As company medicine grew, a more formal approach became prevalent. This was the mutual benefit association, less commonly known as the "establishment fund." One major difference was that instead of providing a company doctor, the companies disbursed funds with which workers could pay for private doctors, hospitals, and medicine. A second main distinction was the method and scope of financing. Instead of the dollar/half-dollar worker fees of the miner systems, dues varied from ten to twenty-five cents a week, averaging about fifty cents a month. More importantly, employers frequently contributed—30 percent of them in 1907, two-thirds in 1926, then slightly less than half in 1931, in the early part of the depression. Some of these contributions were extremely munificent: Eastman Kodak began its fund with a million-dollar contribution; Andrew Carnegie donated four million to begin the fund at Carnegie Steel, and when that became part of United States Steel Corporation, the parent company added another eight million. But these were rarities; to a great extent, company contribution was quite small, averaging in 1907 only $1.81 per member per year. While the Public Health Service did find one company in a 1916 survey that paid the entire cost of its fund, it was the only one of 425 that did. Most companies simply bore the cost of administration—doing the paperwork and giving association officers time off for association tasks.[4]

A third main difference between many mutual benefit associations and the miner system was the business of selective membership. A substantial minority of these plans had restrictive qualifications. Some allowed employees to join only after being employed for a length of time that could extend up to six months; the most frequent waiting period was thirty days. Twenty-two percent had minimum age limits, while 29 percent had maximum-age requirements which prevented middle-aged employees from joining. Some required physical examinations to certify good health, while others charged entrance fees. In 1916, 12 percent excluded women and 8 percent excluded Negroes, the latter figure decreasing to 2 percent in 1931. A few discriminated against foremen, noncitizens, apprentices, union members, or certain nationalities. In addition, in nearly every plan members who resigned their jobs also lost their health coverage. Although other motives are obvious, the overriding one, and the one mentioned most often, was economic. Aside from the debatable assertion that women, Negroes, or noncitizens lost more time by sickness than did young white men, clearly older people got sick more often than younger ones, untrained youngsters were apt to have more accidents than seasoned veterans, and a health certificate was some insurance against early or frequent claims of illness.[5]

The majority of associations, however, had no restrictions on membership, and between 10 and 15 percent even made membership compulsory. Paradoxically, the essential reason for full membership was also economic. The larger the membership, it was reasoned, the cheaper the cost of administration; also, since the purpose of the associations was to distribute the risks of industrial accidents and illnesses more widely, it would appear that the more members there were, the better the principle would operate. Perhaps the reason that there was division on the question of membership was that few of the associations made an actuarial study to determine the proper balance of membership, dues, and company expenses. In any case, those companies which opted for compulsory membership had to wrestle in their corporate consciences with the businessman's creed of individualism, for most businessmen would have felt bound to utter a public "amen" to Stanley McCormick's advice to his brother Cyrus that International Harvester's association ought to be voluntary so as not to affect an employee's wages "independently of his own will." After all, foolish heads might be tempted to draw a parallel between an employee's wages and the businessman's own income. The attempts to resolve the contradiction led to some amusing semantic acrobatics. Some companies simply made membership in the mutual association a condition of employment. That way, an employee joined both the firm and the association "voluntarily." Rather than take that approach, which perhaps smacked a little too much of compulsion, Samuel M. "Golden Rule" Jones delivered this message to his employees: "I believe that I am speaking for a great big majority when I say that any man who works for the Acme Sucker Rod Company ought voluntarily to go into this effort.... I think every fellow should join the Cooperative, or, if he is unwilling to do so, he should quit and let some one have his place who is willing to cooperate."[6]

What made the mutual benefit association so much more complex than the check-off or dues system of the miners was its coverage. Rather than giving a member the cost of medical treatment, it provided a set sum—in 1916 an average of $6.93 a week, which rose to $8.79 by 1931. This usually required a one-week waiting period and, more important, was paid only if the injured person could not work. It covered a duration of from five weeks to three years, with an average of thirteen weeks. A few funds were much more generous—in 1933 the combine of American Telephone and Telegraph, Western Electric, and Western Union, with its $11 million fund, allowed full pay for thirteen weeks in cases of disability and half-pay for thirteen more—but many paid at a very low rate.[7]

The assocations also became the chief medium for paying benefits in case of death. Eighty-three percent paid some kind of death benefit, ranging from $10 to $2000. The American Telephone combine paid a year's wages to the family of the deceased worker, and the few large-scale systems like this one brought the 1917 average to almost $210, but most associations chose the somewhat arbitrary figure of $100 as the appropriate sum, which in 1917 was about enough for a spartan funeral. About a fifth of the associations also granted a payment on the death of a member's wife, at an average of about $63.[8]

After a rather slow start which saw the mutual benefit association adopted by a handful of companies before 1870 and some two dozen by 1880, the idea caught fire. Meager as the benefits sometimes were, they offered considerably better prospects in general than the worker had confronted before, particularly in certain industries such as railroading, with its large and highly transient work force laboring under very hazardous conditions. During the late seventies and eighties, at a time when the total of accidental deaths among railroad employees had passed the 30,000 mark, much of the industry adopted association plans. Association businesses, like Baldwin Locomotive Works and Westinghouse Air Brake, also joined, along with some light industries, like the department stores of Strawbridge and Clothier of Philadelphia and Macy's of New York. By 1887 most of the large companies of Pennsylvania provided medical care of one kind or another, and by 1890 there were 120 mutual benefit associations in the United States.[9]

Instead of declining after the institution of workmen's compensation laws, associations proliferated even more rapidly for three main reasons. First, the laws required benefits without regard to cause. Second, while workmen's compensation pertained primarily to accidents, the funds were for both accidents and sickness. Finally, and perhaps most importantly, the compensation required by law was seldom enough and there was usually a waiting period, so the additional funds were very welcome. Thus, by 1908, according to the U.S. Commissioner of Labor, the number of associations had increased to 500 and included about 640,000 members. Although the number of funds apparently declined to 425 in 1916 and 398 in 1931, the number of members increased to 749,000 in 1916 and 825,000 in 1931, according to studies by the U.S. Public Health Service and the National Industrial Conference Board. The main reason for the increased membership was the growth in proportion of eligible employees; in 1916 it had been only about 60 percent of the average work force, but by 1931 the figure was about 74 percent. Perhaps the largest single fund was the joint venture by fourteen automobile manufacturers in Flint, Michigan; it included 40,000 members, three-fourths of Flint autoworkers.[10]

Mutual benefit associations obviously had their drawbacks, particularly from the perspective of the employee. For one thing, while they paid for accidents regardless of fault, that practice did not thereby lead to a greater management concern for accident prevention since the payments were largely supported by workers' funds. For another, since the terms required that recipients be unable to work, even minor accidents resulted in workers staying at home, which in turn led to attempts to reduce malingering, including waiting periods and inspection committees (usually fellow employees) who visited the home. Then, aside from the discrimination based on age, sex, race, and nationality, there were factors which tended to manipulate employee behavior and independence. For instance, when company administrators dispersed association funds, they would tend to be lenient in payments to valued employees and tightfisted toward marginal ones. Moreover, in a few instances, payments of high death benefits created a feudalistic tie that bound employees to their employers thereby decreasing their mobility and diminishing their bargaining power. The worst shortcoming, however, was the meagerness of the benefits paid out. Even had the average been doubled, it would scarcely have covered the wages lost by unskilled workmen (assuming a $600 a year income) let alone pay for medical expenses. The simple fact is that the funds were too small; employer subsidization was at a very low level, and workers' incomes did not allow for sufficient employee funding. Thus the growth of mutual benefit associations was due not to their positive strength but to the nonexistence or inadequacy of other means of health and accident insurance.[11]

After 1911 an alternative to mutual benefit associations appeared in the form of group insurance policies. Initially, these were written to insure against loss of life only (thus in some instances freeing the employer from the custom of taking up a collection for the widow). Beginning in 1922 and 1923, however, some companies began to add sickness and accident benefits, the latter being most common in states which lacked workmen's compensation laws. Acceptance of the group insurance plan—in which at least 75 percent of a company's employees had to enroll—grew from thirty-two companies in 1916 to 186 in 1926. By then, approximately 404,000 employees in a wide variety of industries were covered.[12]

The popularity of this concept was in no small part the result of effective salesmanship on the part of the underwriters, such as the Equitable Life Assurance Company and the Traveler's Insurance Company. The underwriters argued that commercial insurance was a more effective antidote to the problem of rapid labor turnover than private payments because from the employee's standpoint the former seemed more secure. Many firms, on the other hand, believed that delegating the administrative costs of medical protection to a commercial, profit-making underwriter would be significantly more expensive than continuing to bear those costs themselves. At least one employer objected to commercial insurance on the commendable (if weak) ground that such a company would be interested only in the reduction of industrial accidents but would not be inclined to pursue their complete eradication.[13]

Whether an employer used a mutual benefit association or group insurance, employees contributed. In a typical group insurance plan of 1926, an employer deducted thirty-five cents from a worker's weekly envelope. In return, the employee received $1000 in case of death or $10 per week for thirteen weeks (after a one-week grace period) in case of sickness or accident.[14] These benefits, like those of mutual benefit associations, were of course much better than nothing. In comparison to the need, however, they were woefully small.

The company doctor idea grew along with mutual benefit associations and group insurance, although at a different rate. It was particularly popular in nineteenth-century mining industries and in the railroad industry, where company-built hospital cars could be easily transported from one remote construction site to another.

Although company doctoring grew rapidly after 1900, the idea still lagged far behind mutual benefit associations by 1916. One reason was the attitude of some workers. Whether the company contracted with an independent doctor or actually put one on the payroll, the choice was always the company's (though some companies claimed that the doctor would be dismissed if the employees disliked him). Not only did this affect the question of the patient's choice of physician, it raised the suspicion against the doctor as a "company man." It was a suspicion not without foundation. For one thing, the determination of the nature of the illness might have a direct bearing on who would pay for it. For instance, a Procter and Gamble plant superintendent declared that his company would pay disability benefits only in case of "bona fide sickness," which he defined as "real sickness due to no willful act of [the employee's] own, or to his misbehavior," and specifically excluding illness as a result of "going out and getting drunk." Even more important was the threat constituted by the company doctor to the employee's job. With a doctor on the premises, for instance, or when doctors were assigned to visit absent workers, a foreman no longer needed to take an employee's word on his health problems. Thus not only would malingerers think twice before reporting themselves ill, but those with legitimate debilities might also be frightened into staying on the job longer than they should. Then of course there were the physical examinations, which, though logically should have been a welcome exercise, were subjects of great suspicion. Older workers in particular feared that they would be unable to pass an examination and thus were timid about changing jobs or becoming involved in activities which might force such change, like striking. They had reason: one Massachusetts foundry used the examination as a means "of weeding out men whom the insurance companies classify as bad risks on account of a persistent tendency to get hurt," and a prospective employee could also lose his job opportunity if the doctor's questions revealed "a tendency on [the applicant's] part to make a great deal out of small [health] matters." No wonder that workers in Boston believed company physicians kept records that could jeopardize an individual's job and refused to participate in a medical clinic jointly established by several firms unless the doctors explicitly agreed not to keep any written records of visits.[15]

A second reason that there was not a greater degree of company medicine was the matter of cost. Hospitals, clinics, and medical equipment were expensive items and even without them the cost of a full-time doctor alone could be prohibitive to a company. One physician with extensive personal experience in industrial practice felt that only a firm having at least 750 workers could profit from having a physician, and though many companies smaller than that had doctors, a lower limit most certainly did exist.[16]

Nevertheless, between 1916 and 1926 company medicine almost equaled the spread of mutual benefit associations: by 1926 more than 400 companies having at least 300 employees each provided medical care for employees, according to the Bureau of Labor Statistics. The total number of employees covered was 1,908,000. Moreover, the large majority went beyond the barest elements: while 8 percent had only first-aid facilities and 16 percent had attendants trained in first aid, 70 percent had nurses, 92 percent had hospitals or emergency rooms, and 63 percent were staffed by physicians, mainly young men fresh from medical school. Although some "hospitals" were not worthy of the name (for one Coeur d'Alene, Montana, mining company in 1890, it was simply a cabin—and part of a bloody union fight), they sometimes became extensive affairs.

There were, for example, the Carnegie hospitals, so many of them that a standard blueprint was developed, calling for a floor plan of 46-by-32 feet, containing a ward, operating room, waiting room, redressing room, X-ray room, and nurse's room. Each cost $10,500, and each was staffed by a doctor, three nurses, and four auxiliary personnel. The grandest affair was built by an unidentified company which had plants in two adjoining towns and employed 17,000 men. Designed to serve at least 50,000 people, the hospital had a staff of twenty-nine physicians, sixty nurses, and sixty other personnel. Besides general practitioners, it had three surgeons, an eye specialist, two ear, nose, and throat specialists, and a foot doctor. It even employed a company masseur.[17]

Such specialists were not unique but they were not plentiful. One company which employed a large number of clerical workers had a psychiatrist. More numerous were dentists and optometrists, who were a particular luxury for many employees. Workers who would not otherwise spend money on dental care or on eyeglasses would go to a company dentist or optometrist where the out-of-pocket expenses were very low (usually the cost of the materials). Since dentistry is largely an American profession, it proved to be a form of acculturation for immigrants to American ways. Industrial dentists sometimes found that foreign-born workers had no idea what a toothbrush was and so kept one on their desks for demonstration purposes. Thus did businessmen, inadvertantly perhaps, add one more element in their campaign of Americanization, quite likely for the immigrant one of the more unpleasant and painful, even if more beneficial ones.[18]

This great growth in company medicine was due in large part to two factors: the military experience during the world war and the effects of workmen's compensation laws; together they underscored the value of preventive medicine and medical examinations. Companies discovered they could save a great deal of time, trouble, and money by preventing health problems or catching them early. Among the other advantages was the company doctor's (and nurse's) usefulness in combating malingering, the dentist's aid in Americanizing immigrant workers, and an added force in controlling certain kinds of behavior, such as drinking. In fact, attitude control became an explicit part of company medicine. For example, the Dennison Manufacturing Company explained that its medical department "increases good will of employees and gives one a sense of security because they know that immediate facilities are available for treatment of injuries and sudden illness." Mark M. Jones, supervisor of the Edison interests in Orange, New Jersey, enjoined his department to work actively toward that goal: the department ought to "occupy the position of the grandmother to whom the youngster may go when indisposed, or when he cuts a finger and needs a bandage. He should receive treatment that causes him to wish to return, and the sympathy that causes him to feel that after all it is a good thing to work in a plant that takes such good care of him." It was even possible for the company in some cases to make a bit of a profit on company medicine. One form of the mining check-off system was for the company to keep the difference between miners' fees and the doctors' salaries and to put it into the general fund as part of the profits.[19]

And the worker? Company medicine clearly posed a set of threats to his independence and even his well-being. Yet it generally provided him with health care usually beyond his own means. In some cases it was rather meager to be sure, but in others it was outstanding, far above national standards. More important, even the average seemed to be adequate by the standards of the day. Consider a 1923 Department of Labor survey of medical care in West Virginia coal mining towns. The check-off fee had risen by then to $.75-$1.25 for single men and $1.50-$2.00 for married men, with an additional charge of $7-$25 for maternal care. Each physician usually covered an area of riverbed homes from one to three miles long housing fewer than 200 families. In one section of eleven company towns there were three hospitals and two of the towns were served by a public health nurse. More than 90 percent of the mothers had a doctor in attendance at births, and infant mortality figures (ninety-four deaths per thousand live births before age one) were in line with contemporary national rates. Even though the towns were less crowded than cities, considering the poor sanitation, lack of fresh milk, incomplete diets, and high incidence of immigrant families with poor health habits, the mortality rates seem surprisingly low. No wonder, then, that John Brophy, a high official in the United Mine Workers union, recalled the check-off system with some affection, calling it "a boon to miners." In most cases, company medicine provided better care than would otherwise have been available; in some, it provided care where there would have been little or none.[20]

Taken all in all, then, in spite of the abuses and threats to the employee, company involvement in health care was needed by both employee and employer. Yet that involvement, even at its height, never covered more than 60 percent of American manufacturing companies.[21] The reason was the level of funding. Employees simply could not afford to support a completely adequate system on their own, and employers' commitments had to conform to the larger context of the balance sheet. In a system governed by economic priorities, medical care was provided for the most productive rather than for everyone.

11 Pensions

"Now, what are we going to do with these men?" asked one employer in 1928. "It is easy to say that we owe them nothing and that when we are through with them we will simply cast them adrift. But you know and I know that we don't do anything of the kind—not if we are running a large company or one that is much under public scrutiny. . . . If we admit that we are not going to scrap the aged employee, we find ourselves still facing the question: What are we going to do with him?"[1] It was an ancient question, one which has tested and troubled most cultures. But for the employer in early twentieth-century America, the problem took on deeper meaning: not only did he have the care of his own family entrusted to him, but in a very real sense he had the livelihood of dozens or hundreds or thousands of superannuated citizens under his control. For employers of large numbers of workers, the problems of old age were magnified many times. As with so many of the other social problems attendant to industrialization, production-oriented executives (like virtually everyone else) understood only dimly why suddenly it should become their problem and were ill-equipped to deal with it. Nevertheless, wrestle with it they must, and wrestle with it they did.

Of course, employees had become old and unproductive in the nineteenth century, so the problem was not entirely new. But the nineteenth-century solution was becoming increasingly outdated. Then the custom was simply to assign an aged employee to routine, physically undemanding tasks. Even though his productivity had declined, he continued to receive a partial wage. The size and duration of such payments were totally at the discretion of the employer and they were never granted except for long and faithful service. Surveys of hundreds of American companies disclosed that no more than a half-dozen semiformal pension programs existed before 1900. None limited the discretion of the employer.[2]

The informal, arbitrary system of dealing with aged employees remained in vogue well into the twentieth century and to some extent still persists. But increasingly, many of the same factors which led employers to adopt other welfare programs brought forth a re-evaluation of the customary practice. Gradually, the informal approach gave way to more formal, systematized procedures.

Companies had become much larger. By 1910 it was often no longer convenient for an executive personally to deal with what might be tens or hundreds of retirements each year. With dozens on the retirement rolls, moreover, pensions could become a major expense. Technology was becoming increasingly sophisticated and older employees often found difficulty mastering it. Sophisticated technology, moreover, was often expensive, and a mistake could do costly damage. As a consequence, railroads were among the first to develop formal pension programs. Not only were they among the largest American corporations but also the most dangerous. A locomotive was hardly the best place for one whose reactions had slowed.[3]

The dilemma an employer faced was difficult indeed. On the one hand, a superannuated employee could be a real detriment to his company even if lives were not at stake, as in the railroad case. If he performed a supervisory role, inefficiency could spread, perhaps, to an entire department. A corps of aged workers could become a bottleneck to promotion which could destroy the morale and initiative of younger workers. "The man who is kept on in his old position after his efficiency has departed is a drag on the whole concern," argued one company president in 1908. "As a rule, he is simply in the way. . . . For the corporation's sake, it would be better to get him entirely out of the factory than to have him there setting an example of inefficiency, or occupying a position which the younger men deserve."[4]

On the other hand, wholesale elimination of elderly workers could wreak havoc on an organization. It could destroy the reputation of a firm, making it difficult to attract new employees or to hold valued ones. It could ruin morale, leading to inefficiency and disloyalty. As a result, many employers continued to pay workers well after their productive lives were over. A constructive solution would be welcome indeed.

The crucial fact was that even if a company had no formal pension program, it still had to bear at least some of the cost of a pension plan. "Many employers . . . delude themselves with the thought that they have no pension expense," wrote one exponent of formal pension plans. "As a matter of fact, it is quite conceivable that these employers are expending in an overloaded payroll, in increased accident hazards, and in the blocking of promotion for younger men, far more than they would pay to retired employees under moderate pension plans." Since the expense could not be evaded, it made good sense to rationalize the payment of pensions. With the kind of logic his associates understood, one Plymouth Cordage executive argued that "as a mere question of expense a pension system will be, in the long run, cheaper than the present custom of paying full wages for a comparatively small return."[5]

A host of other benefits, it became apparent, accrued to the payer of pensions. First, a pension plan was a valuable weapon in the war against labor turnover. As with so many other welfare programs, employers hoped to eliminate the transient employee in favor of one who gave a lifetime of service. A pension at the end of a career was an ideal inducement to long service, and the employee might even produce more during his working life if freed from care about his future as well. Pensions also fought competition in the labor market; an employee who wished to maintain his stake in a future pension would be unlikely to succumb to the blandishments of prospective employers who offered a few pennies per hour more.

Like so many other welfare programs, pension plans were enlisted in the struggle against unions. Advocates of formal pension plans were well aware that the function of pensions was to bind the employee ever more closely to the company. Since unions were in effect competitors in a struggle for the loyalty of workers, pension plans served to undermine them.

In fact, pensions often were designed with just that purpose in mind. Almost invariably, they contained clauses like the following:

> If an employee, after leaving the service, voluntarily, or by participating in a strike, shall be reemployed, he shall be considered in his relation to the Pension System as a new employee.
>
> Employees who leave the service of their own volition or under stress of influence inimical to the company . . . , thereby lose all benefits of the pension system.[6]

In short, if an employee went on strike, he did so at the peril of sacrificing his future security. This was not of great consequence to the young or new employee but it was important to the mature one.

Pension plans, accordingly, served to divide the labor movement along age lines. Divided, it could be conquered.

Another benefit derived from pension plans, employers stated, was its salutory effect on public relations. A manufacturing firm in New England reported that its retirement plan "satisfies our consciences and creates some little favorable impression on the community." A southern public service company awarded each retiree a framed "pension certificate," of which it wrote: "We have received a lot of publicity in neighborhoods where these certificates are hung on the wall of the homes and people visiting have been attracted by it and a general discussion ensues, which in most cases is favorable to the public." The value of an attractive public image could never be precisely measured, but it was nonetheless real. Such a reputation could be crucial in winning public support in a strike, in warding off tax increases, and in forestalling legislation to establish universal and compulsory old-age pensions.[7]

By 1910 weighty arguments supported the introduction of more formal pension programs instead of the more arbitrary, informal variety. Some cost had to be borne in either case, and it was very possible that a formal program was the least expensive. Unquestionably this was true in the two dozen instances in which a retirement fund was established to which employees were required to contribute. Besides, a more formalized system paid highly desirable dividends in the areas of labor turnover, union control, and public relations. And finally, pensions discharged the moral obligation most employers felt to assist and care for employees who had served them for up to six decades.

Employers, accordingly, began to move quickly to establish pension programs. Between 1900 and 1910 at least forty-two new programs appeared, and in the next fifteen years firms added at least 181 more. Estimates of the total number of pension plans in operation by 1925 varied from 245 to 310, while one observer claimed that by 1928 more than 500 existed. Similarly, estimates of the number of employees covered varied from 2,815,000 (by the National Industrial Conference Board) to 3,500,000. Firms in virtually every industry adopted pension programs, but they were most numerous in metals, railroads, public utilities, and banking. Since most pension plans required long periods of service to qualify, however, and since most plans had been in operation for relatively brief periods, only a small number of pensioners had as yet begun to receive benefits. The 1924 National Industrial Conference Board survey of 245 companies discovered only 35,953 pensioners out of 2,816,000 employees, or only 1.3 percent. The average pensioner received slightly more than $500 per year.[8]

It could be argued that by 1925 industrial pension plans were still so new that their effectiveness was as yet untested. Close scrutiny of their provisions suggests, however, that employer-operated pension plans could never have become a very satisfactory means of supporting elderly workers in an industrial society.

Industrial pension plans of the 1920s were of three basic types. First, there was the completely arbitrary or informal program. This meant that an employer decided, more or less on an ad hoc basis, every feature: who was to receive a pension, how large it was to be, and how long it would last. Slightly more systematic was the "formal-discretionary" type. The employer still retained full authority to grant, deny, abandon, or alter in any way every pension. But he now established more or less fixed regulations for eligibility and delegated administration of the program to a committee of subordinates. More advanced yet was the "limited-contractual" type. In such a plan employers surrendered none of their discretionary rights to determine eligibilty or to fix the size of a pension; in fact, they assumed no legal obligation whatsoever. They did promise, however, not to reduce a pension once it had been granted, though that promise rested on the integrity of the company alone. Fully contractual plans in which firms assumed a legal obligation were not totally unknown, but were so rare as to be negligible. Approximately 72 percent of the plans were of either the informal or the formal-discretionary type; about 25 percent were of the limited-contractual variety.[9]

Nothing brought out the limited nature of the employers' obligation so forcefully as a careful reading of the fine print in the wording of the pension plans. Almost all contained clauses such as this:

> This Pension System has been established voluntarily by the Company; and it may be amended, suspended or annulled at any time at the pleasure of the Company. It is also expressly understood that every pension hereunder will be granted only in the discretion of the Company, will be continued only in its pleasure, and may be revoked by it at any time.

Other clauses stated that pensions might be withheld not only for "misconduct," but for any other reason.[10]

In practice such caveats were rarely invoked, but they could be if necessary. In 1921 a meatpacking company with 400 pensioners on its rolls went bankrupt. It liquidated its pension fund (to which employees had contributed) by making payments to each pensioner, but the amounts they received were inadequate to sustain payment of their monthly stipend. The pensioners sued for $7 million—the amount necessary to continue their payments—but the courts upheld the company's argument that a qualifying clause absolved them of any obligation.[11]

The conditions which employees had to fulfill in order to become eligible for a pension were stringent enough to limit the system from becoming an effective solution to the problems of the aged. The chief consideration from the standpoint of most employers was to avoid retiring the productive employee while retaining the ability to release the unproductive one. There were, accordingly, different ages for retirement at the company's discretion than for retirement at the employee's request. In 63 percent of the pension programs in 1924, firms reserved the option to compel male employees to retire at age sixty or lower. In 54 percent of the companies male employees could not retire by request until age sixty-five or higher. For male employees seventy years of age, retirement was compulsory in nearly two-thirds of the companies.[12]

Futhermore, a worker had to establish a long record of service to qualify. Nearly a third of the companies required thirty years of continuous service, and 87 percent required at least twenty years. This requirement was in addition to the age requirement; both had to be met. An employee hired after age forty could never hope to qualify in a company whose minimum requirement was thirty years of employment. As a practical matter companies then established upper age limits for hiring; most would not hire anyone over forty-five so that no one would reach retirement age without having served the requisite number of years.[13] This practice served to restrict union activity. A prospective striker over forty would be faced not only with the loss of his pension rights but also with finding himself unemployable in the event that his company failed to rehire him.

Some employees qualified for pensions because of disability. Again, industrial programs fell short of meeting the need. Although occasionally partial incapacity was acceptable, most specified that a worker had to be totally incapacitated. Though a few programs specified that the disability had to occur *away* from work, another condition commonly applied was that the injury be suffered while at work. Injuries had to be immediate; damage slow to appear or coming from obscure sources was not acceptable. Age and length of service requirements were frequently imposed as additional conditions which had to be met.[14]

The generosity of employers in pensioning their employees varied widely. A number of formulas were used to compute the size of the stipend, but the most common method was to select a percentage of the employee's salary, usually 1-2 percent, and to multiply this times the years of service, often with a maximum stipend allowed. Thus, an employee who received 1 percent of his annual salary for each year of service might receive 25 percent of his wage as his pension. The average salary for the final ten years' work was normally used.[15]

The adequacy of the pension is perhaps open to question. But the weight of the evidence attests to the scantiness of the benefits. A conference of experts held under the auspices of the Metropolitan Life Insurance Company in 1923 revealed a consensus that the benefits were much too low. This was further suggested by the tiny percentage of workers who were receiving benefits; while there is no way to determine precisely how many workers refused to retire because of the inadequacy of the payments, this was the case in a number of companies.[16]

The fact that few people had retired under the industrial pension system in the mid-twenties indicates that it had little appeal to most workers. The response to pensions varied with age, with young workers either indifferent or opposed and with middle-aged employees somewhat more favorable. Organized labor, as a competitor for the loyalty of labor, generally looked askance at company pensions by the 1920s. One labor critic was particularly caustic, but his analysis of the weaknesses of industrial pension programs was not far off the mark:

> If you remain with this company throughout your productive lifetime; if you do not die before retirement age; if you are not discharged, or laid off for an extended period; if you are not refused a pension as a matter of discipline; if the company is in business; and if the company does not decide to abandon the plan, you will receive a pension of______, subject to the contingency of its discontinuance or reduction after it has been entered upon.[17]

But it must be remembered that businessmen operated under severe restrictions in devising their programs. It was right, of course, to provide aid for those who had become old in a company's service. But as the experience of the 1930s was to demonstrate, it was also right to avoid making commitments on which one might be unable to deliver. In the 1920s pensions were usually funded as an operating expense. In the event of a business downturn, revenues might well be incapable of sustaining large payments. The solution was the establishment of a permanent pension fund, but in the absence of compelling pressure that was a cost most businessmen were unprepared to bear. Like most other Americans, they believed that old age care ought to remain an individual and family responsibility. They were loath to repeal such an old and hallowed tradition, particularly since to do so would entail a significant cost to themselves.[18]

12 Social Work

Much of welfare capitalism does not fit the modern American's conception of the term "welfare work." Such items as the company store, recreation programs, religious activities—these do not, for most Americans, come to mind when welfare is mentioned. But there was one element of welfare capitalism that would register at once in almost any American's vision of welfare: the figure of the social worker. Mention the social worker and one immediately envisages that inquisitorial arm of authority, bearing in one hand aid and comfort and in the other disaffection and condemnation. The image fits welfare capitalism's version of the social worker at least as well as it does the modern, governmental one. But the familiar picture is narrow, as it was then, particularly at the beginning.

The beginnings of industrial social work are rooted in what might well be considered a form of sexism. Nineteenth-century America was a country of rather clearly defined sex roles, and the world of business was the world of men. Consequently, as businesses grew and employers faced growing numbers of female employees, they found themselves at a loss about treating their workers' peculiar "female" problems; one answer was the hiring of "specialists." Probably the first was Mrs. Aggie Dunn, who was hired in 1875 as "social secretary" for the H. J. Heinz Company of Pittsburgh. For the next fifty years, "Mother" Aggie Dunn interviewed, hired, counseled, and generally watched over her 1,200-girl brood at the picklepacking firm. In 1901 a similar position went to Gertrude Beeks, whose assignment was to "adjust" the problems of 400 girls employed by the McCormick Harvesting Machine Company, where she immediately made a great hit with the girls—and thus fulfilled her main function—by having more mirrors installed in their dressing room.[1]

The instructions to Miss Beeks—to adjust problems—reflected the ephemeral and indefinite nature which would always characterize industrial welfare work. Diana Hirschler, who became "social secretary" at Wm. Filene Sons, the Boston department store, recalled that when she took the position, her employers had "no definite plans" but only "two general ideas": to place an "impartial person" in the store to see that "just and fair conditions existed" and to improve efficiency, if possible. She thus had free rein to do whatever she could think of to improve labor relations; efficiency, it was felt, would come as a consequence. As this area of welfare work extended to include males, men who entered the field received equally imprecise guidelines. One owner of an iron foundry simply told the young man he hired to "go about the works; get acquainted with the men. Meet them while at work; meet them out of hours. Find out if they are dissatisfied with anything. Tell me about it and make suggestions as to what can be done to take away the cause. When we agree on what to do, you do it."[2]

Yet, cloudy as these instructions were, their implementation carried the seeds of developing method and purpose; gradually, as social work was carried on, a coherent purpose and system evolved out of what were seen to be its possibilities. The social worker's earliest function, as we have seen, was to bridge a communications gap caused by sex. But growth and distance and complexity could also lead to faulty relations and impaired communications. Businessmen believed that close and friendly personal relationships were being undermined by rapid expansion; they were losing touch with their employees. Consequently, an early and key instruction to welfare workers was simply to establish contact. This could be done by following the foundryman's advice: "Meet them while at work; meet them out of hours." And meet them the social workers did, sometimes through an ambitious schedule: Clara Kenyon of the Olympia Mills of Columbia, South Carolina, took as her first task the meeting with every employee at his home; the expedition required her to visit 500 houses. Regular contact was built into the instructions: Edgar Adams, general superintendent of the Cleveland Hardware Company, instructed his welfare worker to visit each employee within a week after the employee began work, and at least once a year thereafter.[3]

But obviously it was not simply contact that the businessmen wanted, it was contact of the right sort—fruitful contact. Thus Elizabeth Wheeler, a Rhode Island industrial welfare worker, explained that a welfare worker's proper role was "to tell her employer how he may establish a desired point of contact between himself and his immediate staff and the rank and file of his industrial army." One of the desired elements, of course, was the establishment or restoration of a friendly relationship. "Our real vocation," observed Isabella Nye, welfare worker of Siegel Cooper, a New York department store, "is rather that of a diplomat in endeavoring to bring the employer and employee to a point of view which will lead to mutual trust and satisfaction." Jane Williams, who held a similar position at a Massachusetts printing firm, held similar views: "When [a welfare worker's] vision is broad, she brings about a sympathy between the viewpoints of the employer and employee."[4]

One way of creating a friendlier attitude toward the employer on the part of the employee was that suggested in the words of the foundry owner and the actions of Gertrude Beeks: determine the causes of irritation and alleviate them through management action. Thus Miss Beeks could have more mirrors installed, some might suggest other improvements in toilet facilities or lighting, or Diana Hirschler could recommend promotions in pay or positions, and at least one company granted its welfare worker the power not only to recommend but actually to set wages.[5]

The hand of friendship might be extended even further when there was no particular grievance with the company or when the troubles came from outside. Some welfare workers acted as travel agents, arranging employees' vacations, or as personal shoppers, helping them to make purchases, or as real estate agents, seeking out appropriate living accommodations. Some became recreation leaders, classroom teachers, or library supervisors. Special instructors at U.S. Steel and elsewhere taught wives and daughters of employees how to prepare foods, to care for babies, to sew dresses, and even how to make a bed. These instructions often took place in "model cottages," specially selected buildings in the neighborhood of company housing which served as model housing for employees, "object lessons," as they were referred to by U.S. Steel. The Niagara Falls Power Company operated a typical one. Each room in the cottage was furnished with modest essentials, the price of each article clearly marked, the purpose being to give employees an idea of how they could make a pleasant home out of inexpensive furniture. A woman engaged by the company lived in the house and gave advice on problems of home life, making her, in essence, a resident home economist.[6]

On a more serious level, company nurses, besides treating injury and illness at the company, were often dispatched to absentees' homes on a regular basis where they dispensed such services as extending convalescence of those likely to be carrying communicable diseases or perhaps tracing the causes of some physical illnesses to social problems. Sometimes they were involved in various forms of relief work. The staff of the Industrial Nurses Department of Amoskeag Manufacturing, the Manchester, New Hampshire, textile firm, visited homes thought to be in need of food or fuel, and if the Amoskeag nurses deemed the home actually to be in need of help, and if some connection with the company could be substantiated, they requisitioned from local suppliers a "$5 order of groceries," and perhaps "5 boxes of kindling wood," or half a ton of coal. In December, 1920, the Amoskeag nurses had twenty-four families on their relief list, most of them widows or relatives of employees. U.S. Steel claimed that it distributed "thousands of dollars" in coal, groceries, and clothing during the depression of 1907–8.[7] Ill and injured employees or relatives and survivors of employees sometimes got outright grants-in-aid to tide them over until better times. Rather than outright handouts, some companies developed remedial types of relief which ranged from counsel, as when Mrs. B. Toklatine of Homestead Steel advised widows to stay with their children, to services, such as Carnegie Steel's day nursery, which allowed widows to find work. Mrs. Toklatine placed delinquent children and aged or mentally retarded children in proper institutions. Colorado Fuel and Iron set up an "Industrial Home" for crippled employees and for widows and orphans of employees killed in the company's service; in 1909 the home produced mattresses (presumably for use in company rooming houses) and had plans to make brooms, brushes, rugs, and other lightweight household products. A few companies instructed their welfare workers to refer cases of this type to appropriate governmental relief agencies.[8]

This extension of the employer's friendly hand did have its limits of course. Aside from costs, the important factor was couched in moral terms: workers must not be coddled. One welfare worker was fired for involving herself too deeply in improving working conditions; it "went to her head," complained her employer, a textile manufacturer. "It got so she thought the mill was run chiefly to provide her with people to entertain. She interfered with the work . . . [and] grew outrageously extravagant." As for relief, only if need was thoroughly established, explained Homestead's Mrs. Toklatine, could relief be given out "without serious damage to the character of the dependent person."[9]

This attitude leads us to the other side of the coin. Friendliness is a two-way street; the employer who was willing to extend himself in the interest of his employees expected a friendly demeanor in return. Sometimes this would simply mean a lessening of tensions, an easing of friction, a smoothing of troubled waters; but very often it developed into another form of behavorial engineering—the transformation of laborers into the kinds of people closer to the company's heart's desire.

The social worker was an excellent instrument in this movement; in frequent direct contact with the workers both at work and in their homes, the social secretary or industrial nurse could be a prime conduit of important information to the employer. In some instances this would be relatively informal, as in the gathering of gripes through conversations, while in the cases of determining need for relief or the reason for absence the investigation might take on a much more formal tone. Also, the investigation was quite likely to range much beyond conditions of finance and health—Elizabeth Wheeler, for instance, whose company employed many girls, made a careful investigation into the character and reputation of the young men who wooed her firm's employees. A much more central concern for many companies was union activity: the company-paid truant officer in the company town of Cravens, Louisiana, for example, was ordered to keep a careful watch for union organizers. Whether the object was to bring aid and relief or to control behavior, the first step was to gather information, and the welfare worker, particularly in the guise of the trusted nurse, was about as good a tool as one could find.[10]

It is significant that the chosen tool was not passive; even the act of gathering information made an impact on the laborer. As with governmental social workers, there was always at least an implicit understanding that a home visit was something of an inspection. This could not but create some apprehension on the part of the worker even when he had no consciousness of wrongdoing. Companies sometimes made clear the consequences of misbehavior; as an executive of the Dennison Manufacturing Company of Framingham, Massachusetts, explained: "if there is reason for his [an employee's] being out she [the company nurse] will help him and if there is not, he will have to change his habits if he is to remain in our employ."

There is little doubt, then, that even the possibility of a visit gave pause to would-be malingerers. It was this situation which led the "service director" of a Massachusetts firm to assert that the visiting nurse system "acts as a tracing system in returning men to work at the earliest possible date, and preventing them from becoming malingerers."[11]

As a contact, as an instrument of communications, the social worker was a two-way set; his job of transferring messages from employer to employee was not incidental—indeed, it was a critical factor which went far beyond the "subtle" hints of fact-gathering visits. "My job," said welfare worker Charles Marshall of Plymouth Cordage, "is giving a point of view." He could have been talking of giving the worker's view to the employer; in fact, he was talking of the opposite. Besides being ambiguous, his statement is not quite correct, for the proper function was not simply to give the point of view but to persuade the worker toward that point of view, toward a proper attitude. This is made clear in a comment on the unsuccessful attempt to undercut a union by means of a company-sponsored grievance at the Stanley Electric Company of Pittsfield, Massachusetts, when Dexter Kimball, the company manager, bemoaned the lack of a welfare worker: "If we had had a good 'Social Secretary' . . . he could have gone in there and brought those men to see the thing in the right light." It is hardly surprising that many welfare workers expressed anti-union sentiments or that not one case could be found of a company hiring a pro-union welfare worker.[12]

Persuasion toward the "right light" did not always involve such things as union activity or malingering. It encompassed a wide variety of domestic affairs, including the premarital investigations of Elizabeth Wheeler or the marital counseling of a company welfare worker in Buffalo, New York, who earned high praise from her employer for her ability at reconciling the differences of estranged couples. There was also the abiding businessman's interest in Americanizing his immigrant workers. Commonwealth Steel, for example, hired Edna Haas for her ability to gain rapport with immigrant families, whom she artfully guided toward American customs during her home visits. A more interesting example was the visiting nurse employed by New Jersey Zinc who regularly dressed the scrapes and scratches of workers' children so that she might use them as "an entering wedge for righting wrong conditions." She would follow the children into their homes where she would then begin a program of instruction in American ways. "There is no surer way of getting a hold upon the foreign homes," she reported. "American ways" could mean forms of housing and furniture, hygiene, child care, cooking, finances—the whole range of personal life-styles to which, of course, even many native Americans did not conform.[13]

The moralistic overtones are unmistakable. Indeed, there was an unabashed involvement in the workers' moral attitudes. Complaints by a creditor who was owed a debt by an employee might bring a home visit no less quickly than a foreman's complaint about laxness on the job. Asserting that it was "no longer a debatable question that elaborate clothes and jewelry and powder and paint have a demoralizing effect on the character and ability of a working girl," Mary Gilson, of Joseph and Feiss Company, reported that she visited girls at home "for the sake of securing cooperation on the subject of simplicity of dress."[14] Taken as a whole and dressed in the fineries of rhetoric, this was known as uplifting the worker. One company, which sought a "college girl" for its welfare worker, put it this way: "She influences [the employees] to be honest, to keep well and strong, to live right." More poetic is the language of Elizabeth Wheeler, who urged her colleagues "to study the science of human progress" to learn how to inculcate "noble aspirations and pure living" and how "to get the confidence of a girl whose breeding has been of the 'tumbled-up' variety, and to reveal to her the 'vision splendid.' "[15]

Persuasion took a variety of forms. In some instances, such as the missed opportunity to foil the union at Stanley Electric or Edna Haas's work with immigrants, it doubtless called for a nimble mind and a wise tongue. In others, it might be the role itself—the inquisitor creating apprehension, the comfort of a nurse, the bringer of needed goods, or a new skill developed by a teacher—all likely to induce a feeling of gratitude. Sometimes employers tried to create a special eminence for the welfare worker; in 1919 the Studebaker Corporation hired Reverend Charles A. Lippincott, pastor of the First Presbyterian Church of South Bend, to be, as Studebaker's president put it, "guide, counselor, and friend" to the employees, and in addition their "Great White Father."[16] Presumably, the pastor's presence alone was to serve as an example to employees of what uplift meant.

But behind the pastor's frock and the nurse's skill and the social worker's persuasive tongue lay the true persuader—the power of the company to give or to deny. In most cases this power was suggested or symbolized, though seldom subtly; in some it was put to direct and immediate use. For instance, one industrial nurse at Youngstown

Sheet and Tube went beyond simple advice on budgeting and distributed an employee's paycheck to his creditors until the family was out of debt. The Joseph and Feiss Company of Cleveland went further; it charged its industrial nurse with responsibility for the " 'spirit' of the institution" and gave her the right to discharge any employee "who runs counter to this spirit."[17] Apparently, she could with some justification have been dubbed the "Great White Mother."

It is no wonder that industrial welfare work became a popular kind of welfare capitalism. By 1906, according to one estimate, there were twenty-seven welfare workers in the United States, divided about evenly between men and women, and paid between $720 and $2500 annually. Professor Graham Taylor, whose course of study at the Chicago Commons was the chief source of welfare workers with special training, reported that in 1906 the demand for graduates was so great that he had difficulty in keeping a staff of instructors. By 1925 the Southern Textile Social Service Association, a trade organization for welfare workers and welfare capitalists, reported that it had about 400 members. Many industrial nurses were also welfare workers, and one 1920 study found 560 nurses employed by 460 firms in the United States. By 1927, according to the Bureau of Labor Statistics, nurses could be found in almost every company-owned coal mining town, many of them devoting their entire time to welfare work.[18] Partly because of its relief aspect, social work was one of the few aspects of welfare capitalism maintained during economic depressions.

The company social worker: inquisitor, advisor, teacher, nurse, dispenser of rewards or of punishment, spreader of the "right light." Edgar Adams of Cleveland Hardware described his company's welfare worker: "she is simply the agent that carries out the interest of the corporation in the home and in connection with the living conditions of the employee."[19]

13 Employee Representation

Oh, the company is good to me,
I belong to the company-union;
They cut my pay and I agree,
I belong to the company-union;
My wages they are up so high
My family's starving, so am I;
But sooner than complain, I'd die,
I belong to the company-union.

. . . .

I get the fairest pay on earth,
I belong to the company-union;
I'm paid exactly what I'm worth,
I belong to the company-union;
I think the company is fair,
They lay me off, but I don't care,
My kids object, but I don't dare,
I belong to the company-union.

We never talk of workers' rights
I belong to the company-union;
They tell me that it leads to fights,
I belong to the company-union;
The company has always said
That men who talk like that are red,
We listen to the boss instead,
I belong to the company-union.[1]

The song represents one worker's view of the company union. Another, however, thought it was a fine thing: before it was instituted where he worked, he said he felt like "a servant of the family" but with a company union, "I feel that I am a real honest-to-goodness member of the family and that I can sit down at the same table with the rest of the family." But the songwriting worker remarked about that as well:

Each year we have a swell affair,
I belong to the company-union;
The bosses and their wives are there,
I belong to the company-union.
They give us food, they give us beer,
But one thing does seem mighty queer,
We eat that good just once a year,
I belong to the company-union.[2]

Some employers felt that any negotiation with more than one employee at a time was anathema, smacking of socialism, while others were nearly ecstatic in praise of employee representation. Colonel Stewart of Standard Oil of Indiana claimed that because of it, "in our company we have the world's greatest democracy," and he looked forward to the day when all the company's directors would be elected by employees. Charles Schwab, board chairman of Bethlehem Steel, told a congressional committee about Bethlehem's representative meetings: "I have never attended a meeting in which I have seen such complete harmony, such complete happiness, such complete understanding, as I have seen in ours."[3]

Samuel Gompers called the idea a "semblance of democracy," a "pretense admirably calculated to deceive," and (rather contrarily) a "counterfeit of the flimsiest, most transparent character." The 1919 convention of his American Federation of Labor passed a resolution denouncing company unions as undemocratic. On the other hand, Matthew Woll, a vice-president of the AFL, referred to shop committees as being "not alone favored but recommended," although only as a supplement to unions. He reasoned that they helped to secure teamwork and access to high company officials and were useful in dealing with minor problems and grievances.[4]

The company union, more objectively known as the work council and more generally as the employee representation plan, was a compromise of sorts. The question was, what voice would the worker have in determining his working conditions and his rewards? One answer was, none at all; those whose money had paid for the lands and buildings and machinery would decide these questions by right of ownership. Another was, a total voice—the dictatorship of the proletariat. Between these extremes was labor's answer: the union.

It was an answer unacceptable to almost all businessmen. For one thing, the idea of dealing with professional union men was abhorrent to them. Not only were such men impolite and contemptuous of authority, businessmen felt, but they were actually evil men who brought harm to both business and labor for purely personal gain. To the businessmen, the union organizer was a "labor agitator" who entered a plant uninvited, created unrest where none had existed before by making false charges, signed up members through intimidation, pocketed part of the dues he collected, and forced strikes mainly for recognition—largely personal recognition. In exchange for performing such services—which produced no goods; indeed, were destructive—the union leader ironically enjoyed a comfortable salary. An executive of Plymouth Cordage spoke for almost all businessmen when referring to labor leaders: "Unseen and spiritual forces are today swaying America as reeds are swayed by the wind. There are some good leaders; many poor ones."[5] Another objection was a philosophic divergence: employers' central conception of the business world was that the interests of employer and employee were mutual; that which benefited a business benefited all who worked in it. But unionists believed that the interests were essentially divergent; the money a company made was divided into profits and salaries as determined by the relative bargaining strength of employer and employee. It seemed an irreconcilable—and to both sides a critical—difference. Finally, there was the crucial factor of the professional unionist's—and the union's—independence. Employee representation through unions would mean a significant shift in power and control over business.

If there was to be a collective employee voice in business affairs—and events were forcing employers to the conclusion that it was a possible solution to labor problems—then it would have to be something other than unions, if they had anything to say about it. Working as a labor conciliator for John D. Rockefeller, Jr., William Lyon Mackenzie King, later a prime minister of Canada, made the point precisely: "Between the extreme of individual agreements on the one side, and an agreement involving recognition of unions of national and international character on the other, lies the straight acceptance of the principle of Collective Bargaining."[6] Indeed, it was precisely to ward off that "other alternative" that businessmen took to employee representation.

Although shop committees existed as early as 1833 and the "shop council" was put forward as an antidote to the labor strife of 1886, no important American company adopted employee representation until almost the turn of the century. Then in 1898, Wm. Filene Sons, the

Boston department store, organized a committee of employees to assist in the administration of a medical clinic and insurance plan. Other committees followed, and by 1905 the Filene company had organized the Filene Cooperative Association Council, a legislative body. Modeled after the United States government, the Filene organization included an elected lower house composed of representatives of the workers, an upper house or senate appointed by the company president, and the president's cabinet, a group of high company officials.[7]

Meanwhile, a similar organization developed at the Nernst Lamp Company, a small manufacturer of electrical appliances located in Pittsburgh. It was the brainchild of Nernst vice-president and general manager Holbrook FitzJohn Porter, a deeply religious executive who spoke of a "higher law in the industrial world" which transcended personal economic interest. Believing as he did, Porter sponsored a wide range of very typical educational and recreational welfare activities and proclaimed their success in a series of articles. A central part of the Nernst welfare program was its "factory committee" which included workers, clerical employees, and foremen. Though the Nernst committee, which was organized in the winter of 1903–4, was informal and purely advisory, it anticipated much of what was to come. Between 1907 and 1913 similar committees developed at several other companies.[8]

The representation plan at the Packard Piano Company was particularly important. During the fall of 1912 the company experienced serious labor difficulties and consequently called in a consultant, John Leitch, to find a remedy. The system he devised was an enlargement of the Filene system. Leitch consciously modeled the Packard Piano organization after the United States government on the assumption that it was the most successful governing body in the world. Packard Piano thus had a house of representatives elected by workers, a senate elected by foremen, and a cabinet composed of executives. Either house could initiate a proposal, but both houses as well as the cabinet had to approve it before it became "law." Management thus retained veto power over any labor proposal, though in practice this was seldom used.[9]

Like many welfare capitalists, there was an evangelical quality about John Leitch. After the Packard Piano experience, he traveled to several other companies where he installed similar organizations. In 1919 he published a book which cataloged in glowing terms the success of his plan at Packard Piano. It was an immediate success. Leitch found himself swamped with job offers. His system of employee representation—the "industrial democracy" type—became known as the Leitch Plan and a total of twenty companies adopted it. The Goodyear Tire and Rubber Company was the best-known example. Goodyear added to the characteristic house of representatives and senate the concept of industrial citizenship. To vote for a representative or senator, an employee had to gain the status of "Goodyear Industrian"; this meant one had to be eighteen years of age, an American citizen, able to understand English, and to have worked for the company for six months. But any industrian who absented himself for seven days lost his status. A further Goodyear innovation was the meeting place of the Goodyear Industrial Assembly. The two chambers were patterned after the house and senate chambers in Washington.[10]

But the Leitch Plan, for all its democratic pretensions, proved cumbersome. At the Durham Hosiery Mills of North Carolina, each legislative body had five standing committees: justice, cooperation, economy, energy, and service. A bill originating in either body had to pass the other and then be submitted to the cabinet for approval. A vetoed bill had to be re-passed by two-thirds majorities in both houses and then still could not take effect if, according to the constitution, it would "radically affect the finances, working hours, or the progressive policy of the corporation." Some companies even added a supreme court. Most businessmen perceived that the Leitch Plan duplicated the clumsiness of bicameral government and it never became very popular. Even Goodyear privately recognized the plan's shortcomings. The company paid employee representatives to handle grievances, and according to one executive this became a "nightmare." Apparently the representatives preferred to spend their time handling grievances rather than doing their normal tasks, with the result that they seemed to seek out grievances. Few if any companies installed the Leitch Plan after 1920.[11]

The other principal type of employee representation plan was introduced at Colorado Fuel and Iron in 1915. It had a curious background. The man most responsible for its conception was William Lyon Mackenzie King. As a young man, King had a brief career in the United States. Canadian born and educated, he eventually received a Ph.D. in economics from Harvard. Deeply impressed by the work of Jane Addams at Hull House in Chicago, with whom he was personally acquainted, King addressed much of his graduate work to the problem of industrial relations; his doctoral thesis was a comparative study of sweatshops.

After Harvard, King returned to Canada where he entered politics and by 1909 became minister of labour. Two years later his party met defeat and he found himself unemployed. In September, 1913, the United Mine Workers struck the Colorado Fuel and Iron Company, then under control of the Rockefeller family. A Harvard acquaintance suggested King's name to John D. Rockefeller, Jr., as a possible conciliator and Rockefeller hired him at the handsome salary of $12,000 a year. The two became close friends, but King's brilliant mind so dominated his employer that Rockefeller later recalled that "I was merely King's mouthpiece. I needed education." With Rockefeller's blessing King went to Colorado and constructed what became famous as the Rockefeller Plan.[12]

Mackenzie King later recalled that his purpose was to use Colorado "as a laboratory in which to demonstrate what could be done as a result of applying certain principles in which I firmly believed." King was not an entirely dispassionate social scientist; but neither was he simply a hack advisor sent to pacify a turbulent situation. His outlook was certainly acceptable to young Rockefeller, but it was also advanced beyond nineteeth-century industrial autocracy.[13]

King saw the world as a continual struggle between good and evil. World War I had just broken out and he likened it to the industrial strife in Colorado—in each case good men sought to end the struggle and evil men refused. "The solution of the problem," King wrote, "will of necessity be much the same in the case of both. It will be necessary to devise means whereby the forces seeking aggressive and destructive action shall not be permitted to gain the upper hand, thereby destroying the effective working of those forces which are making for peace and works and health." This, as King put it, was "the underlying idea in my mind."[14]

The difficulty with such a theory was to separate the aggressors from the men of good will. In Colorado, King found the line discernible. The main demand of the United Mine Workers was for recognition of the union, but King regarded recognition as a superficial issue; improved working conditions were the only rightful goal. Unionism was only a means to an end, and a fight for recognition per se was misdirected and ought to be resisted. The problem, then, was to devise a mechanism which would avoid recognition (which was also Rockefeller's chief desire) and which would allow for collective bargaining of a different kind. A program to carry out the latter principle must "afford opportunity of easy and constant conference between employer and employed with reference to matters of concern to both," and also must provide "a guarantee of fair play" in determining wages and working conditions.[15] This doctrine of compromise between industrial autocracy and union recognition was the central philosophy behind not only the Rockefeller Plan but also almost all employee representation plans.

The Rockefeller Plan, in its Colorado Fuel and Iron incarnation, bore some resemblance to American governmental experience. Only wage earners who had been employed for three months could vote. At least one representative was elected for each 150 employees, which meant that most of the twenty-five mines had two representatives, but the constitution stipulated that each mine must have at least one. Only employees were eligible for the post of representative, and all representatives had to stand for reelection each year in primary and final elections held by secret ballot. Immediately after election and every four months thereafter the president of the company called a conference. The company was divided into five mine fields and separate conferences were held in each one. Four "joint committees on industrial relations" composed of three company and three employee representatives met in each district to discuss such questions as safety and accidents; sanitation, health, and housing; recreation and education; and industrial cooperation and conciliation. The latter committee was the most important as it dealt with matters of wages and working conditions. In addition, each year the president of the company called a meeting of all representatives to discuss the work of the committees. The basic structure of the Rockefeller Plan was that of a unicameral legislature.[16]

A channel thus existed through which an employee could take his grievance, either personally or through his representative. He first discussed it with his mine foreman or superintendent. If he received no satisfaction there, he went to the president's industrial representative. This individual visited each mine at least every three months and, speaking for the company president, sought to iron out disagreements. His decision, however, could be appealed directly to the president, or ultimately, to the Joint Committee on Industrial Cooperation and Conciliation in each district. Its decision bound all parties, but since labor and management were equally represented, provision existed for arbitration in case of a tie vote. The members might select an umpire, or if that were impossible, a board of three arbitrators, with each side choosing one and the two so chosen selecting the third. In either case the decision was final. Representatives who felt discriminated against for their activities in behalf of their constituents could also take their case to the Colorado State Industrial Commission.[17]

The Rockefeller Plan was hardly revolutionary. Though it was less cumbersome and included more appellate features than the Leitch Plan, it still retained much of the essence of the latter. But when Colorado Fuel and Iron offered it for approval in October, 1915 (nearly a year after the collapse of the miners' strike), it marked the first acceptance of the principle by a major American corporation. (The total vote cast at the ratification election was only 64.5 percent of the eligible employees, but fully 84 percent of those voting favored it.) Most other employee representation systems were less elaborate than either the Leitch or Rockefeller plans, but they differed more in detail than in fundamental principle.[18]

World War I provided the greatest stimulus for the spread of employee representation plans. In order to keep peace in the shipyards (which were critical to the war effort) the Wilson administration created an adjustment board as an arbitrator of disputes. It quickly found itself swamped and ordered the formation of shop committees in several yards. A similar situation developed in the railroads. The director general of the U.S. Railroad Administration created the General Board of Railway Wages and Working Conditions composed of three management and three labor representatives. Since this board could hardly handle all the railroad labor disputes in the country, it ordered establishment of local shop committees and decided to hear only their appeals. The U.S. Fuel Administration extended the use of shop committees to the coal industry.[19]

In the fall of 1917 severe strikes in other critical industries threatened to cripple war production. An investigating commission sent by Wilson reported that American labor relations were unhealthy because employers refused to bargain on other than an individual basis. In April, 1918, by presidential proclamation Wilson established the National War Labor Board, charging it with the responsibility of keeping labor peace.[20]

Wilson's proclamation in effect called for a truce. It guaranteed labor both the right "to bargain collectively through chosen representatives" and immunity from dismissal for doing so. It at once gave employees the right to organize and prevented employers from using "coercive measures" against them. The *quid pro quo*, in other words, was that labor received the right to organize but not to strike. It was up to the War Labor Board to devise machinery that would fit these constraints.[21]

The president's words obviously lacked detail, but by October, 1918, the board had written a standard plan for the selection of shop committees. Many of its features derived from the Rockefeller Plan: one representative was to be elected for each 100 employees; anyone employed three months could vote; representatives had to be American citizens over eighteen, with the ability to speak and write English; and joint committees composed of equal members of management and labor representatives were to be formed. The War Labor Board added the provision that it would supervise elections and established itself as the court of appeal.[22]

The stimulus of the War Labor Board led to a dramatic increase in the number of plans in force. At the close of 1917 there were probably fewer than two dozen employee representation plans of all types in operation in the United States, but War Labor Board directives led to their introduction into at least a hundred firms. Action by other government agencies as well as voluntary introduction brought further increases. By August, 1919, the National Industrial Conference Board reported that there were 225 plans in operation covering 500,000 workers. In the following two and one-half years expansion was startling—by February, 1922, there were approximately 725 plans operating in the country.[23]

There were several reasons for the rapid expansion in the postwar years. Wilsonian rhetoric had its effect; some businessmen felt that they should practice democracy in industry if the United States was to preach democracy abroad. John D. Rockefeller, Jr., commented: "On the battlefields of France this nation poured out its blood freely in order that democracy might be maintained at home and that its beneficent institutions might become available in other lands as well. Surely it is not consistent for us as Americans to demand democracy in government and practice autocracy in industry." The Bolshevik revolution was an even more important foreign event. Paul Litchfield, vice-president and factory manager of Goodyear Tire and Rubber, wrote a little book in praise of employee representation in which he warned of the "alarming state of affairs in Eastern Europe which is gradually spreading westward." "Bolshevism," he added, "is an industrial disease, and a very contagious one," and businessmen ought quickly to find a "remedy" for it.[24]

The economic situation in the United States heightened the fears playing upon the capitalist mind. Wages had risen to unprecedented levels during World War I, and businessmen anticipated an inevitable return to prewar levels. At least some of the employee representation plans, accordingly, were the result of fears of the reaction of labor to imminent wage reductions. Nearly all plans were initiated at the employer's request, and afterward many employers proposed wage reductions to the new committees.[25] There was little point in proposing the introduction of shop committees if one expected shortly to raise wages.

Even more importantly, trade unionists made impressive gains during the war. Membership in the American Federation of Labor increased by more than 50 percent between 1916 and 1920. If Bolshevism was a distant threat, trade unionism was an immediate one, and with employee representation plans businessmen moved to head it off as well.

Rather than the grudging acceptance of a necessary infringement on their rights, businessmen reflected an enthusiastic satisfaction with the results of employee representation, at least in the early years. A 1922 survey of 361 firms having representation plans reported that 356 companies believed that the plans had had beneficial effects on labor relations and that 310 out of 349 felt that they had led to reduced turnover. In other surveys, the Dutchess Bleachery (bleachers of cotton goods) boasted that its model representation plan had "revolutionized the attitudes of operatives toward production," and another dozen companies reported similar results. Twenty-three companies commented on the effectiveness of representation in reducing strike incidence. In four cases the firms reported that their employees declined to join strikes which occurred either in the industry or in the locality. Executives of the Packard Piano Company, which utilized the Leitch Plan, claimed that aside from improving efficiency and reducing turnover, the plan reduced strike incidence. There is some evidence to support these claims: in July, 1918, a severe strike hit the General Electric plant at West Lynn (whose management was later described as "very autocratic" by a company official), and all but a handful of employees joined an affiliate of the AFL. When efforts at mediation failed, the War Labor Board stepped in and introduced a representation plan which succeeded so successfully in replacing the trade union that eight years later even the strike leaders no longer carried union cards.[26]

Underlying these results, businessmen felt, was the "improved understanding" on the part of employees brought about through representation. Not only were such programs effective antidotes for "propaganda put out by organized labor and labor agents" according to Arthur Young of International Harvester; they also, said the Cleveland Chamber of Commerce, taught "sound economics" to employees so that "they may be assisted to consider labor relations from a sound viewpoint"—such "sound economics" being particularly useful in a time of imminent wage cuts. On a more general level, representation would supply the "continuous education" that General Electric averred would bring employee and employer closer together. Previously, the company explained, employees had only "limited information" which led them to "many misunderstandings and narrow views." But with representation they received "a broader viewpoint" and came to have "an increased sympathy with the aims and purposes of management."[27]

But the rank-and-file workers, with some exceptions, were not similarly enthusiastic about the matter. Nor were they antagonistic, except for union sympathizers and some others. In fact, the general mood seemed to be one of apathy. At Colorado Fuel and Iron, for example, the first vote for representatives, in October, 1915, was also the highest in terms of percentage of eligible employees: 64.6 percent. Between 1917 and 1920, only a little more than half cast their ballots, and by 1921 the number voting had declined to 46.6 percent. In only half the mines was there enough interest to hold the annual meeting the constitution required; in the others miners voted on their way to or from work or passed the ballot box around the mines. In 1927 Bethlehem Steel's Charles Schwab stated that "when we started 10 years ago we had great difficulty getting the workmen to take the slightest interest in it." (Schwab added that, by 1927, 93 percent of the employees voted for representatives, but that number is so large as to suggest coercion.) The Durham Hosiery Mills, Procter and Gamble, and Dan River Mills experienced similar employee apathy.[28]

Not that employee representation brought them no benefits. On the contrary, in some instances representatives were able to secure quite significant improvements, even in the vital area of wages. For instance, employees of the Kimberly-Clark Company, a paper-making firm, received a handsome 20 percent wage advance during the first year the mill council operated. An even more notable gain was registered at Colorado Fuel and Iron, where management intended to follow the lead of U.S. Steel, which decided in 1918 to pay time-and-a-half for the last four hours of the regular twelve-hour day. Through the machinery of the Rockefeller plan, however, employees expressed a preference for an actual eight-hour working day, combined with a 10 percent wage increase. Somewhat reluctantly, the company agreed, and though the change decreased the worker's actual income, it cut his workday by a third, brought him home four hours earlier, and put him five years ahead of U.S. Steel employees.[29]

Employee representatives made other meaningful, if less spectacular, contributions. In some instances companies allowed the representation machinery to work out wage relationships between various skills. At Standard Oil of New Jersey, for example, employee representatives compromised disputes about the relative wages of pipefitters and boilermakers. Companies frequently turned over the operation of other forms of welfare capitalism to employee committees, which came to bear some responsibility for medical care, education, and recreation. It seemed wise to some companies to have an employee committee select a physician or determine a school curriculum. A particularly favorite area of involvement was housing, and committees had some success in improving living conditions. At Colorado Fuel and Iron, for instance, porches were screened, walls were painted, roofs were patched, sewers were connected, and evictions became less frequent, all through the mechanics of the Rockefeller Plan.[30]

Representatives were also instrumental in countering some threats to job security. For instance, since most plans provided that each department of the company would have at least one representative, every foreman in these cases was confronted by an elected representative who either had or could get the ear of management, and workers knew that if they were harassed or dismissed, they had at least some recourse. (Little wonder that foremen, next to union officials the top sergeants of industry, became the staunchest opponents of the system.) At Goodyear the plan also dictated that any employee who worked for the company for three years could not be discharged without the approval of his council member, and a five-year employee could not be discharged without the additional approval of the factory manager.[31]

Employee representatives dealt with a broad range of problems and grievances, including shop rules and regulations, piece rates, scientific management schemes, promotion, discharge, suspension, fines, seniority, safety measures, and general working conditions as well as a whole array of welfare matters. Companies never tired of reciting statistics on the number of grievances taken up and settled to show the effectiveness of the plans. During the first month of the industrial relations plan at Standard Oil of Indiana, for example, 236 matters were discussed and 154 settled to the satisfaction of employees, according to the company. An eastern firm with fourteen employee representation plans in operation reported that in the single year of 1920, 4,520 different subjects were discussed by its committees. These were not manufactured at the instigation of the company; when plans were introduced, employee committees were in fact often inundated by a host of complaints which had accumulated for years.[32]

Where, then, was the source of apathy? For one thing, the terrain of representative activity was not an inspiring chain of unending peaks of success; there were many valleys and quite a bit of desert. A great many of the issues dealt with were minor, and some of the gains involved were, as one executive phrased it, "picayune things." In 1925, for example, one of the topics discussed before the employee council of the Pacific Mills of Lawrence, Massachusetts, was the condition of the cats in the mill. A complainant asked that the cats either be fed or disposed of, which led to much debate about the number of rats and mice available in the mill for the cats to catch.[33]

As for the important matters, like wages and hours, the impressive advances at Kimberly-Clark and Colorado Fuel and Iron were the exception rather than the rule. Most of the wage hikes achieved through representative committees were simply adjustments to the prevailing industry rates, many of which might very well have taken place in any case. This was borne out, ironically, at Colorado Fuel and Iron, where the Rockefeller Plan that had done so much for the steelworker did nothing to raise the wages of coal miners. Instead, Colorado Fuel invariably determined wage rates according to the rates prevailing in the coal industry, which were set through negotiations at union mines. Colorado Fuel miners thus received the benefits of the union miner's struggle without facing the hazards, leading one Welsh miner at Colorado Fuel to a wry observation: "the Biblical proverb that 'Thou shalt eat thy bread by the sweat of thy brow' is turned around here. The union miners in other parts of the country sweat and we eat the bread." Furthermore, in spite of the successes, both large and moderate, representative wage negotiations were far from being a source of employee satisfaction. Quite the contrary; wages were the most discussed subject at representative meetings, and, according to the National Industrial Conference Board, wage questions were the type least often decided according to employee wishes.[34] By their fruits shall ye know them.

But also by their faces. If businessmen found satisfaction in the contrast between company committees and independent unions, the worker saw clear evidence in it for suspicion and disappointment. For one thing, there was no nationwide bargaining, so a large company with several plants or mines could transfer production to an alternate site when faced with heavy demands, thereby playing off one set of employees against another. Since employee representatives had to be employed by the parent company, it was highly unlikely that committees would have what the unions had: expert negotiators with independent information about current wages, working conditions, and the cost of living. As part-timers the representatives could hardly be expected to devote their entire attention to labor's interests. Most importantly, while a union leader would likely be fired for not speaking loudly enough in labor's behalf, such aggressiveness (strongly denounced by businessmen as improper boorishness) on the part of a representative was equally likely to get him fired by the company. A former representative at Colorado Fuel and Iron, an immigrant, summed up the situation concisely: "Company officials good, smart educated men. The representative, he only one man, he got no backing, he got to fight everybody. . . . Under union, miners have educated men who no work for company, but give all their time to take up grievances. Pretty hard for man who works for the company to take up grievances because he afraid that if make the boss mad, maybe he be fired, or given bad place [to work]."[35]

Predictably, then, representatives were generally a far cry from union professionals. Surveys disclose that they were more likely than other employees to be married, native-born American citizens who owned property and were employed by their companies for several years. Companies described them to the National Industrial Conference Board as "older employees" or "of mature age." They were said to be educated and held "high standing in the community." Consistently admitted to be "conservative" or "fairly conservative," they were said to be "sanely constructive." Yet even the companies were not generally impressed with their quality. Companies used such terms as "rather lightweight" and "mediocre," and an executive of Goodyear went so far as to say that "we find that the committeemen, in their zeal to prove themselves fairminded and free of radicalism, are most apt to err on the side of being ultra-conservative."[36]

Such men were unlikely to be in close touch with rank-and-file laborers. Once representatives were elected, they communicated infrequently with employees or other representatives until the next election. They seldom held meetings with their constituents for the airing of questions of concern, nor did they often caucus together to form a united labor position. Quite aside from thus fostering apathy, this lack of grassroots discussion and bedrock support left the representatives with little bargaining authority. "The representative, he only one man, he got no backing."

Employers themselves further undercut representative strength and support. Colorado Fuel and Iron, for instance, paid the expenses of representatives and made up for wages lost when they attended regularly scheduled meetings or when a company representative visited, but in an effort to keep grievances at a minimum, the company refused to subsidize a representative who wished to initiate his own investigation.[37] More significant was the widespread "coincidence" of representation programs and wage cuts. It was foolish for businessmen to use representation as a vehicle for smoothing out wage reductions if they wanted it to succeed on a long-term basis. They could hardly expect workers to make labor heroes out of those who had rubber-stamped lower employee income.

The company union did not belong to the employee, and by and large he knew it. He might not go out on strike against it (though this did happen on at least four different occasions), or carry a banner reading "The Collective Bargaining Association Must Go" (as did the Midvale Steel and Ordnance workers in the 1919 Labor Day parade), or even sing nasty songs about it, but he was far less likely to praise and cherish it, for quite aside from what it delivered or failed to deliver, it could not be to him what the union could.[38] One of Rockefeller's lieutenants, Raymond B. Fosdick, discovered this during an inspection of one plant's system:

> There is a psychological appeal in labor unionism which has not yet been analyzed. It seems to give the men a sense not only of power but of dignity and self-respect. They feel that only through labor unions can they deal with employers on an equal plane. They seem to regard the representation plan as a sort of counterfeit, largely, perhaps, because the machinery of such plans is too often managed by the employers. They want something which they themselves have created and not something which is handed down to them by those who pay their wages.[39]

In concert with other aspects of welfare capitalism, representation's ultimate goal for the businessman was the creation of a broadly favorable atmosphere of labor relations. This was to be achieved when labor agitators and autocratic foremen were disarmed, when businessmen's ideas were widely held, and when confidence in management was full and deep. To a company known as "a good place to work" many benefits would accrue: reduced labor turnover, improved productivity, increases in job applicants, even preferential treatment at the hands of political bodies, and, most important, smooth labor waters, untroubled by strikes and agitation which threatened the power and authority of the employer. Employee representation was the main weapon of the welfare arsenal in the businessman's thrust toward this goal, and in most instances he held on to it longer than to any other form of welfare capitalism. Yet even had the New Deal not wrecked it, even had the AFL charges—that independent meetings of labor representatives were banned; that companies influenced elections, prohibited expert assistance, and intimidated representatives; that representatives lacked the power to bargain as equals; and that committees diverted attention from major questions to minor ones—even had all these charges been false,[40] and had the committees not been used to support wage cuts, even then, it is unlikely that businessmen could have achieved their goals with their representative organizations and won the worker to their side. Because the organizations were theirs, not his.

14 Response and Decline

In the mid-1920s welfare capitalism was flourishing and its exponents in the business community were quick to express their pleasure and their pride in its results. As early as 1917 a query conducted by the Bureau of Labor Statistics had disclosed that about five times as many employers reported favorable results from their welfare programs as reported unfavorable results, and this general satisfaction on the part of management continued into the mid-twenties. Labor relations were more placid, employee morale seemed better, and labor turnover was down. None could match the reduction in turnover at the Ford Motor Company, where the rate dropped from 370 percent in 1913 to 54 percent in 1914 and 16 percent in 1915. But other businesses could and did show that turnover decreased in the twenties and this evidence convinced them that welfarism had value.[1]

Many companies reported that welfare work had favorably affected their employees' character. In 1921 a vice-president of the John B. Stetson hatmaking firm remarked that "we are beginning to see decided improvement in the character and general attitude of the men.... They are easier to deal with when questions of work and policy are considered." Seven years later President Harry Fitzgerald of the Riverside and Dan River Cotton Mills reported that his company had "virtually succeeded in transforming the entire community.... [This] has more than repaid all it cost, to say nothing of the infinite satisfaction of having had some small share in the transformation of so many lives."[2]

Other companies reported that the improved loyalty and efficiency were well worth the expense. The treasurer of Wagner Electric of Saint Louis, for example, said his company had been "amply repaid in the better service obtained from our employees." The president of the Waltham Watch Company even found the converse to be true; not only did welfare practices create a feeling of loyalty when begun, but they also created disloyalty when removed. When Waltham reduced wages, stretched out hours, and disposed of costly welfare programs during the depression of 1921, the result was "great dissatisfaction."[3]

In the twenties it also seemed to many that welfarism had achieved success in the crucial areas of preventing strikes and keeping unions out. By the mid-twenties the number of strikes in the United States declined to a third of what it had been in the years just before World War I. Trade union membership also fell off sharply. The decrease has been credited to several factors, including the general prosperity of the times, the conservatism of union leaders, and a general disinclination toward reform. Business strategies were then and have ever since been considered a factor, doubtlessly correctly. Because of the clear evidence of lessening labor militancy at a time when welfare capitalism was on the rise, it would indeed be very difficult to argue that welfarism did not play a part. There was, moreover, a correlation between the presence of welfare capitalism and the absence of militancy in some industries. In the iron and steel and metal industries where welfare programs were very common, there were less than a fifth as many strikes in 1924 as there had been in 1916. Yet in the building trades where little welfarism existed, there were two-thirds as many strikes in 1924 as there had been in 1916.[4]

Despite the often eloquent endorsements of welfare capitalism by its practitioners, one troublesome question remained open, both then and now: had the American workingman genuinely embraced welfare capitalism or did he harbor a smoldering resentment which might burst out at any time? How did employees really feel about the welfare programs their employers provided?

Most students of welfare capitalism have placed great emphasis on its shortcomings and have argued that employees were aware of them. Its main effect, they argue, was to perpetuate a system of labor-management relations in which the distribution of power—and thus of rewards—was uneven. Since the inadequacies and inequities of welfare capitalism were so great, so the argument goes, they must have been obvious. When American workers were finally given an unfettered opportunity—as they were during the New Deal—they shunned welfare capitalism in favor of unionism. To their credit, they opted for industrial democracy.[5]

But a recent critic has concluded that such a paean to the independence of the American workingman is unjustified. Instead, according to David Brody, the evidence suggests that in the 1920s welfare capitalism had succeeded in winning the support of most workers, and if the Great Depression had not rudely intervened, the affection of workers for welfare capitalism would have continued unabated. "It is comforting to think that welfare capitalism never was a success, never persuaded the American workingman that he was best off as a ward of his employer, and never could have survived once wage earners received a free choice protected from employer retaliation," Brody has written. In his estimation, however, the facts do not allow the historian to take any such comfort.[6]

Brody's argument that welfare capitalism had won the heart of the workingman rests on certain indisputable signs of contentment. Without question the incidence of strikes was much lower during the 1920s than during the preceding decade. The rate of labor turnover declined during the 1920s as well. Some informed contemporary observers, like Robert and Helen Lynd, the students of "Middletown," detected no real concern among workers about the imbalance of power between employers and employees, and others attributed this absence less to prevailing economic conditions than to the success of management strategies. Whether the ultimate demise of welfare capitalism resulted from its inherent flaws or, as Brody argues, "from an extraordinary turn in the business cycle" is a subject worth considering.[7]

Unfortunately, the degree of worker acceptance of welfare capitalism in the 1920s cannot be measured with the same exactitude allowed by modern polling techniques. Sufficient data do exist, however, to make Brody's theory seem implausible. Analysis of the decline of welfare capitalism in the 1930s further weakens the argument.

Without question, some workers appreciated welfare programs and to that extent welfarism did combat unions successfully. The employees of the Cleveland Twist Drill Company, for example, unanimously signed a petition thanking management for "the many comforts and conveniences" it had furnished. A substantial number of businessmen reported that employees expressed appreciation, and students who were generally unfriendly to welfare practices interviewed workers in factories and admitted this to be true. Even "Mother" Jones, the eighty-three-year-old matriarch of the American labor movement, shook the hand of John D. Rockefeller, Jr., after he described the welfare programs of the Colorado Fuel and Iron

Company (though she earned the enmity of much of the Left for doing so).[8]

Yet there was another side to the response of employees to welfare work. An element of welfarism was very frequently present in the most violent of American labor disputes. The best-known example was the Pullman strike of 1894, but welfare programs were also in existence at the sites of other violent strikes, such as those in the coal fields of Colorado, West Virginia, and Pennsylvania, in the Michigan copper mines, in the steel industry in 1919, in the textile mills of the North and Southeast, and in several railroad strikes. Important welfare companies struck included (besides the Pullman Company) National Cash Register in 1901, International Harvester on several occasions, Ludlow Manufacturing in 1909, Pressed Steel Car Works the same year, Colorado Fuel and Iron in 1913, Westinghouse Air Brake in 1914, United States Steel in 1919, Riverside and Dan River Cotton Mills in 1930, and the Kohler Company (makers of plumbing goods) in 1934.[9] The correlation between violence and welfarism indicates that a great many workers found welfarism distasteful.

Labor leaders of the 1920s to a man disliked welfarism and clearly hated employee representation. Articles slamming welfarism regularly appeared in the labor press. But ultimately of greater importance was what rank-and-file employees thought of welfare practices. They were certainly not articulate, but occasionally they recorded their feelings. A group of employees of Plymouth Cordage, for example, described their company's profit sharing program as "a sottish or we could say very stupid idea.... [We] are not asking for such as you call it a Bonus. [No!] But are asking for a better condition in wages and ... hours. Other employees similarly reasoned that money spent on welfare work was money that could have fattened their pay envelopes.[10]

A favorite pastime which enlivened conferences of industrial welfare workers was exchanging stories of encounters with unappreciative workers. A young woman in charge of one of the National Tube Company's playgrounds, for example, told of asking a child whose face and hands were dirty to have her mother wash them. The next day the little girl was still unwashed and the playground director inquired whether she had followed her instructions. She had, she insisted, but her mother had sent back counterinstructions to the director—"She said you go to — — —." Jean Hoskins, the "service secretary" of a Maine manufacturing firm, recalled how local newspapers heralded her arrival on a mission of "social uplift." When she reached the plant, workers greeted her with "hard suspicious glances" and dubbed her "Sanitary Jane." On another occasion thirty angry girls descended on her office and declared that they were just as clean as she was and that they would not submit to physical examinations or take off their shoes and stockings for anyone.[11]

Visitors who interviewed factory workers on the job commonly found dissatisfaction with welfarism. Algie M. Simons, a reconstructed socialist who wrote a book-length study of personnel practices, visited the Pullman Company in the late 1890s and reported that "nowhere have I seen such concentrated hatred against an employer." More than a third of Pullman's employees chose to live outside the town, even though they could not duplicate the living arrangements for the same price. A student who canvassed welfare companies in the twenties reported visiting one where employees resented welfare practices so bitterly that they engaged in deliberate sabotage against the company.[12]

Thus some employees indicated that they approved of welfare programs while others indicated (usually more forcefully) that they did not. In only one known instance was a careful survey taken of the opinions of *all* the employees in a factory. In the mid-twenties a Harvard scholar, J. David Houser, circulated a questionnaire in a factory which he did not identify. He asked workers to rate five "incentives" on a five-point scale: job security, remuneration, advancement by ability, opportunity for promotion, and welfare work. An extremely favorably attitude rated 5. Welfare work averaged 2.0 for all the workers in the factory, or in slight disfavor. Among the five incentives tested, welfare work scored lowest or most unfavorably. Houser's impressions gathered in other factories confirmed the data.[13]

As a whole, workers were more likely to respond passively or negatively to welfarism rather than to embrace it openly, but one group supported it with regularity—Afro-American workers. Trade unions in which prejudice was the rule rather than the exception offered little to black men. Black workers, accordingly, frequently supported employee representation even though they were denied equal participation in the plans. They were surprised and flattered when white men asked to confer with them. The *Southern Workman,* the voice of Hampton Institute, praised the welfare capitalism of the Tennessee Coal, Iron, and Railroad Company as "an outstanding example of what can be done to improve the living and social status of the Negro industrial workers."[14]

The key to the varied response to welfare capitalism was its undeniably paternalistic and maternalistic quality. One of its chief strategies, as has been pointed out, was that of strengthening the worker's family life. Through welfare programs, corporations even came to fulfill some of the functions of the family. They provided food and shelter, training, play, comfort during illness or old age, and even discipline. Many businessmen thought of their labor forces as second families. "I was just too stupid to realize," lamented James Inglis, president of the American Blower Company, after belatedly learning of welfarism, "that I had a family in my own works and never did a thing for it."[15]

Some companies carried the homelike "big family" atmosphere to extremes. U.S. Playing Card had separate stairways for men and women. Parke-Davis required that men remove their hats in departments where women were employed. Bausch and Lomb dismissed its female employees ten minutes early so that they could avoid undesirable males. Each of these companies protected its employees' womanhood. "I believe that the people who work for us should be next to us after our family," a Boston welfare capitalist remarked.[16]

Other companies mothered their employees. Certainly this was partially the function of company home economists, social workers, and nurses. A Newark, New Jersey, manufacturer put up white curtains around the factory windows and placed potted plants throughout the factory. Flowers, as noted earlier, decorated a great many factories. A New York manufacturer carefully papered the ceiling and walls of his employees' rest room, placed a rug on the floor, and made sure that easy chairs and a couch were available.[17]

The paternalism and maternalism of welfare capitalism explains why employees responded as they did. Some employees did not resent a company which acted in this manner; indeed, some welcomed it. Certainly there was little reason, for example, for black employees to resent paternalistic practices. White men customarily acted in a patronizing manner toward them and this was simply an additional instance. But employees usually preferred to take charge of their own lives and found paternalism intrinsically demeaning. By regarding himself as a father to his employees and acting accordingly, an employer unavoidably relegated them to an inferior, childlike position. When employers offered services like housing, medicine, and recreation, they did so under the uncomplimentary assumption that employees could not provide them for themselves. When employees accepted those services, they implicitly exposed a weakness. This aspect of welfare capitalism was not so insulting as to provoke outright resistance, but it was enough to induce most employees to remain cool toward the whole system.

By the late twenties the growth of welfare practices slackened measurably—a direct result of this lack of appreciation on the part of employees. A study published by the National Industrial Conference Board in 1931 showed that few companies added new welfare programs between 1925 and 1930 and nearly as many companies dropped them. The types of activities which companies preferred also changed. The more directly practical ones, like medical work, pension plans, or locker rooms replaced educational, recreational, and religious forms.[18]

Several other factors contributed to the leveling off of interest. The popularity of inexpensive automobiles ended the need for company towns. Workers who bought autos first stopped shopping at company stores and then moved out of company houses. Not all of them could afford cars in the twenties, but visitors to company towns reported finding houses left vacant though the residents in other housing remained working for the company. Automobiles also undercut the need for company doctors and company churches.[19]

The general prosperity of the period also contributed. Cities which earlier had found it difficult to provide services like recreation and education expanded their activities into these fields. Consequently, companies located in large cities became less likely to provide community services for their employees.

Some of the factors which contributed to the rise of welfarism, ironically, also contributed to its decline. As corporations became larger and larger, their managements became so distant that they lost all contact with their employees. Managers who had never had contact with employees at all had little desire to restore what they had lost. Improved technology operated in the same way. Industries in which success had come to depend on high-speed precision machinery rather than on a pool of skilled labor had little desire to protect the supply with welfare programs.[20]

Some employers came to believe that the benevolent image which welfarism promoted was counterproductive. In 1930, for example, the AFL selected the Dan River and Riverside Mills in Danville, Virginia, as a place to begin a new campaign to organize southern textile workers. One reason the union chose the Dan River Mills was because the company had acquired a reputation for fair labor practices as a result of its extensive welfare program. It might, accordingly, be expected to yield to labor demands more readily than others. No company wanted to be thought of as a pushover. Other employers believed that welfare measures simply whetted employees' appetites rather than satisfying them. Few companies were willing to give to employees something that would encourage them to ask for more.[21]

One variety of welfare capitalism, however, continued to grow in the late twenties. Businessmen began to rely more heavily on employee representation. This was the most inexpensive and effective means of minimizing the union threat. By the late twenties the art of keeping unions out had progressed to the point where companies would dispense with earlier, less efficient techniques.[22]

While by 1930 the growth of welfare capitalism was thus arrested for all practical purposes, the Great Depression terminated the movement as it had existed. With the deterioration of business conditions after 1929, welfare companies drew their belts ever tighter and reduced or eliminated expenditures on a variety of welfare activities. The great stock market crash quickly made stock purchase plans expendable. When business profits evaporated in the early thirties, profit sharing programs did likewise. Educational and recreational programs were also cut. Many company dentists, education directors, housing supervisors, recreational directors, and social workers joined the swollen ranks of the unemployed. No activity, save employee representation, escaped the cutbacks.[23]

Besides the economic downturn (which had historically slowed the development of welfare capitalism), the Great Depression brought forth a new factor which seriously and adversely affected welfarism—this was aggressively antagonistic government. As early as the famous "hundred days" of the New Deal, government distaste for some kinds of welfare capitalism became apparent. Codes of fair competition drafted in the summer and fall of 1933 by the National Recovery Administration gave the first indications of New Deal attitudes toward welfarism.

The NRA code for the cotton textile industry was the very first one written. In part it read that "there is something feudal and repugnant to American principle in the practice of employer-ownership of employee homes. . . . It is hoped that, with the creation of real industrial self-government and improvement in the minimum wage, an impetus will be given by employers to independent home ownership eventually looking toward home ownership by employees and the conversion of the differential into a wage equivalent." The code required companies to "consider the question of plans for eventual employee ownership of homes in mill villages" and to make a report by 1 January 1934. The code for the bituminous coal industry similarly sought to end the requirement of living in company houses and shopping in company stores.[24]

One section of the National Industrial Recovery Act had the curious effect of discouraging welfarism in theory but encouraging it in practice. Section 7a, NIRA's most famous provision, stipulated "that employees shall have the right to organize and bargain collectively through representatives of their own choosing, and shall be free from the interference, restraint or coercion of employers . . . in the designation of such representatives; . . . [and] that no employee and no one seeking employment shall be required as a condition of employment to join any company union or to refrain from joining . . . a labor organization of his own choosing."[25] This clause was meant to encourage unionism at the expense of employee representation plans. But the language contained an important loophole. The law prevented employers from *forcing* employees to join a company union, but it did not prevent them from *encouraging* employees to join one.

In practice, encouragement worked as well as force. Although most employers preferred not to bargain collectively at all, if they had to they preferred to do so on their own terms. Within nine months of the passage of the NIRA, dozens of companies sought to take advantage of the loophole by introducing employee representation plans. By May, 1934 (less than a year after passage), there were at least 751 employee representation plans in operation in the United States, covering nearly 2.6 million workers.[26]

In May, 1935, employers received a brief respite when the Supreme Court declared the law unconstitutional. But two months later New Deal congressmen approved the National Labor Relations Act, commonly known as the Wagner Act. This law reenacted the labor provisions of the NIRA with more care and force. Section 8 eliminated the loophole that had led to the expansion of employee representation programs. It declared that it was an "unfair labor practice" for business to support a company union or to use hiring and firing to encourage membership in one. To enforce compliance, the Wagner Act created the National Labor Relations Board.

A month after the Wagner Act, the New Deal struck yet another blow at welfare capitalism when it attempted to reenact the then-unconstitutional NRA code for the bituminous coal industry by passing the Guffey-Snyder Coal Conservation Act. This law was known popularly as the "little NRA" because it retained the labor provisions of the old NIRA. It also guaranteed miners the right to peaceable assembly as well as exemption from the requirement of living in a company house or shopping at a company store. But in 1936 the Supreme Court struck down Guffey-Snyder as it had its predecessor.

The decision against Guffey-Snyder gave employee representation a breathing spell. Many employers suspected that the Wagner Act would meet the same fate and delayed compliance until the Court ruled. Two months after the passage of the Wagner Act, in fact, there were still 672 employee representation plans in operation. But the justices ruled in favor of the Wagner Act, which spelled the end of employee representation and, indirectly, of the whole array of welfare practices. Businessmen had come to rely on employee representation, and when it fell by the wayside, the other programs were largely pointless. In 1937, moreover, the Guffey-Snyder Act reappeared in its third incarnation, the Guffey-Vinson Bituminous Coal Act. This struck a telling blow at company housing and stores.

In another way the Wagner Act impaired the operation of other forms of welfarism. In a number of cases the National Labor Relations Board issued cease-and-desist orders to prevent companies from operating social and recreational clubs. It did so whenever it found that any such club operated as a mechanism by which employees reported and discussed grievances with management. The board ruled that such a club was a company-sponsored labor organization and thus illegal under section 8. The board also issued cease-and-desist orders when it found that a company gave credit for a company-sponsored recreation program to a labor organization it liked rather than to a competing organization of which it disapproved. Explained one NLRB spokesman: "Good business, fair play, and good sportsmanship demand that the employer divorce from his recreational programs any attempt to interfere with the serious business of self-organization and collective bargaining."[27]

The Wagner Act and the National Labor Relations Board so actively encouraged the growth of unions that by 1943 membership had tripled over the 1935 level. As far as the nation's large industries were concerned, the question of union shop versus open shop, of trade union versus company union, was decided. Since the struggle against unions had been lost, there was little reason for continuing welfare programs. Gradually companies sold their houses and discontinued their welfare programs.

Three decades after the Wagner Act, in fact, there were but few remnants of welfare capitalism left. A survey of twenty-three Georgia textile mills taken in 1952 showed that while most still maintained housing, only about 40 percent of the employees still lived in company houses. Fully a third of the companies had recently sold all or part of the housing. Company towns, in fact, became rather like decrepit white elephants. In 1968 wishful entrepreneurs listed the towns of Hiawatha, Colorado, and Acme, Wyoming, for sale in their entirety. Their only remaining value consisted of a chance of converting them into successful tourist attractions. The mining town of Montreal, Wisconsin, became a ski resort.

Company houses which remained occupied lost much of their identity when sold to private owners. The aged structures without exception needed repair, and the new owners nearly always repaired them differently. The old architectural uniformity was largely lost, though it could still be observed in the outlines of buildings in the coal towns of Pennsylvania, the copper towns of Michigan, and the textile towns of Massachusetts and North Carolina. A committee was formed to preserve the remnants of the town of Pullman, and, perhaps retaining a hint of past struggles, named itself after the town's architect, Solon J. Beman, rather than after Pullman itself.[28]

Here and there a few companies continued the old programs. International Business Machines maintained company country clubs. Richfield Oil had model homes. E. I. duPont de Nemours had company psychiatrists and Reynolds Tobacco had company chaplains. Recreation remained popular, and Wisconsin Gas announced that "we feel that recreation makes for happy, close-knit families." Testimony taken by the U.S. Civil Rights Commission in 1968 disclosed that the American Can Company then owned and operated the town of Bellamy, Georgia. It still had a company school and a company store with prices substantially higher than in a nearby supermarket. The company still made deductions for rent and food from each paycheck and still had employees who had virtually nothing left to spend. The textile town of Kannapolis, North Carolina, was also reportedly still operated as a company town of the old style. Profit sharing programs continued in many firms and stock ownership in some. Most companies made their factories more pleasant places to work through tasteful architecture and improved locker and lunch rooms. Yet for the most part, by 1970 welfare capitalism in its traditional sense had disappeared, survived only by curious anachronisms.[29]

The swift and nearly complete demise of welfare capitalism makes the Brody hypothesis difficult to accept. The argument that except for the severity of the Great Depression welfare capitalism would have continued indefinitely is, in the first place, quite speculative. Even when that aspect is ignored, it still fails to convince. With the single exception of employee representation plans, employer interest in welfare programs had leveled off by 1930—well before the depression had reached its nadir. While the great economic upheaval which produced the New Deal may well have been aberrant, in the face of even a moderate downturn American businessmen displayed a strong inclination to jettison welfare programs.

Substantial evidence exists, as mentioned, to suggest that even in the mid-twenties a great many employees had serious reservations (to say the least) about the effectiveness and advisability of welfare programs. It is very possible that some circumstance other than a severe depression might have broadened that discontent and translated it into political action. If, for example, the economy had in fact continued to grow in the thirties and forties in much the same way that it grew in the twenties, the gulf between income received by employers and employees would almost certainly have widened. In a society with democratic traditions like the United States, it seems unlikely that such an inequitable distribution of wealth and prerogative could have been protected indefinitely. If industrial unions had not won out, some other counterweight would likely have appeared.

It is hardly plausible, furthermore, to assume that American businessmen sought to maintain their grasp on welfare programs indefinitely. If housing, education, recreation, and social work had remained business functions a great deal longer, they would have grown in scope and complexity to the extent that their administrators would have become encumbered by nearly insurmountable difficulties, not to mention enormous expenses. The greatest likelihood is that businessmen would have become eager to surrender such responsibilities.

If Brody was somewhat off the mark when he suggested that welfare capitalism possessed sufficient vitality to continue indefinitely, he was correct in his assertion that welfare capitalists were far more serious about solving the social problems attendant to industrialization than their critics have been willing to admit.[30] As the critics of business have argued, and as much in the foregoing chapters has confirmed, welfare capitalism left much to be desired. Yet if welfare capitalism was an unpleasant step in the process of American industrialization, it was probably a necessary one.

The fact is that a society making heavy investments in capital goods cannot at once afford good housing, good schools, good medicine, and generous pensions for all its workers. Nor does a society become immediately aware of all the peculiar problems accompanying industrialization, particularly if (as in the United States case) the experience of others is either completely missing or only marginally applicable. Often hard-pressed businessmen were breaking new ground with their welfare programs, and if they did not always see the best possible solution, they were not the only ones. As confused and mixed as the motives of welfare capitalists were, and as ineffective and even devious as their programs sometimes seemed, their critics were often equally myopic.

Welfare capitalism met the human problems of industrialization in a way which at best can be termed only minimally acceptable. But *some* effort had to be made, and in the transitional years workable alternatives were scarce. Welfare capitalism was but a temporary expedient, an interim solution. It was better than nothing at all, but it could never have fulfilled the high hopes of its advocates. Yet if in its substance welfare capitalism was sorely lacking, in its functioning it anticipated the bureaucratic solutions implemented by the critics of business.

The New Deal years, it has often been observed, exhibited numerous inconsistencies. While chastising business for its paternalism, New Dealers built massive bureaucracies aimed at imposing solutions to social problems from above. The small army of social workers fielded by the New Deal, for example, was in one sense a replacement for the industrial welfare workers hired by American corporations. (Businessmen were at least equally inconsistent: although they had been seeking to mold the lives of others for years, their major objection to the New Deal was that it was paternalistic. It could be argued, though, that businessmen learned more rapidly than their critics the difficulty, if not the folly, of imposing social programs from above.)

The record of welfare capitalism suggests, then, that given the continued growth of industrialism, a bureaucratic solution to the concomitant social problems was all but inevitable. The key question was whether the technical elite which would operate the bureaucracy would function under the aegis of business or of government. Viewed in this way, welfare capitalism becomes an important element in the emerging pattern of economic organization. It should not be overlooked by students of organizational history.

The record of welfare capitalism suggests that it does indeed matter whether the bureaucracy dealing with social programs serves a private or a public interest. Although businessmen were hardly less sophisticated than their critics, the fact remains that ultimately the package of programs they offered could not fulfill the aspirations of their employees. While the record of welfare capitalism was not as bad as labor critics sometimes made it out to be, it is true that government-operated welfare programs have resulted in substantial improvement for the labor force. Welfare capitalism, a bureaucratic approach designed for business ends, has not been greatly missed, nor does its return seem likely.

Notes

Chapter 1. The Crisis of Industrial Relations

1. The Bureau of Labor was imprecise in its definition of a strike, but the average of the strikes it discussed involved about 270 workers and lasted about 24 days. G. W. W. Hanger, "Strikes and Lockouts in the United States," *Bulletin of the Bureau of Labor* 9, pt. 2, no. 54 (September 1904) : 1099.

2. *St. Louis Star,* 9 March 1928; U.S., Congress, Senate, Committee on Interstate Commerce, *Hearings, Conditions in the Coal Fields of Pennsylvania, West Virginia, and Ohio,* 70th Cong., 1st sess., 10 February-17 May 1928, p. 947; M. McCusker, "Report on the Colorado Situation," report to the U.S. Commission on Industrial Relations, 3 February 1915, Commission on Industrial Relations Records, State Historical Society of Wisconsin, pp. 18-24; William Zumach, "Report on Investigation of Detective Agencies," report to the U.S. Commission on Industrial Relations, 1 September 1914, pp. 2-3, Commission on Industrial Relations Records; State Historical Society of Wisconsin; B. M. Rastall, "The Cripple Creek Srike of 1893," Colorado College Studies, General Series no. 17, Social Science Series no. 5, vol. 2 (Colorado Springs, Col., 1905), p. 31; Bituminous Operators' Special Committee, "The United Mine Workers in West Virginia," brief submitted to the U.S. Coal Commission, August 1923, reprinted in Senate, *Conditions in the Coal Fields,* p. 2014.

3. Inis Weed, drafts of reports on violence and suppression in industrial disputes [1915], folder 1, p. 18, Commission on Industrial Relations Records, box 7, National Archives; U.S., Congress, Senate, Subcommittee of the Committee on Education and Labor, *Hearings, Conditions in the Paint Creek District, West Virginia,* 63d Cong., 1st sess., 1913, pp. 581-94, 644-46, 666-68, 684-90; U.S., Senate, *Conditions in the Coal Fields,* p. 2480; U.S., Congress, House, *Report on the Miners' Strike in Westmoreland County, Pa. in 1910-11,* 62d Cong., 2d sess., Doc. no. 847, 1912, pp. 110-21; Senate, *Conditions in the Coal Fields,* p. 2644.

4. U.S., Congress, Senate, Committee on Education and Labor, *Hearings, West Virginia Coal Fields,* 67th Cong., 1st sess., 1921, pp. 53-56, 169-73.

5. Henry Winthrop Ballantine, "Martial Law During Strikes, With Special Reference to its Regulation and Restraint," [1914?], report to the U.S. Commission on Industrial Relations Records, file 468, National Archives, p. 1.

6. U.S., *Congressional Record,* 66th Cong., 2d sess., 1920, 44, pt. I, p. 31.

7. Harriet Herring, *Welfare Work in Mill Villages: The Story of Extra-Mill Activities in North Carolina* (Chapel Hill: University of North Carolina Press, 1929) ; *Monthly Bulletin of the American Iron and Steel Institute* 2, no. 1 (January 1914) : passim; *The Hillbilly,* 1922 school yearbook of Tridelphia District Schools, Man,

West Virginia, Records of the U.S. Coal Commission, entry 77, box 41, Federal Records Center, Suitland, Maryland, pp. 73-75.

8. "Expenses of Employee Services Carried on by the United States Steel Corporation," *Industrial Relations* 18, no. 37 (13 September 1924): 2083; Victor H. Olmsted, "The Betterment of Industrial Conditions," *Bulletin of the Department of Labor* 5, no. 31 (November 1900): 1151-53.

9. Otto P. Geier, "Health of the Working Force," *Industrial Management* 54, no. 1 (October 1917): 19; W. D. Earnest (of John Wanamaker Company, New York, New York) to Boston Chamber of Commerce, 14 April 1913, Boston Chamber of Commerce Records, file 332-19, and Dr. R. S. Quimby (service manager, Hood Rubber Company, Watertown, Massachusetts) to E. M. Hood, 29 July 1927, Manufacturers' Research Association Records, Baker Library, Harvard University, Cambridge, Massachusetts.

10. U.S., Congress, Senate, Committee on Education and Labor, *Hearings, Investigation of Strike in Steel Industries,* 66th Cong., 1st sess., 1919, p. 129; Gerald W. Johnson, "Service in the Cotton Mills," *American Mercury* 5 (June 1925): 223; Edward Berman, "Paternalism and the Wage Earner," *American Federationist* 32, no. 5 (May 1925): 360; R. A. Mitchell (agent, Alabama City) to J. Howard Nichols (treasurer, Dwight Manufacturing Company), 16 January 1897, Dwight Manufacturing Company Records, box MH-1, Baker Library.

11. Louis A. Boettiger, *Employee Welfare Work: A Critical and Historical Study* (New York: Ronald Press, 1923), p. 196; Mitchell to Nichols, 14 January 1898, Dwight Manufacturing Company Records, box MH-1; "Expenses of Employee Services Carried on by U.S. Steel," p. 2083; "Sanitary Survey of Kayford, Kanawha County, West Virginia," Coal Commission Records, entry 13, box 7, p. 2; U.S., Bureau of Labor Statistics, *Welfare Work for Employees in Industrial Establishments in the United States,* Bulletin no. 250, 1919, pp. 85-87; Louis E. Van Norman, "Why Not More Beautiful Factories? Some Opinions of Manufacturers as to Attractive Business Plants," *Home and Flowers* 13, no. 1 (1902): 25; J.R. Snavely, "The Industrial Community at Hershey, Pa.," *American Landscape Architect* 3 (1930): 25.

12. Testimony of Ezra Van Horn (vice-president, Clarkson Coal Mining Company), Senate, *Conditions in the Coal Fields,* p. 2254; C. P. Marshall, rough draft of a pamphlet on welfarism, [1920?], Plymouth Cordage Company Records, file H, box 3, "Mr. Marshall's Reports" folder, Baker Library; U.S., Bureau of Labor Statistics, *Health and Recreation Activities in Industrial Establishments, 1926,* Bulletin no. 458, 1928, pp. 54-55; H. J. Heinz Company, "The Home of the '57,'" [ca. 1910], Boston Chamber of Commerce Records, file 332-19, p. 34; Budgett Meakin, *Model Factories and Villages: Ideal Conditions of Labour and Housing* (Philadelphia: George W. Jacobs and Co., 1905), p. 128; Goodyear Tire and Rubber Company, *The Work of the Labor Division* (Akron, Ohio: By the author, 1920), pp. 30-31; Thomas Darlington, "Model Yard Conditions at the Bethlehem Steel Company's Works," *Monthly Bulletin of the American Iron and Steel Institute* 1, no. 1 (January 1913): 17.

13. George W. Eads, "N. O. Nelson, Practical Cooperator, and the Great Work He Is Accomplishing for Human Upliftment," *Arena* 36, no. 204 (November 1906): 473-74; Robert Ozanne, *A Century of Labor-Management Relations at McCormick and International Harvester* (Madison: University of Wisconsin Press, 1967), pp. 36-37; Giselle D'Unger, "The Spirit of Neighborliness in a Great Corporation,"

World To-Day 17, no. 6 (December 1909): 1287; Alfred Lief, *"It Floats": The Story of Procter and Gamble* (New York: Rinehart and Co., 1958), pp. 131-32; Robert Glass Cleland, *A History of Phelps Dodge, 1834-1950* (New York: Alfred A. Knopf, 1952), pp. 92-93, 201.

14. Irving Bernstein, *The Lean Years: A History of the American Worker, 1920-1933* (Boston: Houghton Mifflin Co., 1960; Baltimore, Md.: Penguin Books, 1966), p. 187; Ozanne, *Century of Labor-Management Relations,* p. 245; Milton Derber, *The American Idea of Industrial Democracy, 1865-1965* (Urbana: University of Illinois Press, 1970), pp. 206ff.; Homer J. Hagedorn, "A Note on the Motivation of Personnel Management: Industrial Welfare 1885-1910," *Explorations in Entrepreneurial History* 10, nos. 3-4 (April 1958): 137.

15. Allan Nevins and Frank Ernest Hill, *Ford: Expansion and Challenge, 1914-1933* (New York: Charles Scribner's Sons, 1957), pp. 345, 354. The major works of the business revisionists are discussed in Gabriel Kolko, "The Premises of Business Revisionism," *Business History Review* 38, no. 3 (Autumn 1959): 330-44. See also John Tipple, "The Anatomy of Prejudice: Origins of the Robber Baron Legend," *Business History Review* 33, no. 4 (Winter 1959): 510-23.

16. William Appleman Williams, *The Contours of American History* (Cleveland: World Publishing Company, 1961; Chicago: Quadrangle Books, 1966), pp. 360, 416, 428, 438-39, 470. Others who have written in the same mode include Gabriel Kolko, *The Triumph of Conservatism: A Reinterpretation of American History, 1900-1916* (Glencoe, Ill.: Free Press of Glencoe, 1963; Chicago: Quadrangle Books, 1967), James Weinstein, *The Corporate Ideal in the Liberal State: 1900-1918* (Boston: Beacon Press, 1968), and Stephen J. Scheinberg, "The Development of Corporation Labor Policy, 1900-1940" (Ph.D. diss., Department of History, University of Wisconsin, 1966).

17. Weinstein, *Corporate Ideal,* pp. 3-4; Scheinberg, "The Development of Corporation Labor Policy," pp. 171-73.

18. Robert H. Wiebe, *The Search for Order, 1877-1920* (New York: Hill and Wang, 1967); Louis Galambos, "The Emerging Organizational Synthesis in Modern American History," *Business History Review* 44, no. 3 (Autumn 1970): 280; John Higham, "Hanging Together: Divergent Unities in American History," *Journal of American History* 61, no. 1 (June 1974): 24; Ellis W. Hawley, "Herbert Hoover, the Commerce Secretariat, and the Vision of an 'Associative State,' 1921-1928," *Journal of American History* 61, no. 1 (June 1974): 116-40; James Gilbert, *Designing the Industrial State: The Intellectual Pursuit of Collectivism in America, 1880-1940* (Chicago: Quadrangle Books, 1972).

19. Daniel Nelson and Stuart Campbell, "Taylorism Versus Welfare Work in American Industry: H. L. Gantt and the Bancrofts," *Business History Review* 46, no. 1 (Spring, 1972): 16.

20. Higham, "Hanging Together," 24.

Chapter 2. The Early Days of Modern Welfarism

1. Donald Wilhelm, "Big Business Man as a Social Worker: I. Elbert H. Gary," *Outlook* 107 (22 August 1914): 1005; John Kimberly Mumford, "This Land of Opportunity: 'The Watchword of the Hour—Honest Business and Fair Play,'" *Harper's Weekly* 52, no. 2686 (13 June 1908): 20; Raymond B. Fosdick, *John D.*

Rockefeller, Jr.: A Portrait (New York: Harper and Brothers, 1956), p. 185.

2. The best definition of welfare capitalism is "anything for the comfort and improvement, intellectual or social, of the employees, over and above wages paid, which is not a necessity of the industry nor required by law," U.S., Bureau of Labor Statistics, *Welfare Work for Employees in Industrial Establishments in the United States,* Bulletin no. 250, 1919, p. 8. Other definitions may be found in Irving Bernstein, *The Lean Years: A History of the American Worker, 1920-1933* (Boston: Houghton Mifflin Co., 1960), p. 181; Stephen J. Scheinberg, "The Development of Corporation Labor Policy, 1900-1940" (Ph.D. diss., Department of History, University of Wisconsin, 1966), p. 44; Harriet Herring, *Welfare Work in Mill Villages: The Story of Extra-Mill Activities in North Carolina* (Chapel Hill: University of North Carolina Press, 1929), p. 10; Gertrude Beeks, *Welfare Work,* address before the National Association of Wool Manufactures, 7 February 1906 (By the author, 1906), p. 3; John R. Commons, " 'Welfare Work' in a Great Industrial Plant," *Review of Reviews* 28 (July 1903): 79; and Alexander Fleisher, "Welfare Service for Employees," *Annals of the American Academy* 69 (January 1917): 51.

3. Richard T. Ely, "Industrial Betterment," and "An American Industrial Experiment," *Harper's Monthly* 105 (June and September 1902): 39-45, 548-53; Commons, " 'Welfare Work,' " pp. 79-81; Victor H. Olmsted, "The Betterment of Industrial Conditions," *Bulletin of the Department of Labor* 5, no. 31 (November 1900): 117-56; New Jersey, Bureau of Statistics of Labor and Industries, *Twenty-seventh Annual Report, 1904* (Trenton, 1904); George A. Stevens and Leonard W. Hatch, "Employers' Welfare Institutions," New York, Department of Labor, *Third Annual Report of the Commissioner of Labor,* 1903, pt. 4, in New York, *Assembly Documents, 1904* 22, no. 61 (Albany, 1904); Rhode Island, Commissioner of Industrial Statistics, "Welfare Work in Rhode Island," *Nineteenth Annual Report, 1906* (Providence, 1906).

4. E. H. Cameron, *Samuel Slater, Father of American Manufactures* (Freeport, Me.: Bond Wheelwright Company, 1960), pp. ix-x, 93-95.

5. Louis A. Boettiger, *Employee Welfare Work: A Critical and Historical Study* (New York: Ronald Press, 1923), pp. 116-21; Howard M. Gitelman, "The Waltham System and the Coming of the Irish," *Labor History* 8, no. 3 (Fall 1967): 231; Charles N. Glaab and A. Theodore Brown, *A History of Urban America* (New York: Macmillan Co., 1967), p. 43; George S. White, *Memoir of Samuel Slater, the Father of American Manufactures,* 2d ed. (Philadelphia, 1836), pp. 126-42.

6. "James Montgomery on Factory Management, 1832," *Business History Review* 42, no. 2 (Summer 1968): 224-26.

7. Charles W. Moore, *Timing a Century: History of the Waltham Watch Company* (Cambridge: Harvard University Press, 1945), p. 58; William Howe Tolman, *Industrial Betterment* (New York: Social Service Press, 1900), pp. 52-53.

8. Bernard M. Cannon, "Social Deterrents to the Unionization of Southern Cotton Textile Mill Workers" (Ph.D. diss., Department of Sociology, Harvard University, 1951), p. 397n.; Donald B. Cole, *Immigrant City: Lawrence, Massachusetts, 1845-1921* (Chapel Hill: University of North Carolina Press, 1963), p. 73; William M. Leiserson, *Adjusting Immigrant and Industry* (New York: Harper & Brothers, 1924), pp. 66-70.

9. Sarah Comstock, "A Woman of Achievement: Miss Gertrude Beeks," *World's Work* 26 (August 1913): 445; Lena Harvey Tracy, *How My Heart Sang: The Story of*

Pioneer Industrial Welfare Work (New York: Richard R. Smith, 1950), p. 102.

10. Letter of S. M. Darling to C. W. Price, S. H. Crosby, et al., 18 August 1904, Cyrus H. McCormick, Jr., Papers, series 2C, box 40, State Historical Society of Wisconsin; B. Preston Clark, "Industrial Homes and Gardens," typewritten report in "Housing" folder, file H, drawer 3, Plymouth Cordage Company Records, Baker Library, Harvard University, Cambridge, Massachusetts, p. 7; Louis E. Van Norman, "Why Not More Beautiful Factories? Some Opinions of Manufacturers as to Attractive Business Plants," *Home and Flowers* 13, no. 1 (1902): 25-26.

11. National Civic Federation, *Eleventh Annual Meeting: Welfare Workers' Conference, 1911* (New York: By the author, [1911]), p. 373.

12. Tracy, *How My Heart Sang,* pp. 138-39; S. Thurston Ballard, "Welfare Work and Profit Sharing," *American Industries* 8, no. 2 (1 September 1908): 18; Charles Buxton Going, "Village Communities of the Factory, Machine Works, and Mine," *Engineering Magazine* 21, no. 1 (April 1901): 60-61.

13. Edward Chase Kirkland, *Dream and Thought in the Business Community, 1860-1900* (Ithaca: Cornell University Press, 1956; Chicago: Quadrangle Paperbacks, 1964), pp. 5-6; Samuel Crowther, "We Meet the Problem No Business Ever Escapes," *System* 49, no. 4 (April 1926): 523.

14. Samuel W. Latta, *Rest Houses for Railroad Men: How the Railroad Men Regard Such Conveniences* (New York: Welfare Department of the National Civic Federation, 1906), pp. 3, 15-26; William Menkel, " 'Welfare Work' on American Railroads," *Review of Reviews* 38 (October 1908): 450-51; C. Howard Hopkins, *History of the Y.M.C.A. in North America* (New York: Association Press, 1951), pp. 228-34.

15. Gerald G. Eggert, *Railroad Labor Disputes: The Beginnings of Federal Strike Policy* (Ann Arbor: University of Michigan Press, 1967), pp. 8-9; Menkel, " 'Welfare Work' on American Railroads," p. 451; Hopkins, *History of the Y.M.C.A.,* pp. 228-34; "Practical Altruism in the Shop," *Scientific American Supplement* 51, no. 1236 (1 June 1901), 21251.

16. Jacob Henry Dorn, *Washington Gladden, Prophet of the Social Gospel* (Columbus: Ohio State University Press, 1966), pp. 40-50, 183-200; Washington Gladden, *Working People and Their Employers* (Boston: Lockwood, Brooks and Company, 1876), pp. 44, 138, 194-95; Procter and Gamble, *Seventeenth Semi-Annual Meeting of the Employees of the Procter & Gamble Company, Ivorydale, Ohio, February 3, 1896,* pp. 5-6.

17. Stanley Buder, *Pullman: An Experiment in Industrial Order and Community Planning, 1880-1930* (New York: Oxford University Press, 1967), pp. 33, 42.

18. Ibid., pp. 50-73.

19. George W. Eads, "N. O. Nelson, Practical Cooperator, and the Great Work He Is Accomplishing for Human Upliftment," *Arena* 36, no. 204 (November 1906): 464, 473-74.

20. I. W. Howerth, "Profit-Sharing at Ivorydale," *American Journal of Sociology* 2, no. 1 (July 1896): 44-45; William Howe Tolman, *Social Engineering* (New York: Macmillan Co., 1909), pp. 328-30; Olmsted, "Betterment of Industial Conditions," pp. 1117-56; Oscar W. Nestor, "A History of Personnel Administration, 1890 to 1910" (Ph.D. diss., Department of Economics, University of Pennsylvania, 1954), p. 193.

21. Pennsylvania, Department of Internal Affairs, Bureau of Industrial Statistics,

Fifteenth Annual Report, 1887, in *Annual Report of the Secretary of Internal Affairs* 15, pt. 3 (Harrisburg, 1888); "Theory and Practice of Profit Sharing," *Catholic World* 58 (October 1893): 111-16.

22. Buder, *Pullman,* pp. 168-201, passim.

23. Olmsted, "Betterment of Industrial Conditions," pp. 1117-56; "Theory and Practice of Profit Sharing," p. 116; Boris Emmet and John E. Jeuck, *Catalogues and Counters: A History of Sears, Roebuck and Company* (Chicago: University of Chicago Press, 1950), pp. 140-41.

24. Carroll T. Fugitt, "The Truce Between Capital and Labor," *Cassier's Magazine* 28 (September 1905) : 339-59; Nicholas Paine Gilman, *A Dividend to Labor: A Study of Employers' Welfare Institutions* (Boston: Houghton, Mifflin and Company, 1899), p. 233; Olmsted, "Betterment of Industrial Conditions," pp. 1117-56; Gordon Maurice Jensen, "The National Civic Federation: American Business in an Age of Social Change and Social Reform" (Ph.D. diss., Department of History, Princeton University, 1956), pp. 146-47.

Chapter 3. Spreading the Gospel

1. Samuel M. Jones, *Letters of Labor and Love* (Indianapolis: Bobbs-Merrill Company, 1905), esp. p. 109; Edward A. Filene, *The Way Out: A Forecast of Coming Changes in American Business and Industry* (Garden City, N.Y.: Doubleday, Page and Co., 1924); Gertrude Beeks, "Practical Welfare Work," and "Lines of Practical Welfare Work," *American Industries* 5 (15 June, 1 July 1907): both pp. 3-4; National Civic Federation, Women's Department, Committee on Welfare Work for Employees, *Examples of Welfare Work in the Cotton Industry: Conditions and Progress, New England and the South* (New York, [1910?]), p. 14; letter of Employers' Welfare Underwriting Service to Boston Chamber of Commerce, 19 March 1917, Boston Chamber of Commerce Records, file 332-19, Baker Library, Harvard University, Cambridge, Massachusetts; John H. Patterson, "Altruism and Sympathy as Factors in Works Administration," *Engineering Magazine* 20, no. 4 (January 1901): 577-602.

2. Letter of Waltham Watch Company to C. Ogleby, Ferro Machine and Foundry Company, Cleveland, Ohio, 10 April 1913, Boston Chamber of Commerce Records, file 332-19; Budgett Meakin, *Model Factories and Villages: Ideal Conditions of Labour and Housing* (Philadelphia: George W. Jacobs and Co., 1905), pp. 85, 114; National Civic Federation, *Examples of Welfare Work,* p. 14; Lena Harvey Tracy, *How My Heart Sang: The Story of Pioneer Industrial Welfare Work* (New York: Richard R. Smith, 1950), p. 156.

3. Clarence J. Hicks, *My Life in Industrial Relations: Fifty Years in the Growth of a Profession* (New York: Harper and Brothers, 1941), pp. 41-58; National Civic Federation, *Examples of Welfare Work,* pp. 15-16; Stephen J. Scheinberg, "The Development of Corporation Labor Policy, 1900-1940" (Ph.D. diss., Department of History, University of Wisconsin, 1966), p. 113.

4. James Leiby, *Carroll Wright and Labor Reform: The Origin of Labor Statistics* (Cambridge: Harvard University Press, 1960), pp. 143, 144n.; William Howe Tolman, *Social Engineering* (New York: Macmillan Company, 1909), pp. 44-46; letter of Tolman to Nettie Fowler McCormick, 31 October 1901, Nettie Fowler McCormick papers, series 3B, box 27, State Historical Society of Wisconsin; Josiah

Strong, "What Social Service Means," *Craftsman* 9 (February 1906): 620-21.

5. Letters of Josiah Strong to Nettie Fowler McCormick, 22 August 1900, and Tolman to Nettie Fowler McCormick, 31 October 1901, Nettie Fowler McCormick Papers, series 3B, boxes 24, 27; League for Social Service, "Weekly Letter Service to Commercial Members," 18 and 25 December 1901, Nettie Fowler McCormick Papers, series 3B, box 27; "American Institute of Social Service, Commercial Clients Outside New York City, November 1, 1904," Cyrus H. McCormick, Jr., Papers, series 2C, box 40, State Historical Society of Wisconsin; William Howe Tolman, "The Social Engineer: A New Factor in Industrial Engineering," *Cassier's Magazine* 20, no. 2 (June 1901): 91-107; William Howe Tolman, *Industrial Betterment*, vol. 16 of Herbert B. Adams, ed., *Monographs on American Social Economics* (New York: Social Service Press, 1900); Tolman, *Social Engineering,* pp. 44-46.

6. Gordon Maurice Jensen, "The National Civic Federation: American Business in an Age of Social Change and Social Reform" (Ph.D. diss., Department of History, Princeton University, 1956), esp. p. 35.

7. Marguerite Green, *The National Civic Federation and the American Labor Movement* (Washington, D.C.: Catholic University of America Press, 1956), pp. 267-69, 275-76; National Civic Federation, *Conference on Welfare Work, 1904* (New York: Press of Andrew H. Kellogg, 1904), p. 1.

8. National Civic Federation, Welfare Department, *Welfare Work in Mercantile Houses* (New York: National Civic Federation, 1905); National Civic Federation, *Eleventh Annual Meeting: Welfare Worker's Conference, 1911* (New York: National Civic Federation, [1911]), p. 316; Green, *National Civic Federation,* pp. 269-77.

9. Jensen, "National Civic Federation," pp. 148-49; Green, *National Civic Federation,* pp. 270-74, 292-93.

10. Chicago *Record-Herald,* 3 April 1906, clipping, and letters of M. L. Goss to Cyrus H. McCormick, Jr., Papers, series 2C, box 42; Joseph W. Roe, "How the College Can Train Managers," *Engineering Magazine* 51, no. 4 (July 1916): 541; Robert Ozanne, *A Century of Labor-Management Relations at McCormick and International Harvester* (Madison: University of Wisconsin Press, 1967), p. 169.

11. Elizabeth Lewis Otey, *Employers' Welfare Work,* U.S., Bureau of Labor Statistics, Bulletin no. 123 (Washington, D.C.: Government Printing Office, 1913); U.S., Bureau of Labor Statistics, *Welfare Work for Employees in Industrial Establishments in the United States,* Bulletin no. 250, 1919; U.S., Bureau of Labor Statistics, *Health and Recreation Activities in Industrial Establishments, 1926,* Bulletin no. 458; letters of S. M. Darling to Department of Commerce and Labor, 17 November 1904, and to Winston C. Garrison, chief, Bureau of Statistics, State of New Jersey, 28 December 1904, in the Cyrus H. McCormick, Jr., Papers, series 2C, boxes 40, 41. See Essay on Sources for supplementary government publications.

12. Hicks, *My Life in Industrial Relations,* p. 30; Sarah Comstock, "A Woman of Achievement: Miss Gertrude Beeks," *World's Work* 26 (August 1913): 448.

13. American Institute of Social Service, "Weekly Commercial Letter," 30 November 1904, Cyrus H. McCormick, Jr., Papers, series 2C, box 40; Ozanne, *Century of Labor-Management Relations,* pp. 80-81.

14. Annie E. S. Beard, "Welfare Work for Government Employees," *World To-Day* 13, no. 6 (December 1907): 1273; National Civic Federation, *Proceedings, Twelfth Annual Meeting, 1912* (New York, [1913?]), pp. 285, 349-84.

15. Gerald D. Nash, "Franklin Roosevelt and Labor: The World War I Origins of

Early New Deal Policy," *Labor History* 1, no. 1 (Winter 1960): 41; letter of L. A. Coolidge, chairman, Committee on Welfare, Council of National Defense, to W. S. Gifford, director, Council of National Defense, 22 September 1917, in Chief Clerk's Records, file 119/1, Department of Labor Records, box 125.

16. Chief Clerk's Records, file 16-529, Department of Labor Records, box 52.

17. Daniel Bloomfield, *Labor Maintenance: A Practical Handbook of Employees' Service Work* (New York: Ronald Press, 1920), pp. 309-10; John Nolen, *New Towns For Old: Achievements in Civic Improvement in Some American Small Towns and Neighborhoods* (Boston: Marshall Jones Company, 1927), pp. 89-99; John Ihlder, "Card Houses: Can the Government Afford to Abandon its Industrial Villages?" *Survey* 41 (18 January 1919): 521; Richard S. Childs, "Government's Model Villages," *Survey* 41 (1 February 1919): passim; C. W. Moores, "The Greatest Landlord in America," *House Beautiful* 44, no. 7 (December 1918): 380.

18. U.S., Department of Labor, Working Conditions Service, *Treatment of Industrial Problems by Constructive Methods,* 1919, p. 3; U.S., Department of Labor, Office of the Secretary, *Report of the Working Conditions Service,* 1919, pp. 3, 6, 17-28.

19. Bituminous Operators' Special Committee, *The Company Town,* pamphlet submitted to the U.S. Coal Commission, 8 September 1923, p. 13, in U.S. Coal Commission Records, entry 8, box 3, Federal Records Center, Suitland, Maryland; Harriet L. Herring, *Welfare Work in Mill Villages: The Story of Extra-Mill Activities in North Carolina* (Chapel Hill: University of North Carolina Press, 1929), p. 120.

20. David Brody, *Steelworkers in America: The Nonunion Era* (Cambridge: Harvard University Press, 1960), pp. 180-81, 187-88.

21. Ibid., pp. 189-98; Charlton Edholm, "Why Factory Classes Pay," *Independent,* vol. 96, no. 3646, p. 94.

22. William Thomas Laprade, "Democracy or Disaster," *South Atlantic Quarterly* 18, no. 4 (October 1919): 299; memorandum of C. P. Marshall to F. C. Holmes, 2 February 1922, Plymouth Cordage Company Records, file H, drawer 3, "Mr. Marshall's Reports" folder, p. 2.

23. Joseph G. Rayback, *A History of American Labor* (New York: Free Press, 1959; Paperback ed., 1966), pp. 275, 279, 281-83; Richard B. Morris, ed., *Encyclopedia of American History* (New York: Harper and Row, 1965), p. 554.

24. Ellis W. Hawley, "Herbert Hoover, the Commerce Secretariat, and the Vision of an 'Associative State,' 1921-28," *Journal of American History* 61, no. 1 (June 1974): 118.

25. Abraham Epstein, "Industrial Welfare Movement Sapping American Trade Unions," *Current History Magazine, New York Times* 24, no. 4 (July 1926): 516; U.S., Bureau of Labor Statistics, *Health and Recreation Activities in Industrial Establishments, 1926,* Bulletin no. 458, 1928, p. 86; U.S., Bureau of the Census, *Historical Statistics of the United States: Colonial Times to 1957,* 1960, p. 91; Raynal C. Bolling, "United States Steel Corporation and Labor Conditions," *Annals of the American Academy* 42 (July 1912): 39; "Expenses of Employee Services Carried on by the United States Steel Corporation," *Industrial Relations* 18, no. 37 (13 September 1924): 2083. See also "What Personnel Activities Cost," *Industrial Relations* 2, no. 14 (17 April 1920): 221; U.S., Bureau of Labor Statistics, *Welfare Work for Employees in Industrial Establishments,* Report no. 250, p. 118; National Industrial Conference Board, *Effect of the Depression on Industrial Relations Programs* (New York: By the author, 1934), p. 14.

Chapter 4. Goals and Strategies

1. Letter of Henry Bruére to Stanley Fowler McCormick, 27 July 1903, Cyrus H. McCormick, Jr., Papers, series 2C, box 41, State Historical Society of Wisconsin; National Civic Federation, *Conference on Welfare Work, 1904* (New York: Press of Andrew H, Kellogg, 1904), p. 61; cf. David Brody, *Steelworkers in America: The Nonunion Era* (Cambridge: Harvard University Press, 1960), p. 177, for avowals of philanthropic goals by Elbert H. Gary.

2. Augustus P. Loring, memorandum of 7 February 1912, Plymouth Cordage Company Records, file H. drawer 3, Baker Library, Harvard University, Cambridge, Massachusetts, p. 1; quoted in Robert Ozanne, *A Century of Labor-Management Relations at McCormick and International Harvester* (Madison: University of Wisconsin Press, 1967), p. 86.

3. U.S., Congress, House, *Report of the Industrial Commission on the Relations and Conditions of Capital and Labor Employed in Manufactures and General Business,* 14, 57th Cong., 1st sess., 1901, House Doc. 183, pp. 350-51; Graham Taylor, "The Policy of Being Human in Business," Chicago *Daily News,* 16 June 1906, clipping in the Cyrus H. McCormick, Jr., Papers, series 2C, box 42.

4. Robert Sloss, "Our New Industrial Conservation," *Harper's Weekly* 57, no. 2932 (1 March 1913): 8.

5. "The Commonwealth Steel Company's Fellowship Work," *Monthly Bulletin of the American Iron and Steel Institute* 4, no. 4 (April 1916): 125; J. David Houser, *What the Employer Thinks: Executives' Attitudes Toward Employees* (Cambridge: Harvard University Press, 1927), p. 56; John A. Garraty, "The United States Steel Corporation Versus Labor: The Early Years," *Labor History* 1, no. 1 (Winter 1960): 3; letter of H. P. Judson to faculty members of University of Chicago, 19 October 1905, Cyrus H. McCormick, Jr., Papers, series 2C, box 42; Charles W. Hubbard, "Some Practical Principles of Welfare Work," *Journal of Social Science* 42 (September 1904): 92-93; Alan R. Raucher, *Public Relations and Business, 1900-1929* (Baltimore: Johns Hopkins Press, 1968), pp. 65-68.

6. Donald Wilhelm, "Big Business Man as a Social Worker: I. Elbert H. Gary," *Outlook* 107 (22 August 1914): 1006-8; memorandum of C. P. Marshall to F. C. Holmes, 2 February 1922, Plymouth Cordage Company Records, file H, drawer 3, "Mr. Marshall's Reports" folder, Baker Library; Garraty, "Steel Corporation," pp. 20-21; William Menkel, "'Welfare Work' on American Railroads," *Review of Reviews* 38 (October 1908): 463.

7. Frank T. Carlton, "The Golden Rule Factory," *Arena* 32, no. 179 (October 1904): 408; U.S., Bureau of Labor Statistics, *Proceedings of the Employment Managers' Conference, Philadelphia, Pa., April 2 and 3, 1917,* Bulletin no. 227, 1917, p. 151; Goodyear Tire and Rubber Company, *The Work of the Labor Division* (Akron, Ohio: Goodyear Tire and Rubber Company, 1920), p. 34.

8. *Monthly Bulletin of the American Iron and Steel Institute* 5, no. 1 (January-February 1917): 9, 27-31.

9. Herbert J. Lahne, *The Cotton Mill Worker* (New York: Farrar & Rinehart, 1944), p. 75.

10. Robert Sidney Smith, *Mill on the Dan: A History of Dan River Mills, 1882-1950* (Durham, N.C.: Duke University Press, 1950), pp. 242-43.

11. Philip W. Blake, "Housing the Workers Who Earn $5.00 and $6.00 per Day," *Industrial Management* 60, no. 6 (December 1920): 435; John T. Bartlett, "Guarding

the Employee's Pocketbook," *Industrial Management* 61, no. 5 (1 March 1921): 194; White Motor Company, "The White Motor Company Special Fund for Twelve Months, 1919," Plymouth Cordage Company Records, file H, drawer 3, "Mr. Marshall's Reports" folder, p. 9, Baker Library; National Civic Federation, *Conference on Welfare Work, 1904,* pp. 102-3.

12. For a fascinating account of the conflict between welfare capitalism and scientific management, see Daniel Nelson and Stuart Campbell, "Taylorism Versus Welfare Work in American Industry: H. L. Gantt and the Bancrofts," *Business History Review* 46, no. 1 (Spring 1972): 1-16 (quote, p. 5); cf. Samuel Haber, *Efficiency and Uplift: Scientific Management in the Progressive Era* (Chicago: University of Chicago Press, 1964).

13. Louis Galambos, "The Emerging Organizational Synthesis in Modern American History," *Business History Review* 44, no. 3 (Autumn 1970): 284.

Chapter 5. Housing

1. James B. Allen, *The Company Town in the American West* (Norman: University of Oklahoma Press, 1966), reviewed by Herbert G. Gutman in *Labor History* 9, no. 2 (Spring 1968): 282-85.

2. H. F. J. Porter, "Industrial Betterment," *Cassier's Magazine* 38, no. 4 (August 1910): 312-13; Gertrude Beeks, "Employees' Welfare Work," *Independent* 55, no. 2684 (22 October 1903): 2518; Bernard M. Cannon, "Social Deterrents to the Unionization of Southern Cotton Textile Mill Workers" (Ph.D. diss., Department of Sociology, Harvard University, 1951), p. 393.

3. G. W. W. Hanger, "Housing of the Working People in the United States by Employers," *Bulletin of the Bureau of Labor* 9, no. 54 (September 1904): 1191-243; Leifur Magnusson, *Housing By Employers in the United States,* U.S., Bureau of Labor Statistics, Miscellaneous Series, Bulletin no. 263, 1920. The results of the latter are conveniently summarized in Leifur Magnusson, "Employers' Housing in the United States," *Monthly Review of the U.S. Bureau of Labor Statistics* 5, no. 5 (November 1917): 835-94.

4. John Coolidge, *Mill and Mansion: A Study of Architecture and Society in Lowell, Massachusetts, 1820-1865* (New York: Columbia University Press, 1942), p. 32.

5. Ibid., pp. 37, 187; Magnusson, "Employers' Housing in the United States," p. 872; Joseph H. White, *Houses for Mining Towns,* U.S. Department of the Interior, Bureau of Mines, Bulletin no. 87 (Washington, D.C.: Government Printing Office, 1914), pp. 17-18; Charles W. Hubbard, "Some Practical Principles of Welfare Work," *Journal of Social Science* 42 (September 1904): 87.

6. Magnusson, "Employers' Housing in the United States," 872-73; White, *Houses for Mining Towns,* pp. 17-18.

7. Coolidge, *Mill and Mansion,* pp. 29, 43; Magnusson, "Employers' Housing in the United States," p. 885; Leslie H. Allen, "The Problem of Industrial Housing," *Industrial Management* 54, no. 3 (December 1917): 403; "An Improvement in Poured Concrete Houses for Workingmen," *Square Deal* 13, no. 98 (September 1913): 108.

8. Magnusson, "Employers' Housing in the United States," p. 873; W. Fox, "The 'Company Community' in the American Coal Fields," *New Statesman* 30, no. 755 (15 October 1927): 7; Bituminous Operators' Special Committee, *The Company Town,* brief submitted to the U.S. Coal Commission, 8 September 1923, U.S. Coal

Commission Records, entry 8, box 3, Federal Records Center, Suitland, Maryland, p. 16; U.S., Congress, Senate, *Women and Child Wage Earners in the United States,* vol. 16, *Family Budgets of Typical Cotton Mill Workers,* 61st Cong., 2d sess., Doc. no. 645, 1911, pp. 27-28; U.S., Congress, Senate, Committee on Interstate Commerce, *Hearings, Conditions in the Coal Fields of Pennsylvania, West Virginia, and Ohio,* 70th Cong., 1st sess., 1928, p. 50; U.S., Congress, Senate, *Reports of the Immigration Commission,* vol. 6, *Immigrants in Industries, Part 1: Bituminous Coal Mining, Vol. I,* 61st Cong., 2d sess., Doc. no. 633, vol. 68, 1911, pp. 94-95; U.S., Congress, Senate, *Reports of the Immigration Commission,* vol. 7, *Immigrants in Industries, Part 1: Bituminous Coal Mining,* Vol. II, 61st Cong., 2d sess., Doc. no. 633, 1911, vol. 69, pp. 64-65.

9. Nettie P. McGill, *The Welfare of Children in Bituminous Coal Mining Communities in West Virginia,* U.S. Department of Labor, Children's Bureau, Publication no. 117, 1923, pp. 15-16.

10. Magnusson, "Employers' Housing in the United States," p. 888; Bituminous Operators' Special Committee, *The Company Town,* pp. 21-22; "Agents 'Write-ups' of Coal Towns," [1922?], Ethelbert Stewart Papers, Bureau of Labor Statistics Records, National Archives, Washington, D.C.; George Korson, *Coal Dust on the Fiddle: Songs and Stories of the Bituminous Industry* (Hatboro, Penn.: Folklore Associates, 1965), p. 33; "Address of Rt. Rev. Joseph F. Busch, Bishop of Lead [South Dakota]," 11 August 1913, reprinted in U.S. Commission on Industrial Relations, "Company Owned Towns," typewritten report in State Historical Society of Wisconsin; White, *Houses for Mining Towns,* p. 38; McGill, *Welfare of Children,* p. 11.

11. Korson, *Coal Dust on the Fiddle,* p. 33; McGill, *Welfare of Children,* p. 11.

12. Jeannette Paddock Nichols, "Does the Mill Village Foster Any Social Types?" *Journal of Social Forces* 2, no. 3 (March 1924): 353.

13. U.S., Congress, Senate, *Immigrants in Industries, Part 2: Iron and Steel Manufacturing, Report of the Immigration Commission, IX,* 61st Cong., 2d sess., 1911, Doc. no. 633, p. 187; McGill, *Welfare of Children,* p. 9; Budgett Meakin, *Model Factories and Villages: Ideal Conditions of Labour and Housing* (Philadelphia: George W. Jacobs and Co., 1905), p. 392; Anna Rochester, *Labor and Coal* (New York: International Publishers, 1931), p. 89; William B. Gates, *Michigan Copper and Boston Dollars: An Economic History of the Michigan Copper Mining Industry* (Cambridge: Harvard University Press, 1951), p. 110; Senate, *Conditions in the Coal Fields,* p. 78; Magnusson, "Employers' Housing in the United States," 870.

14. U.S., Congress, Senate, Committee on Education and Labor, *Investigation of Strike in Steel Industries,* 66th Cong., 1st sess., 1919, p. 268; McGill, *Welfare of Children,* p. 11.

15. Magnusson, "Employers' Housing in the United States," p. 871.

16. White, *Houses for Mining Towns,* pp. 47, 49; Bituminous Operators' Special Committee, *The United Mine Workers in West Virginia,* brief submitted to the U.S. Coal Commission, August 1923, reprinted in Senate, *Conditions in the Coal Fields,* p. 1987; Senate, *Report of the Immigration Commission, IX,* p. 187; McGill, *Welfare of Children,* pp. 14-15.

17. U.S. Public Health Service, "Memorandum relative to Sanitary Rating of Certain Industrial Communities in the United States," prepared for the U. S. Coal Commission, 18 September 1923, Coal Commission Records, entry 37, box 17; manuscripts of Public Health Service sanitary surveys of coal communities, 1923,

"Summarized Report on the Sanitation of 123 Communities in the Bituminous Coal Districts of 9 States," 24 July 1923, esp. p. 57, Coal Commission Records, entry 13, box 7.

18. Alexander M. Daly, "The Fulton Bag & Cotton Mills, Atlanta, Georgia," typewritten report [1915?], records of the U.S. Commission on Industrial Relations, file 46, National Archives, Washington, D.C., pp. 1-4; U.S., Congress, House, Committee on Labor, *Hearings, To Rehabilitate and Stabilize Labor Conditions in the Textile Industry of the United States,* 74th Cong., 2d sess., 1936, p. 165; Senate, *Conditions in the Coal Fields,* pp. 2529, 2540; Marie L. Obenauer, "Progress Report on Living Conditions and Cost of Living of Mine Workers," typewritten report, 8 January 1923, Coal Commission Records, entry 68, box 38, p. 16.

19. Magnusson, *Housing By Employers in the United States,* p. 20.

20. Ibid., p. 26.

21. See, for example, Bituminous Operators' Special Committee, *The Company Town,* pp. 6-8.

22. William S. Eaton to the shareholders of the Shawmut Village Company, 12 February 1862, Pennsylvania Coal Company Records, case 2, Baker Library, Harvard University, Cambridge, Massachusetts; H. K. Hathaway, "Report to the Plymouth Cordage Company, Plymouth, Mass.," Plymouth Cordage Company Records, file H, drawer 3, Baker Library; Arthur Pound, *The Turning Wheel: The Story of General Motors Through Twenty Years, 1908-1933* (Garden City, N.Y.: Doubleday, Doran and Co., 1934), p. 413. It has been argued, conversely, that poor housing was indicative of weak competition for labor. See Paul McGouldrick, *New England Textiles in the Nineteenth Century: Profits and Investment* (Cambridge: Harvard University Press, 1968), p. 35.

23. Magnusson, "Employers' Housing in the United States," p. 890; Magnusson, *Housing By Employers in the United States,* p. 14. For other cases where housing brought a similar gross return see David Brody, *Steelworkers in America: The Nonunion Era* (Cambridge: Harvard University Press, 1960), pp. 88-89; E. R. L. Gould, *The Housing of the Working People,* eighth special report of the Commissioner of Labor, U.S., Congress, House, Executive Document no. 354, 53d Cong., 3d sess., 1895, pp. 321, 327; letter of Luke Grant to W. Jett Lauck, 27 February 1914, in Luke Grant, "Papers in relation to the Michigan copper strike," Commission on Industrial Relations Records, State Historical Society of Wisconsin, pp. 2-3.

24. Upkeep, insurance, and taxes on houses owned by six companies in the anthracite district of Pennsylvania averaged 5 percent of the original cost; often the cost was higher (Magnusson, *Housing By Employers in the United States,* pp. 111, 172-74, 176-77; Edward L. Kellogg, "Improved Housing in a Mining Town," *American City* 12, no. 2 [February 1915]: 165-67; H. G. Lee, "Welfare Work Conducted by Representative Employers throughout the United States," typewritten report, 25 January 1915, Commission on Industrial Relations Records, State Historical Society of Wisconsin, pp. 73-74; National Civic Federation, *Eleventh Annual Meeting: Welfare Workers' Conference,* 1911 [New York, 1911], pp. 73-74). Only when housing was new or very substantially constructed was it less (Magnusson, *Housing By Employers in the United States,* pp. 174-75, 193).

25. Letters of F. C. Holmes to Augustus P. Loring, 22 April 1920, and Loring to Holmes, 23 April 1920, Plymouth Cordage Company Records, file H, drawer 3, "Housing" folder; letter of Luke Grant to W. Jett Lauck, 27 February 1914, in Grant,

"Papers in relation to the Michigan copper strike," pp. 2-3; "Pocasset Worsted Company, Providence, R.I.," 15 June 1904, Cyrus H. McCormick, Jr., Papers, Series 2C, box 40, State Historical Society of Wisconsin; Gould, *Housing of the Working People,* pp. 327, 334-35; Stanley Buder, *Pullman: An Experiment in Industrial Order and Community Planning* (New York: Oxford University Press, 1967), pp. 89-91; Robert Sidney Smith, *Mill on the Dan: A History of Dan River Mills, 1882-1950* (Durham, N.C.: Duke University Press, 1960), p. 258; George A. Stevens and Leonard W. Hatch, "Employers' Welfare Institutions," State of New York, Department of Labor, *Third Annual Report of the Commissioner of Labor,* 1903, pt. 4, in State of New York, *Assembly Documents* 22, no. 61 (1904): 243-44; Meakin, *Model Factories and Villages,* pp. 392-405; Gates, *Michigan Copper,* p. 111; Brody, *Steelworkers in America,* pp. 88-89; U.S., Congress, Senate, Subcommittee of the Committee on Education and Labor, *Hearings, Conditions in the Paint Creek District, West Virginia,* 63d Cong., 1st sess., 1913, pp. 1325-26, 1333-34, 1360; U.S., Congress, House, *Hearings, United States Steel Corporation,* 62d Cong., 2d sess., 1912, vol. 5, p. 3330; U.S., Congress, House, *Report on the Miners Strike in Bituminous Coal Field in Westmoreland County, Pa. in 1910-11,* 62d Cong., 2d sess., Doc. no. 847, 1912, pp. 202-9.

26. Charles B. Fowler, Daniel Bloomfield, and Henry P. Dutton, "Report of the Committee on the Economic and Social Implications of the Company Store and Scrip System," March 1936, pp. 18, 73n., Work Materials no. 4, Records of the National Recovery Administration, group 9, National Archives; Ole S. Johnson, *The Industrial Store: Its History, Operations and Economic Significance* (Atlanta: Division of Research, School of Business Administration, University of Georgia, 1952), p. 25; Senate, *Conditions in the Coal Fields,* p. 862; Bituminous Operators' Special Committee, *United Mine Workers in West Virginia,* p. 2014.

27. Johnson, *Industrial Store,* esp. p. 92; Fowler, Bloomfield, and Dutton, "Economic and Social Implications of the Company Store"; Bituminous Operators' Special Committee, *Memorandum on Variation of Living Costs in the Bituminous Coal Fields,* 17 September 1923, passim, esp. pp. 14, 36, Coal Commission Records, entry 8, box 4.

28. Ohio, General Assembly, *Proceedings of the Hocking Valley Investigation Committee* (Columbus: Westbote Company, 1893), p. 83; John Brophy, *A Miner's Life* (Madison: University of Wisconsin Press, 1964), p. 35; David J. Saposs, "Self Government and Freedom of Action in Isolated Industrial Communities," [1914?], typewritten report, Commission on Industrial Relations Records, State Historical Society of Wisconsin, p. 52; Fowler, Bloomfield, and Dutton, "Economic and Social Implications of the Company Store," p. 62; Johnson, *Industrial Store,* p. 91; Senate, *Conditions in the Coal Fields,* p. 939; U.S., Congress, Senate, Committee on Education and Labor, *Hearings, West Virginia Coal Fields,* 67th Cong., 1st sess., 1921, pp. 67-68.

29. David J. Saposs, handwritten notes of interviews with residents of Fullerton, Louisiana, Ray, Arizona, and Taft and Gregory, Texas, Commission on Industrial Relations Records, box 2, National Archives.

30.U.S. Senate, *Report of the Immigration Commission,* 9, p. 190; Korson, *Coal Dust on the Fiddle,* p. 68.

31. Ohio, *Hocking Valley Investigation,* pp. 90, 113; letter of Durham Cotton Manufacturing Company to A. D. Ezell, East Durham, North Carolina, May 23,

1910, Durham Cotton Manufacturing Company Records, 1910 Copybook, Duke University Library, Durham, North Carolina.

32. Ohio, *Hocking Valley Investigation,* p. 113.

33. Cannon, "Social Deterrents," pp. 60-61; letter of forty petitioners to Secretary of Labor Frances Perkins, 29 July 1933, Chief Clerk's File 167/2439, Department of Labor Records.

34. In 1927 the Pittsburgh Coal Company, which owned twenty company stores, wrote off $40,507.12 due to bad debts. Assuming that half the annual payroll (excluding management) was spent in company stores (and some evidence indicates that this is a low figure), losses due to bad accounts must have been substantially below 1 percent of annual sales. See Senate, *Conditions in the Coal Fields,* pp. 36-37, 874, 955, 2567, 2578, 2583, 2649, 2715, 2724, 2731.

35. Jerold S. Auerbach, *Labor and Liberty: The La Follette Committee and the New Deal* (Indianapolis and New York: The Bobbs-Merrill Company, 1966), p. 118; ibid., pp. 1822-23, 2862-63; U.S., Senate, Subcommittee of the Committee on Education and Labor, *Hearings, Conditions in the Paint Creek District,* West Virginia, 63d Cong., 1st sess., 1913, pp. 382, 1366-67; House, *Report of the Industrial Commission,* 12, p. 15; Johnson, *Industrial Store,* p. 72. The trade associations were the National Industrial Stores Association, National Coal Association, National Lumber Manufacturer's Association, American Cotton Manufacturer's Association, American Mining Congress, Alabama Mining Institute, Coupon Book Manufacturer's Association, American Farm Bureau Federation, and National Association of Manufacturers. See also letter of John Turner to William Nelson Page, 13 July 1882, Page Papers, Southern Historical Collection, University of North Carolina, Chapel Hill, box 1.

36. House, *Report of the Industrial Commission,* 12, p. 277; Saposs, handwritten notes of interview with Superintendent Tuxworth, Pickering Land and Lumber Company, Craven, Louisiana, 27 August 1914, Commission on Industrial Relations Records, box 2, National Archives; Senate, *Conditions in the Paint Creek District,* p. 382; Ohio, *Hocking Valley Investigation,* p. 223; supplement to *The Hillbilly,* 1922 school yearbook of Triadelphia District Schools, Man, West Virginia, pp. 61-63, Coal Commission Records, entry 77, box 41.

37. "Tenement Survey, 1935," dated 6 November 1935, and "Tenement Survey, 1935," dated 31 January 1936, case CD-1, Amoskeag Manufacturing Company Records, Baker Library.

38. House, *Miners' Strike in Westmoreland County, Pa.,* pp. 210-14; Senate, *Conditions in the Coal Fields,* pp. 34n., 345, 1131, 1249-52, 1517, 1918, 2057, 2258-59, 2269, 2339, 2343, 2419, 2442.

39. Barron B. Beshoar, *Out of the Depths: The Story of John R. Lawson, A Labor Leader,* 3d ed. (Denver: Colorado Labor Historical Committee of the Denver Trades and Labor Assembly, 1957), p. 62; Senate, *West Virginia Coal Fields,* pp. 15, 23, 181, 186; Brophy, *Miner's Life,* p. 186.

40. Senate, *Conditions in the Coal Fields,* pp. 1251, 2258; House, *Miners' Strike in Westmoreland County, Pa.,* pp. 210-15.

41. Senate, *Conditions in the Coal Fields,* pp. 1415, 1992-93, 1999-2003, 2082-87; Senate, *West Virginia Coal Fields,* p. 504.

42. Senate, *Conditions in the Coal Fields,* pp. 224-26, 943, 950, 1217-18, 1447.

43. M. McCusker, "Report on the Colorado Situation," 3 February 1915, type-

written report to the U.S. Commission on Industrial Relations, State Historical Society of Wisconsin, pp. 3-5; John J. Cornwell, "Governor's Message," State of West Virginia, *Senate Journal*, Regular and Extraordinary Sessions, 1921, appendix A, p. 44; Saposs, "Self Government and Freedom of Action in Isolated Industrial Communities," p. 38; Cannon, "Social Deterrents," pp. 62-63.

44. Senate, *Conditions in the Coal Fields,* pp. 104-5, 149-50, 524-25, 943.

45. Cannon, "Social Deterrents," pp. 62-63; W. C. Chanler, "Civil Liberties in the Soft Coal Fields: The Point of View of the Operators," *Independent* 111, no. 3853 (13 October 1923): 163; Bituminous Operators' Special Committee, *Company Town,* p. 33. It is possible that the last statement was by Chanler also.

46. McCusker, "Report on the Colorado Situation," pp. 3-5.

Chapter 6. Education

1. Thomas W. Dyott, *An Exposition of the System of Moral and Mental Labor, Established at the Glass Factory of Dyottsville* (Philadelphia, 1833), p. 1.

2. Berenice M. Fisher, *Industrial Education: American Ideals and Institutions* (Madison: University of Wisconsin Press, 1967), pp. 110-11; William Howe Tolman, *Industrial Betterment,* Monographs on Social Economics, vol. 16 (New York: Social Service Press, 1900), pp. 53-54; Pennsylvania, Department of Internal Affairs, Bureau of Industrial Statistics, *Fifteenth Annual Report,* 1887, in *Annual Report of the Secretary of Internal Affairs* 15, pt. 3 (Harrisburg, 1888), p. E14; New Jersey, Inspector of Factories and Workshops, *Fourth Annual Report, 1886,* Legislative Document no. 24 (Trenton, 1887), pp. 58-64.

3. *Social Service* 3, no. 4 (April 1901): 95-96; supplement to *The Hillbilly,* 1922 school yearbook of Triadelphia District Schools, Man, West Virginia, U.S. Coal Commission Records, entry 77, box 41, p. 59, Federal Records Center, Suitland, Maryland; letter of Henry Bruére to John G. Wood, 5 September 1903, Cyrus H. McCormick, Jr., Papers, series 2C, box 41, State Historical Society of Wisconsin.

4. Report of the Committee on Industrial Betterment, Health and Safety, National Association of Manufacturers, *Proceedings of the Twenty-Seventh Annual Convention* (New York, 1922), p. 5; Edward Chase Kirkland, *Dream and Thought in the Business Community, 1860-1900* (Chicago: Quadrangle Paperbacks, 1964; Ithaca: Cornell University Press, 1956), p. 57; U.S., Congress, Senate, Committee on Education and Labor, *Hearings, Investigation of Strike in Steel Industries,* 66th Cong., 1st sess., 1919, pp. 275-76.

5. U.S., Bureau of Labor Statistics, Bulletin no. 458, *Health and Recreation Activities in Industrial Establishments,* 1926, p. 90; Howard K. Wilson, " A Study of Paternalism in the Colorado Fuel and Iron Company Under John C. Osgood: 1892-1903" (A.M. thesis, Department of History, University of Denver, 1967), pp. 65-67.

6. "Making Good American Citizens," *Monthly Bulletin of the American Iron and Steel Institute* 2, no. 9 (September 1914): 246; Florence Hughes, *Sociological Work, The New Jersey Zinc Co.* (Palmerton, Pennsylvania: New Jersey Zinc Co., 1914), p. 7, in the New York Public Library.

7. Harriet L. Herring, *Welfare Work in Mill Villages: The Story of Extra-Mill Activities in North Carolina* (Chapel Hill: University of North Carolina Press, 1929), pp. 33, 57.

8. U.S., Congress, Senate, Committee on Education and Labor, *Hearings, West Virginia Coal Fields,* 67th Cong., 1st sess., 1921, pp. 869-71, 911, 1027-28; Ohio, General Assembly, *Proceedings of the Hocking Valley Investigation Committee* (Columbus: Westbote Company, 1893), p. 238.

9. Richard T. Ely, "An American Industrial Experiment," *Harper's Monthly* 105 (June 1902): 42; U.S., Congress, House, *Report of the Industrial Commission on the Relations and Conditions of Capital and Labor Employed in Manufactures and General Business* 7, 56th Cong., 2d sess., Doc. no. 495, 1901, p. 484; Edgar Gardner Murphy, *Child Labor in Alabama: The Nichols-Sears-Murphy Correspondence* (Montgomery: Alabama Committee on Child Labor, [1902?]), p. 3.

10. Wilson, "Paternalism in the Colorado Fuel and Iron Company," p. 72; William H. Tolman, *Social Engineering* (New York: Macmillan Co., 1909), pp. 258-60; *Social Service* 4, no. 6 (December 1901): 225. The latter article was reprinted in the company magazine as "Social Betterment in the Rocky Mountains," *Camp and Plant* 1, no. 12 (1 March 1902): 177-82. Not to be outdone in the pursuit of efficiency, Jones and Laughlin Steel operated their schools twelve months a year. See Tom M. Girdler, *Boot Straps* (New York: Charles Scribner's Sons, 1943), p. 172.

11. House, *Report of the Industrial Commission* 7, pp. 486, 489, 494.

12. Holland Thompson, *From the Cotton Field to the Cotton Mill: A Study of the Industrial Transition in North Carolina* (New York: Macmillan Company, 1906), pp. 173-74; L. A. Williams, "The Intellectual Status of Children in Cotton Mill Villages," *Social Forces* 4, no. 1 (September 1925): 184-85.

13. Thompson, *From Cotton Field to Cotton Mill,* p. 120; House, *Report of the Industrial Commission* 7, pp. 482, 492, 504; Bernard M. Cannon, "Social Deterrents to the Unionization of Southern Cotton Textile Mill Workers" (Ph.D. diss., Department of Sociology, Harvard University, 1951), p. 551.

14. Bituminous Operators' Special Committee, *The United Mine Workers in West Virginia,* pamphlet submitted to the U.S. Coal Commission, August 1923, reprinted in U.S., Congress, Senate, Committee on Interstate Commerce, *Hearings, Conditions in the Coal Fields of Pennsylvania, West Virginia, and Ohio,* 70th Cong., 1st sess., 1928, pp. 1986-87; cf. Senate, *Conditions in the Coal Fields,* pp. 1840-41; *Labor Advocate* (Birmingham, Ala., 5 August 1916); James Bowron, unpublished autobiography, entry for 28 August 1915, vol. 2., p. 409, James Bowron Papers, University of Alabama Library; letter of William Butterworth to J. L. Simmon, 21 June 1922, Deere & Co. Records, box 400-2, file 472, Moline, Illinois; *ACIPCO News* 32, no. 12 (December 1947): 9-21.

15. Bituminous Operators' Special Committee, *The Company Town,* pamphlet submitted to the U.S. Coal Commission, 8 September 1923, pp. 24-25, U.S. Coal Commission Records, entry 8, box 3; letter of C. W. Price to Manufacturing Department, 22 March 1906, Cyrus H. McCormick, Jr., Papers, series 2C, box 41.

16. Homer Lawrence Morris, *The Plight of the Bituminous Coal Miner* (Philadelphia: University of Pennsylvania Press, 1934), p. 93; David J. Saposs, "Self Government and Freedom of Action in Isolated Industrial Communities," report to the U.S. Commission on Industrial Relations [1914?], p. 42, State Historical Society of Wisconsin; David J. Saposs, "Company Towns—Louisiana, Arizona, and Texas," [1914?], p. 3, Records of the United States Commission on Industrial Relations, Record group 174, General Records of the Department of Labor, National Archives, Washington, D.C.

17. U.S. Commission on Industrial Relations, *Report on the Colorado Strike,*

prepared by George P. West (Washington, 1915), p. 71; Saposs, "Self Government and Freedom of Action," p. 29; Senate, *West Virginia Coal Fields,* p. 936; U.S., Congress, Senate, Committee on Manufactures, *Hearings, Conditions in Coal Fields in Harlan and Bell Counties, Kentucky,* 72d Cong., 1st sess., 1932, p. 190.

18. H. W. Foght, *A Half-Time Mill School,* U.S., Bureau of Education, Bulletin no. 6, 1919, p. 9; letter of John E. Warren, Cumberland Mills, Maine, to James E. McKibben, Boston, Massachusetts, 7 April 1913, Boston Chamber of Commerce Records, File 332-19, Baker Library, Harvard University, Cambridge, Massachusetts.

19. Budgett Meakin, *Model Factories and Villages: Ideal Conditions of Labour and Housing* (Philadelphia: George W. Jacobs and Company, 1905), p. 261; Isabella Chilton Wilson, "Welfare Work in a Mining Town," *Journal of Home Economics* 11, no. 1 (January 1919): 22; National Civic Federation, *Conference on Welfare Work, 1904* (New York: Press of Andrew H. Kellogg, 1904), pp. 15-16; Wilson, "Welfare Work in a Mining Town," p. 22; National Civic Federation, *Conference on Welfare Work, 1904,* pp. 15-16; Meakin, *Model Factories,* p. 261; Tolman, *Social Engineering,* p. 268; Senate, *Investigation of Strike in Steel Industries,* p. 276.

20. L. Grace Powell Sitzer, "Wrigley Doesn't Apologize for Welfare Work," *Factory and Industrial Management* 77, no. 3 (March 1929): 502; Senate, *Investigation of Strike in Steel Industries,* p. 262; "Report from W. E. C. Nazro, 8/1/20 to 8/1/21," Plymouth Cordage Company Records, file H, drawer 3, pp. 12-13, 24, Baker Library.

21. Lawrence Lewis, "Uplifting 17,000 Employees," *World's Work* 9 (March 1905): 5943; supplement to *The Hillbilly,* p. 61.

22. William M. Leiserson, *Adjusting Immigrant and Industry* (New York: Harper and Brothers, 1924), pp. 121-22; John Nolen, *New Towns for Old: Achievements in Some American Small Towns and Neighborhoods* (Boston: Marshall Jones Co., 1927), p. 73; Louis A. Boettiger, *Employee Welfare Work: A Critical and Historical Study* (New York: Ronald Press, 1923), p. 147; Daniel Bloomfield, *Labor Maintenance: A Practical Handbook of Employees' Service Work* (New York: Ronald Press, 1920), pp. 140-47, 152.

23. "Rep't of W. E. C. Nazro, 8/1/19 to 8/1/20," and memorandum of Marshall to F. C. Holmes, 2 February 1922, Plymouth Cordage Company Records, file H, drawer 3, Baker Library; Cannon, "Social Deterrents," p. 384.

24. Pennsylvania, Bureau of Industrial Statistics, *Fifteenth Annual Report,* p. E13; Stanley Buder, *Pullman: An Experiment in Industrial Order and Community Planning, 1880-1930* (New York: Oxford University Press, 1967), p. 63; U.S., Bureau of Labor Statistics, Bulletin no. 260, *Welfare Work for Employees,* pp. 95-96.

25. Meakin, *Model Factories,* p. 290; M. S. Rossy, "Cost of an Employee Service Department," *Industrial Management* 70, no. 1 (July 1925): 5; U.S., Bureau of Labor Statistics, *Welfare Work for Employees,* pp. 95-96; "Rep't from W. E. C. Nazro, 8/1/11 to 8/1/12," Plymouth Cordage Company Records, file H, drawer 3, p. 8; American Gas Association, *Report on Eduation of Gas Company Employees* (New York, 1928), p. 9.

26. U.S., Bureau of Labor Statistics, Bulletin no. 227, *Proceedings of the Employment Managers' Conference,* pp. 87, 148; letter of H. J. Montgomery to S. M. Darling, 11 August 1904, Cyrus H. McCormick, Jr. Papers, series 2C, box 40; Hester A. Wetmore, "How Can a Company Library Increase Public Appreciation of Industry?" in National Association of Manufacturers, *Proceedings of the Thirty-third Annual Meeting* (New York, 1928), pp. 395-97.

27. Meakin, *Model Factories,* pp. 287, 295; Pennsylvania, Bureau of Industrial

Statistics, *Fifteenth Annual Report,* pp. E13, E34-35; *Social Service* 2, no. 2 (February 1900): 12-13; House, *Report of the Industrial Commission* 7, pp. 482-83, 14, pp. 353, 659; National Civic Federation, *Conference on Welfare Work,* 1904, p. 67; U.S., Congress, Senate, *Report on Conditions of Employment in the Iron and Steel Industry in the United States* 3, 62d Cong., 1st sess., Doc. no. 110, 1911-13, p. 471; "Rep't of W. E. C. Nazro, 8/1/13 to 8/1/14," and H. K. Hathaway, "Report to the Plymouth Cordage Company, Plymouth, Mass.," section L, both in Plymouth Cordage Company Records, file H, drawer 3; R. E. Phillips, "The Betterment of Working Life," *World's Work* 1 (December 1900): 159; letter of Montgomery to Darling, 11 August 1904, Cyrus H. McCormick, Jr., Papers; letters of Gertrude Beeks to F. A. Flather, 2 December 1902, and to Stanley McCormick, 15 December 1902, Nettie Fowler McCormick Papers, series 3B, box 30, State Historical Society of Wisconsin. Cf. American Gas Association, *Report of Committee on Education of Employees,* p. 9.

28. Elizabeth C. Wheeler, "Opportunities of the Social Secretary," in *Employers and Employees: Full Text of the Addresses Before the National Convention of Employers and Employees. . . , September 22-25, 1902* (Chicago: Public Policy, n.d.), p. 173; U.S., Congress, Senate, Subcommittee of the Committee on Education and Labor, *Hearings, Conditions in the Paint Creek District, West Virginia,* 63d Cong., 1st sess., 1913, pp. 2199-200.

29. M. McCusker, "Report on Colorado Situation," report to the U.S. Commission on Industrial Relations, 3 February 1915, pp. 14-17, State Historical Society of Wisconsin.

30. National Industrial Conference Board, *Employee Magazines in the United States* (New York: By the Author, 1925), pp. 1-3; Oscar W. Nestor, "A History of Personnel Administration, 1890-1910" (Ph.D. diss., Department of Economics, University of Pennsylvania, 1954), pp. 157-60; Edwin A. Hunger, "Making the Plant Paper Pay," *Industrial Management* 60, no. 5 (November 1920): 341; Alan R. Raucher, *Public Relations and Business, 1900-1929* (Baltimore: Johns Hopkins Press, 1968), pp. 68-69.

31. National Industrial Conference Board, *Employee Magazines,* pp. 29-31, 38; Hunger, "Making the Plant Paper Pay," p. 343.

32. Jean Atherton Flexner, " 'Selling the Company,' " *New Republic* 38 (9 April 1924): 172; letter of S. M. Darling to G. F. Steele, 17 December 1904, Cyrus H. McCormick, Jr., Papers, series 2C, box 39; "The Commonwealth Steel Company's Fellowship Work," *Monthly Bulletin of the American Iron and Steel Institute* 4, no. 4 (April 1916): 149 (the italics are mine).

33. R. W. Fleming and Edwin E. Witte, "Marathon Corporation and Seven Labor Unions," *Causes of Industrial Peace Under Collective Bargaining,* Case Study no. 8 (Washington, D.C.: National Planning Association, 1950), p. 12; D. C. Vandercook, "Teaching Economics Through the Employees Publication," *Industrial Management* 69, no. 5 (May 1925): 308; W. R. R. Winans, "What Employee Publications Are Doing to Improve Industrial Relations," *Industrial Management* 69, no. 4 (April 1925): 213.

34. Bloomfield, *Labor Maintenance,* p. 295; Paul H. Giddens, *Standard Oil Company (Indiana): Oil Pioneer of the Middle West* (New York: Appleton-Century-Crofts, 1955), p. 345; John T. Bartlett, "The Dramatic Gesture and the Photo: Two Ways to Personalize Management," *Industrial Management* 62, no. 5 (November 1921): 273-74.

35. *Filene Co-operative Association Echo* 1, no. 1 (1 July 1902): 8; Bartlett, "Dramatic Gesture," 273-74; *Borden Eagle* 2, no. 1 (January 1922): 7-9.

36. *Filene Co-operative Association Echo* 1, no. 1 (1 July 1902): 8; Hunger, "Making the Plant Paper Pay," p. 341; Vandercook, "Teaching Economics," p. 309.

37. Vandercook, "Teaching Economics," pp. 309-10; John T. Bartlett, "Naming the Employees' Magazine," *Industrial Management* 61, no. 1 (1 January 1921): 16; "List of Employee Magazines in New York State and Their Editors," *Industrial Relations* 4, no. 5 (28 August 1920): 356; National Industrial Conference Board, *Employee Magazines,* pp. 65-86, passim.

38. Flexner, " 'Selling the Company,' " p. 171-72; G. G. Kingsley, "How the Employees Magazine Promotes Safety," *Industrial Management* 62, no. 4 (October 1921): 243; John T. Bartlett, "Guarding the Employee's Pocketbook," *Industrial Management* 61, no. 5 (March 1921): 193; Boris Emmet and John E. Jeuck, *Catalogues and Counters: A History of Sears, Roebuck and Company* (Chicago: University of Chicago Press, 1950), p. 145.

39. Flexner, " 'Selling the Company,' " p. 172; Hunger, "Making the Plant Paper Pay," p. 342; Frank H. Williams, "Make 'Em Read the Plant Paper," *Industrial Management* 60, no. 1 (July 1920): 71.

Chapter 7. Religion

1. John Coolidge, *Mill and Mansion: A Study of Architecture and Society in Lowell, Massachusetts, 1820-1865* (New York: Columbia University Press, 1942), p. 42.

2. Stanley Buder, *Pullman: An Experiment in Industrial Order and Community Planning, 1880-1930* (New York: Oxford University Press, 1967), pp. 66-67.

3. National Civic Federation, *Conference on Welfare Work, 1904* (New York: Press of Andrew H. Kellogg, 1904), pp. 78-80. A description of YMCA work is in U.S., Congress, Senate, Subcommittee of the Committee on Education and Labor, *Hearings, Conditions in the Paint Creek District, West Virginia,* 63d Cong., 1st sess., 1913, pp. 2195-202.

4. David Brody, *Steelworkers in America: The Nonunion Era* (Cambridge: Harvard University Press, 1960), p. 116.

5. *Social Service* 2, no. 2 (February 1900): 5, and no. 3 (March 1900): 16-17.

6. Letter of Thomas Lynch, president, Frick Coal Company, to J. A. Farrell, president, United States Steel Corporation, 16 September 1911, reprinted in U.S., Congress, House, *Hearings, United States Steel Corporation,* 62d Cong., 2d sess., 1912, vol. 5, p. 3282; William Howe Tolman, *Social Engineering* (New York: Macmillan Co., 1909), p. 42.

7. Harriet Herring, *Welfare Work in Mill Villages: The Story of Extra-Mill Activities in North Carolina* (Chapel Hill: University of North Carolina Press, 1929), p. 99.

8. Bernard M. Cannon, "Social Deterrents to the Unionization of Southern Cotton Mill Workers" (Ph.D. diss., Department of Sociology, Harvard University, 1951), pp. 524-25.

9. F. Ray Marshall, *Labor in the South* (Cambridge: Harvard University Press, 1967), p. 342.

10. Cannon, "Social Deterrents," pp. 433-34n., 483-85; Holland Thompson, *From the Cotton Field to the Cotton Mill: A Study of the Industrial Transition in North*

Carolina (New York: Macmillan Co., 1906), pp. 174-76.

11. Thompson, *From Cotton Field to Cotton Mill,* p. 176; National Civic Federation, *Eleventh Annual Meeting: Welfare Worker's Conference, 1911* (New York: National Civic Federation, [1911]), p. 377; James Myers, *Representative Government in Industry* (New York: George H. Doran Company, 1924), p. 218; remarks of William Cooper Procter, Profit Sharing Dividend Celebration, 27 February 1915, Procter & Gamble Records, box A-7, Cincinnati, Ohio.

12. Herring, *Welfare Work in Mill Villages,* p. 28; Bituminous Operators' Special Committee, *The United Mine Workers in West Virginia,* report to the U.S. Coal Commission, August 1923, reprinted in U.S., Congress, Senate, Committee on Interstate Commerce, *Hearings, Conditions in the Coal Fields of Pennsylvania, West Virginia, and Ohio,* 70th Cong., 1st sess., 1928, p. 1986; Budgett Meakin, *Model Factories and Villages: Ideal Conditions of Labour and Housing* (Philadelphia: George W. Jacobs and Co., 1905), p. 393; George F. Paul, "Welfare Work on a Delta Plantation," *Southern Workman* 54, no. 7 (July 1925): 317; Herring, *Welfare Work in Mill Villages,* pp. 101-4; James B. Allen, *The Company Town in the American West* (Norman: University of Oklahoma Press, 1966), pp. 100-1; Senate, *Conditions in the Coal Fields,* pp. 1455-56; letter of O. B. Tilton, Alabama City, Alabama, to J. Howard Nichols, 1 August 1896, Dwight Manufacturing Company Papers, box MH-1, Baker Library, Harvard University, Cambridge, Massachusetts.

13. U.S., Congress, House, Committee on Labor, *Hearings, To Rehabilitate and Stabilize Labor Conditions in the Textile Industry of the United States,* 74th Cong., 2d sess., 1936, p. 281; James B. Allen, "The Company Town: A Passing Phase of Utah's Industrial Development," *Utah Historical Quarterly* 34, no. 2 (Spring 1966): 150.

14. William P. Few, "Constructive Philanthropy of a Southern Cotton Mill," *South Atlantic Quarterly* 8, no. 1 (January 1909): 82; David J. Saposs, "Self Government and Freedom of Action in Isolated Industrial Communities," report to the U.S. Commission on Industrial Relations [1914?], pp. 16, 29, State Historical Society of Wisconsin.

15. Brody, *Steelworkers in America,* p. 116; Saposs, "Self Government and Freedom of Action," pp. 32, 49. Cf. U.S., Congress, Senate, Committee on Manufactures, *Hearings, Conditions in Coal Fields in Harlan and Bell Counties, Kentucky,* 72d Cong., 1st sess., 1932, pp. 189-90.

16. Senate, *Conditions in the Coal Fields,* pp. 1014-15; U.S., Congress, House, *Report on the Miners' Strike in Bituminous Coal Field in Westmoreland County, Pa. in 1900-1,* 62d Cong., 2d sess., Doc. no. 847, 1912, pp. 89-90.

17. U.S., Commission on Industrial Relations, *Report on the Colorado Strike,* by George P. West (Washington, D.C.: Government Printing Office, 1915), p. 55, quoted in Allen, *Company Town,* p. 60.

18. Senate, *Conditions in the Coal Fields,* pp. 1026-30, 2749-50.

19. John R. Commons, "Suggestions and Recommendations on Basis of Investigations and Hearings at Lead," report to the U.S. Commission on Industrial Relations, 2 September 1914, p. 6, and George P. West and William P. Harvey, "General Situation in Lead, S.D.," report to the Commission on Industrial Relations [1914?], both in the Commission on Industrial Relations Records, box 2, National Archives; William P. Harvey, "Industry in the Black Hills," report to the Commission on Industrial Relations, 7 July 1915, p. 71, State Historical Society of Wisconsin;

"Address of Rt. Rev. Joseph F. Busch, Bishop of Lead [South Dakota]," 11 August 1913, reprinted in U.S. Commission on Industrial Relations, "Company Owned Towns," n.d., p. 2, State Historical Society of Wisconsin.

20. Ibid.

21. Saposs, "Self Government and Freedom of Action," p. 32.

Chapter 8. Recreation

1. Broadus Mitchell, *William Gregg, Factory Master of the Old South* (Chapel Hill: University of North Carolina Press, 1928), p. 85.

2. U.S., Bureau of Labor Statistics, *Welfare Work For Employees in Industrial Establishments in the United States,* Bulletin no. 250, 1919, pp. 8, 73, 89; U.S., Bureau of Labor Statistics, *Health and Recreation Activities in Industrial Establishments, 1926,* Bulletin no. 458, 1928, pp. 32, 45; Nettie P. McGill, *The Welfare of Children in Bituminous Coal Mining Communities in West Virginia,* U.S., Department of Labor, Children's Bureau, Publication no. 117, 1923, pp. 58-60; Bituminous Operators' Special Committee, *The United Mine Workers in West Virginia,* report to the U.S. Coal Commission, August 1923, reprinted in U.S., Congress, Senate, Committee on Interstate Commerce, *Hearings, Conditions in the Coal Fields of Pennsylvania, West Virginia, and Ohio,* 70th Cong., 1st sess., 1928, p. 1986.

3. Louis A. Boettiger, *Employee Welfare Work: A Critical and Historical Study* (New York: Ronald Press, 1923), p. 196; Daniel Bloomfield, *Labor Maintenance: A Practical Handbook of Employees' Service Work* (New York: Ronald Press, 1920), pp. 224-25; David Brody, *Steelworkers in America: The Nonunion Era* (Cambridge: Harvard University Press, 1960), p. 169; letter of Ludlow Manufacturing Associates to Boston Chamber of Commerce Records, file 332-19, Baker Library, Harvard University, Cambridge, Massachusetts; Edward Kirk Titus, "An Instructive Factory Village," *World's Work* 9 (January 1905): 5753; George P. West and William P. Harvey, "General Situation in Lead, S.D.," report to the U.S. Commission on Industrial Relations [1914?], p. 1, Records of the Commission on Industrial Relations, box 2, National Archives, Washington, D.C.

4. Stanley Buder, *Pullman: An Experiment in Industrial Order and Community Planning, 1880-1930* (New York: Oxford University Press, 1967), pp. 124-25; New Jersey, Bureau of Statistics of Labor and Industries, *Sixth Annual Report, 1883,* pp. 160-61; Ralph W. Hidy and Muriel E. Hidy, *Pioneering in Big Business, 1882-1911: History of Standard Oil Company (New Jersey)* (New York: Harper and Brothers, 1955), p. 590.

5. Arthur H. Cole, assisted by Dorothy Lubin, "Perspectives on Leisure-Time Business," *Explorations in Entrepreneurial History,* 2d series, 1, no. 3, Supplement (1964): 24-35; Fritz Redlich, "Leisure-Time Activities: A Historical, Sociological, and Economic Analysis," *Explorations in Entrepreneurial History,* 2d series, 3, no. 1 (Fall 1965): 18-19; E. E. Bach, "Musical Organizations of the Ellsworth Collieries Company, Ellsworth, Pa.," *Monthly Bulletin of the American Iron and Steel Institute* 3, no. 1 (January 1915): 27.

6. Bloomfield, *Labor Maintenance,* p. 214; Buder, *Pullman,* p. 69; Charles Frederick Weller, "Recreation in Industries," *Playground* 11 (August-September 1917): 251-52; letter of R. C. Clark to G. H. Duling, 13 April 1949, Community Relations file XIR/xc, Eli Lilly and Company Records, Indianapolis, Indiana.

7. U.S., Bureau of Labor Statistics, *Health and Recreation Activities*, p. 41; U.S., Congress, Senate, Committee on Interstate Commerce, *Hearings, Conditions in the Coal Fields of Pennsylvania, West Virginia, and Ohio*, 70th Cong., 1st sess., 1928, p. 1845; M. McCusker, "Report on Colorado Situation," report to the U.S. Commission on Industrial Relations, 3 February 1915, Commission on Industrial Relations Records, State Historical Society of Wisconsin, p. 14; James Myers, *Representative Government in Industry* (New York: George H. Doran Company, 1924), p. 17.

8. C. B. Lord, "Athletics for the Working Force," *Industrial Management* 54, no. 1 (October 1917): 48.

9. U.S., Bureau of Labor Statistics, *Health and Recreation Activities*, p. 92; Robert Sidney Smith, *Mill on the Dan: A History of Dan River Mills, 1882-1950* (Durham, N.C.: Duke University Press, 1960), p. 252, n.14; *Monthly Bulletin of the American Iron and Steel Institute* 2, no. 7 (July 1914): 203-7; Howard K. Wilson, "A Study of Paternalism in the Colorado Fuel and Iron Company Under John C. Osgood: 1892-1903" (A.M. thesis, Department of History, University of Denver, 1967), pp. 98-99; George Korson, *Coal Dust on the Fiddle: Songs and Stories of the Bituminous Industry* (Hatboro, Penn.: Folklore Associates, Inc., 1965), p. 17; Robert W. Dunn, *The Americanization of Labor: The Employers' Offensive Against the Trade Unions* (New York: International Publishers, 1927), p. 194.

10. U.S., Bureau of Labor Statistics, *Health and Recreation Activities*, pp. 37-39, 46-51; Holland Thompson, *From Cotton Field to the Cotton Mill* (New York: Macmillan Co., 1906), p. 202; Harriet L. Herring, *Welfare Work in Mill Villages: The Story of Extra-Mill Activities in North Carolina* (Chapel Hill: University of North Carolina Press, 1929), pp. 134-41; Dunn, *Americanization of Labor*, p. 223; W. Irving Clark, "The Place of Athletics in the Industrial Scheme," *Industrial Management* 71, no. 6 (June 1926): 386; James B. Allen, "The Company Town: A Passing Phase of Utah's Industrial Development," *Utah Historical Quarterly* 34, no. 2 (Spring 1966): 153-54; Jack Petrill, *After the Whistle Blows: A Guide to the Field of Recreation in Industry* (New York: William-Frederick Press for the Industrial Recreation Bureau, 1949), p. 62.

11. U.S., Bureau of Labor Statistics, *Proceedings of the Employment Managers' Conference, Philadelphia, Pa., April 2 and 3, 1917*, Bulletin no. 227, 1917, p. 148; Mary Barnett Gilson, "Recreation of the Working Force," *Industrial Management* 54, no. 1 (October 1917): 53-55; "Measurable Effects of Welfare Work in Industry," *Playground* 12, no. 10 (January 1919): 433; New Jersey, Bureau of Statistics of Labor and Industries, *Twenty-Seventh Annual Report, 1904*, p. 322; Lena Harvey Tracy, *How My Heart Sang: The Story of Pioneer Industrial Welfare Work* (New York: Richard R. Smith, 1950), pp. 127-29; Smith, *Mill on the Dan*, p. 252; U.S., Bureau of Labor Statistics, *Welfare Work for Employees*, p. 88; Goodyear Tire and Rubber Company, *Work of the Labor Division*, pp. 37-38; U.S., Bureau of Labor Statistics, *Health and Recreation Activities*, p. 48; Budgett Meakin, *Model Factories and Villages: Ideal Conditions of Labour and Housing* (Philadelphia: George W. Jacobs & Co., 1905), p. 224; *Monthly Bulletin of the American Iron and Steel Institute* 2, no. 2 (February 1914): "Editorial Notes."

12. *Social Service* 2, no. 9 (September 1900): 14-19; Smith, *Mill on the Dan*, p. 252.

13. U.S., Bureau of Labor Statistics, *Health and Recreation Activities*, p. 41; Smith, *Mill on the Dan*, p. 252, n. 14; letter of R. A. Mitchell, Alabama agent, to J.

Howard Nichols, 10 August 1897, Dwight Manufacturing Company Records, box MH-1, Baker Library; U.S., Department of Labor, Working Conditions Service, *Safeguarding Workers in the Tanning Industry*, 1919, figs. 17, 47, 60; New Jersey, Bureau of Statistics of Labor and Industries, *Twenty-Seventh Annual Report, 1904,* pp. 379-81.

14. U.S., Bureau of Labor Statistics, *Welfare Work for Employees,* p. 133; U.S., Bureau of Labor Statistics, *Health and Recreation Activities,* p. 54; New Jersey, Bureau of Statistics and Industry, *Twenty-Seventh Annual Report, 1904,* pp. 379-81; Goodyear Tire and Rubber Company, *Work of the Labor Division*, p. 40; Bloomfield, *Labor Maintenance*, p. 221.

15. Charles R. Hook, "Musical Organizations of the American Rolling Mill Company, Middletown, Ohio," *Monthly Bulletin of the American Iron and Steel Institute* 3, no. 1 (January 1915): 9.

16. Letter of W. F. Straw to Amoskeag men and women, regarding "Amoskeag Song Contest," 21 May 1928, and "Amoskeag, Old Amoskeag," words by William C. Swallow [1928?], Amoskeag Manufacturing Company Records, case CD-1, Baker Library (cf. Program, Borden Glee Club, First Concert and Dance, 16 December 1938, p. 1, Borden and Company Records, New York, New York).

17. Schoolfield and Riverside were the locations of the company's main mills. Smith, *Mill on the Dan,* p. 273.

18. Letter of S. M. Darling to Cyrus H. McCormick, Jr., 31 October 1903, Cyrus H. McCormick, Jr., Papers, series 2C, box 39, State Historical Society of Wisconsin; Henry Bruére, "Recommendations for Dealing with Social Betterment Problem at Reaper Works," June 1903, Nettie Fowler McCormick Papers, series 3B, box 34, State Historical Society of Wisconsin.

Chapter 9. Profit Sharing and Stock Ownership Plans

1. Nicholas Paine Gilman, *Industrial Partnership of Profit Sharing: A Word to the Employer* (Boston: Press of George H. Ellis, 1890), p. 6; New Jersey Bureau of Statistics of Labor and Industries, *Third Annual Report, 1880,* pp. 125-29.

2. I. W. Howerth, "Profit Sharing at Ivorydale," *American Journal of Sociology* 2, no. 1 (July 1896): 44-45; "Profit Sharing in the Pillsbury Mills," *Review of Reviews* 4 (September 1891): 172-73; Daniel Bloomfield, *Labor Maintenance: A Practical Handbook of Employees Service Work* (New York: Ronald Press, 1920), p. 376; Gilman, *Profit Sharing,* pp. 296-330; Dwight T. Farnham, "Some Experiences with Profit Sharing," *Industrial Mangement* 52, no. 6 (March 1917): 760; National Civic Federation, *Profit Sharing by American Employers* (New York: Profit Sharing Department, National Civic Federation, 1920), p. 1; Borris Emmet, *Profit Sharing in the United States,* U.S., Bureau of Labor Statistics, Bulletin no. 208, December 1916, p. 9; National Industrial Conference Board, *Employee Stock Purchase Plans,* pp. 2, 33-40; U.S., Congress, Senate, Committee on Interstate Commerce, *Hearings, Conditions in the Coal Fields of Pennsylvania, West Virginia, and Ohio,* 70th Cong., 1st sess., 1928, p. 1306; Abraham Epstein, "Industrial Welfare Movement Sapping American Trade Unions," *Current History Magazine* 34, no. 4 (July 1926): 519.

3. John A. Garraty, *Right-Hand Man: The Life of George W. Perkins* (New York: Harper and Brothers, 1960), p. 112; Andrew Carnegie, "Capital and Labour Harmony: Partnership and Profit Sharing Plans," *Cassier's Magazine* 34, no. 3 (July

1903): 184–86; "Carnegie on Employees as Partners," *Outlook* 74 (16 May 1903): 148; National Industrial Conference Board, *Employee Stock Purchase Plans,* p. 44n.; Alfred Lief, *The Firestone Story: A History of the Firestone Tire and Rubber Company* (New York: McGraw-Hill Book Co., 1951), p. 84.

4. Robert Sidney Smith, *Mill on the Dan: A History of Dan River Mills, 1882–1950* (Durham, N.C.: Duke University Press, 1960), pp. 284–89.

5. "Profit Sharing in the Pillsbury Mills," pp. 172–74; diary entry for 28 April 1903, Cyrus H. McCormick, Jr., Papers, series 4C, box 6, State Historical Society of Wisconsin; Arthur Goodrich, "The United States Steel Corporation's Profit-Sharing Plan," *World's Work* 5 (February 1903): 3058; George Perkins, "Let Workers Share in Profits," *American Employer* 2, no. 3 (October 1913): 151; Howerth, "Profit-Sharing at Ivorydale," p. 53; Boyd Fisher, "Where Profit Sharing Fails and Where it Succeeds," *System* 29, no. 4 (April 1916): 382–83; U.S., Congress, Senate, Committee on Education and Labor, *Investigation of Strike in Steel Industries,* 66th Cong., 1st sess., 1919, p. 278.

6. U.S., Congress, House, *Report of the Industrial Commission on the Relations and Conditions of Capital and Labor Employed in Manufactures and General Business, vol. XLV,* Doc. no. 183, 57th Cong., 1st sess., 1901, pp. 385–89; *Cincinnati Enquirer,* 20 April 1887; *Chicago Daily News,* 19 December 1888; remarks of William Cooper Procter, Profit Sharing Dividend Celebration, 27 February 1915, Procter and Gamble Company Records, box A-7, Cincinnati, Ohio.

7. H. G. Lee, "Welfare Work Conducted by Representative Employers throughout the United States," report to the U.S. Commission on Industrial Relations, 27 January 1915, Commission on Industrial Relations Records, State Historical Society of Wisconsin, p. 68, quoting Perkins in the *Boston Evening Transcript,* 2 July 1913; Arthur O. Lovejoy, "Profit-Sharing and International Peace," *International Journal of Ethics* 31 (April 1921): 242; National Civic Federation, *Tenth Annual Meeting, 1909* (New York: By the author, 1910), p. 145; Farnham, "Some Experiences with Profit Sharing," p. 761.

8. John A. Garraty, "The United States Steel Corporation Versus Labor: The Early Years," *Labor History* 1, no. 1 (Winter 1960): 19.

9. Nicholas Paine Gilman, *A Dividend to Labor: A Study of Employers' Welfare Institutions* (Boston: Houghton, Mifflin & Company, 1899), pp. 380–88; Emmet, *Profit Sharing in the United States,* p. 17; Oscar W. Nestor, "A History of Personnel Administration, 1890 to 1910" (Ph.D. diss., Department of Economics, University of Pennsylvania, 1954), p. 110; David Brody, *Steelworkers in America: The Nonunion Era* (Cambridge: Harvard University Press, 1960), pp. 153–54; Senate, *Investigation of Strike in Steel Industries,* p. 246; Clarence J. Hicks, *My Life in Industrial Relations: Fifty Years in the Growth of a Profession* (New York: Harper and Brothers, 1941), p. 108.

10. Robert W. Dunn, *The Americanization of Labor: The Employers' Offensive Against the Trade Unions* (New York: International Publishers, 1927), pp. 157–60; William M. Leiserson, *Adjusting Immigrant and Industry* (New York: Harper and Brothers, 1924), p. 167.

11. Thomas G. Plant Company, *Profit Sharing, Relief and Saving Fund Department,* n.d., pamphlet in Cyrus H. McCormick, Jr., Papers, series 2C, box 40; George A. Stevens and Leonard W. Hatch, "Employers' Welfare Institutions," in New York, Department of Labor, *Third Annual Report of the Commissioner of Labor,* 1903, pt.

4, in New York, Assembly Documents, 1904, 22, no. 61, p. 271; "Industrial Betterments," *Massachusetts Labor Bulletin* no. 30 (March 1904), pp. 68-69; Frank W. Blackmar, "Two Examples of Successful Profit-Sharing," *Forum* 19 (March 1895): 59.

12. Pennsylvania, Department of Internal Affairs, Bureau of Industrial Statistics, "Welfare Work and Co-operation as Means to Create More Cordial Relations," *Forty-First Report of the Bureau of Industrial Statistics,* 1913-14, in *Annual Report of Secretary of Internal Affairs* 41, pt. 3, p. 48; Ordway Tead, "The Rise of Employee Stock-Ownership," *Industrial Management* 71, no. 3 (March 1926): 157-58; Alfred Lief, "It Floats"; *The Story of Proctor and Gamble* (New York: Rinehart and Company, 1958), pp. 131-32; Herbert Feis, *Labor Relations: A Study Made in the Procter and Gamble Company* (New York: Adelphi Company, 1928), p. 32; remarks of Thomas G. Plant, minutes of meeting of the Committee on Industrial Relations, Boston Chamber of Commerce, 11 June 1909, p. 19, Boston Chamber of Commerce Records, file 332-19, Baker Library, Harvard University, Cambridge, Massachusetts.

13. National Civic Federation, *Profit Sharing By American Employers,* pp. 283-92; Edward A. Rumely, "Mr. Ford's Plan to Share Profits," *World's Work* 27 (April 1914): 668; Emmet, *Profit Sharing in the United States,* pp. 97, 108.

14. Emmet, *Profit Sharing in the United States,* pp. 99-108; Keith Sward, *The Legend of Henry Ford* (New York: Rinehart & Co., 1948), pp. 55-63; Allan Nevins and Frank Ernest Hill, *Ford: Expansion and Challenge, 1915-1933* (New York: Charles Scribner's Sons, 1957), pp. 324-49.

15. Garraty, *Right-Hand Man,* pp. 29, 109-13; Robert Ozanne, *A Century of Labor-Management Relations at McCormick and International Harvester* (Madison: University of Wisconsin Press, 1967), p. 73.

16. Garraty, *Right-Hand Man,* pp. 29, 109-13; National Industrial Conference Board, *Employee Stock Purchase Plans,* pp. 91-92; Senate, *Investigation of Strike in Steel Industries,* pp. 276-78.

17. Lovejoy, "Profit Sharing and International Peace," 254-55; National Civic Federation, *Practical Experience With Profit Sharing,* p. 41.

18. Howerth, "Profit-Sharing at Ivorydale," p. 45; "Profit Sharing in the Pillsbury Mills," p. 173; letter of N. O. Nelson to James A. McKibben, 16 April 1913, Boston Chamber of Commerce Records, file 332-19; Ida Tarbell, *New Ideals in Business: An Account of Their Practice and Their Effects* (New York: Macmillan Company, 1916), pp. 254-55.

19. U.S., Federal Trade Commission, *National Wealth and Income,* 69th Cong., 1st sess., Senate Doc. no. 126, 25 May 1926, p. 160.

Chapter 10. Medical Care

1. Carl A. Auerbach et al., *The Legal Process* (San Francisco: Sandler Publishing Company, 1961), pp. 401-3; David Brody, *Steelworkers in America: The Nonunion Era* (Cambridge: Harvard University Press, 1960), p. 92.

2. Auerbach, *Legal Process,* p. 534.

3. William B. Gates, Jr., *Michigan Copper and Boston Dollars: An Economic History of the Copper Mining Industry* (Cambridge: Harvard University Press, 1951), p. 104; Vernon H. Jensen, *Heritage of Conflict: Labor Relations in the Nonferrous Metals Industry up to 1930* (Ithaca: Cornell University Press, 1950), p. 28; U.S.,

Congress, Senate, *Immigrants in Industries, Part 17 . . . Part 20, Report of the Immigration Commission,* vol. 16, 61st Cong., 2d sess., Senate Doc. vol. 78, 1911, p. 333; U.S., Congress, Senate, Subcommittee of the Committee on Education and Labor, *Hearings, Conditions in the Paint Creek District,* West Virginia, 63d Cong., 1st sess., 1913, pp. 914-17; U.S., Congress, Senate, *Report on Conditions of Employment in the Iron and Steel Industry in the United States,* vol. 4, Doc. no. 110, 62d Cong., 1st sess., 1911-13, p. 246; U.S., Congress, Senate, *Report of the Industrial Commission on the Relations and Conditions of Capital and Labor Employed in the Mining Industry,* vol. 12, Doc. no. 181, 57th Cong., 1st sess., 1901, p. lxxii.

4. Robert Ozanne, *A Century of Labor-Management Relations at McCormick and International Harvester* (Madison: University of Wisconsin Press, 1967), p. 81; Nicholas Paine Gilman, *A Dividend to Labor: A Study of Employers' Welfare Institutions* (Boston: Houghton, Mifflin and Company, 1899), pp. 106-88; Edwin L. Shuey, *Factory People and Their Employers* (New York: Lentilon and Co., 1900), pp. 181-87; U.S., Commissioner of Labor, *Workmen's Insurance and Benefit Funds in the United States, Twenty-Third Annual Report,* 1908, pp. 448-87 (averaging column 16 and excluding funds 459-61); Abraham Epstein, "Industrial Welfare Movement Sapping American Trade Unions," *Current History Magazine* 24, no. 4 (July 1926): 519; National Industrial Conference Board, *The Present Status of Mutual Benefit Associations* (New York: National Industrial Conference Board, 1931), p. 93; Edgar Sydenstricker, "Existing Agencies for Health Insurance in the United States," U.S., Bureau of Labor Statistics, *Proceedings of the Conference on Social Insurance,* Bulletin no. 212, 1917, p. 456; J. B. Erskine, "United States Steel and Carnegie Pension Fund," U.S., Bureau of Labor Statistics, *Proceedings of the Conference on Social Insurance,* p. 742; letters of Eastman Kodak Company to James A. McKibben, 22 April 1913, and Baldwin Locomotive Works to McKibben, 4 April 1913, Boston Chamber of Commerce Records, file 332-19, Baker Library, Harvard University.

5. W. L. Chandler, "The Employees' Mutual Benefit Association," *Industrial Management,* nos. 1-4, 6, January-April, June 1918, pp. 38, 111; National Industrial Conference Board, *Present Status of Mutual Benefit Associations,* pp. 48-50; U.S., Commissioner of Labor, *Workmen's Insurance and Benefit Funds,* pp. 429-39; Sydenstricker, "Existing Agencies for Health Insurance," pp. 453-54.

6. National Industrial Conference Board, *Present Status of Mutual Benefit Associations,* p. 41; Boris Emmet, "Operation of Establishment and Trade-Union Disability Funds," *Monthly Review of the Bureau of Labor Statistics* 5, no. 2 (August 1917): 219; letter of Stanley McCormick to Cyrus H. McCormick, Jr., 21 April 1902, Cyrus H. McCormick, Jr., Papers, series 2C, box 41, State Historical Society of Wisconsin; Senate, *Conditions of Employment in the Iron and Steel Industry* 4, p. 250; Chandler, "Employees' Mutual Benefit Association," pp. 37-38; Samuel M. Jones, *Letters of Labor and Love* (Indianapolis: Bobbs-Merrill Co., 1905), pp. 88-89.

7. Emmet, "Operation of Establishment and Trade-Union Disability Funds," pp. 219-30; Chandler, "The Employees' Mutual Benefit Association," passim, esp. 220; National Industrial Conference Board, *Present Status of Mutual Benefit Associations,* pp. 12, 72-74; Sydenstricker, "Existing Agencies for Health Insurance," pp. 456-57; letter of Harry J. Brandt to James A. McKibben, 1 May 1933, Boston Chamber of Commerce Records, file 332-19, Baker Library.

8. Chandler, "Employees' Mutual Benefit Association," pp. 222, 294-95.

9. U.S., Commission of Labor, *Workmen's Insurance and Benefit Funds,* pp. 276–77, 429–39; National Civic Federation, *Tenth Annual Meeting,* 1909 (New York: National Civic Federation, 1910), p. 284; National Civic Federation, *Conference on Welfare Work, 1904* (New York: Press of Andrew H. Kellogg, 1904), p. 51; Pennsylvania, Department of Internal Affairs, Bureau of Industrial Statistics, "Alleviation of Distress Among Workingmen," *Fifteenth Annual Report,* 1887, in *Annual Report of the Secretary of Internal Affairs* 15, pt. 3, pp. B9-B46, E16; U.S., Bureau of Labor Statistics, *Proceedings of the Employment Managers' Conference, Philadelphia, Pa., April 2 and 3, 1917,* p. 168; Jerome L. Schwartz, "Early History of Prepaid Medical Care Plans," *Bulletin of the History of Medicine* 39, no. 5 (September–October 1965): 453.

10. Selig Perlman, "Second Preliminary Report on Welfare Work and Social Insurance," report to the U.S. Commission on Industrial Relations, 7 November 1914, p. 7, State Historical Society of Wisconsin; U.S., Commissioner of Labor, *Workmen's Insurance and Benefit Funds,* pp. 271, 389; Sydenstricker, "Existing Agencies for Health Insurance in the United States," p. 453; National Industrial Conference Board, *Present Status of Mutual Benefit Associations,* pp. 35, 46. See also W. L. Chandler, "Benefit Funds: A Summary and Analysis of Benefit Funds in 461 Industrial Establishments," *System* 25, no. 3 (March 1914): 257–61, and U.S., Bureau of Labor Statistics, *Health and Recreation Activities in Industrial Establishments, 1926,* Bulletin no. 458, 1928, pp. 59–65; W. H. Winans, "Mutual Benefit Associations," in National Association of Manufacturers, *Proceedings of the Thirty-Third Annual Meeting* (New York, 1928), p. 352; Franklin V. Swan, "Industrial Welfare Work in Flint, Michigan," *Survey* 32 (18 July 1914): 411; Jack Petrill, *After the Whistle Blows: A Guide to the Field of Recreation in Industry* (New York: William-Frederick Press for the Industrial Recreation Bureau, 1949), pp. 10–15.

11. Selig Perlman, "Digest of Mr. Perlman's Report on Welfare Work and Social Insurance," report to the U.S. Commission on Industrial Relations, 24 February 1915, Commission on Industrial Relations Records, State Historical Society of Wisconsin, pp. 2–5.

12. U.S. Bureau of Labor Statistics, *Health and Recreation Activities,* pp. 66–68.

13. Report of W. C. Swallow, director of Employees' Service Department, Amoskeag Manufacturing Company, on proposed insurance plan, 1 August 1916, Amoskeag Manufacturing Company Records, case CD-1, Baker Library, p. 4; Robben W. Fleming and Edwin E. Witte, "Marathon Corporation and Seven Labor Unions," in *Causes of Industrial Peace Under Collective Bargaining,* Case Study no. 8 (Washington, D.C.: National Planning Association, 1950), p. 13; Selig Perlman, "Preliminary Report on Welfare Work and Social Insurance," report to the U.S. Commission on Industrial Relations, 1 September 1914, appendix 3, Commission on Industrial Relations Records, National Archives, Washington, D.C.

14. U.S., Bureau of Labor Statistics, *Health and Recreation Activities,* pp. 68–73.

15. "Summary of Answers to Inquiry on Medical Aid," unpublished report, 2 April 1914, Boston Chamber of Commerce Records, file 332-19, Baker Library; Sydenstricker, "Existing Agencies for Health Insurance," pp. 452–53; Norman J. Wood, "Industrial Relations Policies of American Management, 1900–1933," *Business History Review* 34, no. 4 (Winter 1960: 411; "Medical and Hospital Service for Industrial Employees," *Monthly Labor Review* 24, no. 1 (January 1927): 7; remarks of A. E. Anderson, Profit Sharing Dividend Celebration, 27 February 1915, Procter and

Gamble Company Records, box A-7, Cincinnati, Ohio; J. W. Plaisted, "Memorandum for Committee on Industrial Relations," unpublished report, 17 December 1914, Boston Chamber of Commerce Records, file 332-19, Baker Library; Bernard M. Cannon, "Social Deterrents to the Unionization of Southern Cotton Textile Mill Workers" (Ph.D. diss., Department of Sociology, Harvard University, 1951); statement of Walworth Manufacturing Company on medical and dental clinics, [1927?], Manufacturers' Research Association Records, file 432, case 2.

16. William Turnblazer (president, District 19, United Mine Workers of America), "Words of Warning to the Coal Miners and Citizens of Southeastern Kentucky and Tennessee," leaflet dated 28 July 1931, Collective Bargaining Agreements, box 23, Records of the Bureau of Labor Statistics, National Archives, Washington, D.C.; Otto P. Geier, "Health of the Working Force," *Industrial Management* 54, no. 1, (October 1917): 19.

17. "Medical and Hospital Service for Industrial Employees," pp. 9-13; Jensen, *Heritage of Conflict,* p. 28; William O'Neill Sherman, "Carnegie Steel Company Standard Emergency Hospital," *Monthly Bulletin of the American Iron and Steel Institute* 1, no. 12 (December 1913): 347; U.S., Bureau of Labor Statistics, *Welfare Work for Employees in Industrial Establishments in the United States,* Bulletin no. 250, 1919, pp. 21-26. See also *Co-operation,* December 1928, p. 22, Kimberly-Clark Company Records, Neenah, Wisconsin, and U.S., Congress, Senate, Committee on Manufactures, *Hearings, Conditions in Coal Fields in Harlan and Bell Counties, Kentucky,* 72d Cong., 1st sess., 1932, pp. 200-1, for descriptions of company hospitals.

18. Kimberly-Clark Company, Safety Bulletin, no. 23, August 1915, p. 2, Kimberly-Clark Records, Neenah, Wisconsin; Sanford DeHart, "The Industrial Dentist," *Industrial Management* 73, no. 2 (February 1927): 90; "Dental Work in Factories a Success," *Industrial Relations* 11, no. 11 (8 July 1922): 1172; "Employees' Teeth Kept in Shape by Pittsburg Firm," *Square Deal* 11 (January 1913): 539; letter of Dr. R. S. Quimby, service manager, Hood Rubber Company, Watertown, Massachusetts, to E. M. Hood, Manufacturers' Research Association, Boston, Massachusetts, 29 July 1927, Manufacturers' Research Association Records, file 432, case 2, Baker Library; Daniel Bloomfield, *Labor Maintenance: A Practical Handbook of Employees' Service Work* (New York: Ronald Press, 1920), p. 197; annual report of the Efficiency Division, 1931, p. 6, Eli Lilly and Company Records, Indianapolis, Indiana; "Summary of Nationality and Age of Patients visiting and receiving treatment [*sic*] . . . For two years ending April 30th, 1915," unpublished report, "Dental & Medical Service" folder, Amoskeag Manufacturing Company Records, case CD-1, Baker Library.

19. Letter of Martin F. Carpenter, Dennison Manufacturing Company, Framingham, Massachusetts, to Elsie M. Hood, Boston, Massachusetts, 8 August 1927, Manufacturers' Research Association Records, file 432, case 2; Mark M. Jones, "Development of the Health Department of Thomas A. Edison Interests," *Industrial Management* 55, no. 6 (June 1918): 491; John Brophy, *A Miner's Life* (Madison: University of Wisconsin Press, 1964), p. 70; Jones, "Development of the Health Department," p. 493; George Korson, *Coal Dust on the Fiddle: Songs and Stories of the Bituminous Industry* (Hatboro, Penn.: Folklore Associates, 1964), pp. 58-59; Senate, *Conditions in Kentucky Coal Fields,* p. 200.

20. Nettie P. McGill, *The Welfare of Children in Bituminous Coal Mining Communities of West Virginia,* U.S., Department of Labor, Children's Bureau,

Publication no. 117, pp. 48-52; Korson, *Coal Dust on the Fiddle,* pp. 58-59; David J. Saposs, "Company Towns—Louisiana, Arizona, and Texas," report to the U.S. Commission on Industrial Relations, [1914?], Commission on Industrial Relations Records, National Archives, p. 13; Brophy, *Miner's Life,* p. 70.

21. The most ambitious study was made in 1916 by the Public Health Service. It mailed questionnaires to 6,500 companies and received 2,300 replies. Of those replying, 425 had mutual benefit associations and "about 100" had other types of medical care. The study assumed that those who failed to reply offered no medical care and concluded that as a result "a conservative estimate would probably be that only between 10 and 12 percent of the manufacturing and mining establishments in the United States" offered any medical benefits. Also in 1916, the Bureau of Labor Statistics surveyed the welfare work of 431 companies. Rather than mailing questionnaires, however, it sent investigators into the fields. It found that 61 percent provided medical care beyond first aid. The sample may nevertheless have been biased toward those companies that the bureau knew conducted welfare work. Ten years later the bureau conducted another study, this time disregarding mutual benefit associations. Though it did not report its sampling technique, it found 407 companies, most of which were very large, that provided medical service. A decade after that, in 1936, the National Industrial Conference Board conducted a mail survey. Then under serious criticism from New Dealers and others, businessmen were much more eager to respond than they had been in 1916, particularly to a business-sponsored organization that was likely to write a rejoinder. The Industrial Conference Board accordingly could report that of 2,075 manufacturing companies surveyed, 1,292, or 62.3 percent offered medical programs. The proportion for 377 nonmanufacturing firms was even higher: 81.2 percent. The Bureau of Labor Statistics and National Industrial Conference Board figures are thus reasonably close, and there is evidence that the Public Health figures are low. See Sydenstricker, "Existing Agencies for Health Insurance," pp. 452-53; U.S., Bureau of Labor Statistics, *Welfare Work for Employees in Industrial Establishments,* pp. 7-8, 15; "Medical and Hospital Service for Industrial Employees," p. 9; National Industrial Conference Board, *What Employers Are Doing for Employees: A Survey of Voluntary Activities for Improvement of Working Conditions in American Business Concerns* (New York: National Industrial Conference Board, 1936), pp. 5, 44-45.

Chapter 11. Pensions

1. Edward S. Cowdrick, "Industrial Pension," in National Association of Manufacturers, *Proceedings of the Thirty-third Annual Meeting* (New York, 1928), p. 346.

2. "Pension Plans in American Industry," *Industrial Relations* 8, no. 7 (15 October 1921): 858; Abraham Epstein, "Industrial Welfare Movement Sapping American Trade Unions," *Current History Magazine, New York Times* 24, no. 4 (July 1926): 519; National Industrial Conference Board, *Industrial Pensions in the United States* (New York: By the author, 1925), p. 5.

3. William Menkel, " 'Welfare Work' on American Railroads," *Review of Reviews* 38 (October 1908): 458; Selig Perlman, "Digest of Mr. Perlman's Report on Welfare Work and Social Insurance," typewritten report to the U. S. Commission on Industrial Relations, 24 February 1915, pp. 8-9, State Historical Society of Wisconsin.

4. Remarks of Augustus P. Loring, president, Plymouth Cordage Company, in National Civic Federation, [*Proceedings of the*] *Ninth Annual Meeting, 1908* (New York: By the author, 1909), p. 124.

5. Cowdrick, "Industrial Pension," p. 346; memorandum of C. P. Marshall, [1922?], Plymouth Cordage Company Records, file H, drawer 3, Baker Library, Harvard University, Cambridge, Massachusetts.

6. National Industrial Conference Board, *Industrial Pensions,* pp. 28, 64; L. D. Wood, "Industrial Pension Plans," *American Federationist* 33, no. 7 (July 1926): 859; National Civic Federation, *Proceedings, Twelfth Annual Meeting, 1912* (New York: By the author, [1913?]), p. 277.

7. National Industrial Conference Board, *Industrial Pensions*, p. 37.

8. Ibid., pp. 5-8; Epstein, "Industrial Welfare Work," p. 519; "Pension Plans in American Industry," p. 858.

9. National Industrial Conference Board, *Industrial Pensions,* pp. 14-15, 41-60.

10. Ibid., pp. 49-50.

11. Wood, "Industrial Pension Plans," p. 859.

12. National Industrial Conference Board, *Industrial Pensions*, p. 72.

13. Ibid., p. 74.

14. Ibid., pp. 79-82.

15. Ibid., pp. 85-92; cf. "Applications for Pensions," Plymouth Cordage Company Records, file H, drawer 3.

16. National Industrial Conference Board, *Industrial Pensions,* p. 91.

17. Luther Conant, "A Critical Analysis of Industrial Pension Systems," quoted in Robert W. Dunn, *The Americanization of Labor: The Employers' Offensive Against the Trade Unions* (New York: International Publishers, 1927), p. 185.

18. Cowdrick, "Industrial Pensions," p. 346; National Industrial Conference Board, *Industrial Pensions*, p. 43; S. P. Bush, general manager, Buckeye Steel Castings Company, "Special Report on Old-Age Pensions," in National Association of Manufacturers, *Proceedings of the Twenty-second Annual Convention* (New York, 1917), p. 48.

Chapter 12. Social Work

1. Frank B. Miller and Mary Ann Coghill, "Sex and the Personnel Manager," *Industrial and Labor Relations Review* 18, no. 1 (October 1964): 35; Robert Ozanne, *A Century of Labor-Management Relations at McCormick and International Harvester* (Madison: University of Wisconsin Press, 1967), p. 32.

2. National Civic Federation, *Conference on Welfare Work, 1904* (New York: Press of Andrew H. Kellogg, 1904), pp. 26-27; *Chicago Daily News,* 20 June 1906, clipping in the Cyrus H. McCormick, Jr., Papers, series 2C, box 41, State Historical Society of Wisconsin; Daniel Nelson and Stuart Campbell, "Taylorism Versus Welfare Work in American Industry: H. L. Gantt and the Bancrofts," *Business History Review* 46, no. 1 (Spring 1972): 8.

3. National Civic Federation, Women's Department, Committee on Welfare Work for Employees, *Examples of Welfare Work in the Cotton Industry: Conditions and Progress, New England and the South* (New York, [1910?]), pp. 164-65; *Monthly Bulletin of the American Iron and Steel Institute* 5, no. 1 (January 1917): 5.

4. *Employers and Employees: Full Text of the Addresses Before the National Convention of Employers and Employees, ... September 22-25, 1902* (Chicago: Public Policy, n.d.), pp. 164-65; *Social Service* 10, no. 1 (July 1904): 10; U.S., Bureau of Labor Statistics, *Proceedings of the Employment Managers' Conference, Philadelphia, Pa., April 2 and 3, 1917,* Bulletin no. 227, 1917, p. 83.

5. National Civic Federation, *Conference on Welfare Work, 1904,* pp. 26-27; "Usefulness of the Social Secretary," *Review of Reviews* 34 (August 1906): 223-24 (an abridgement of Mary Rankin Cranston, "The Social Secretary—An Opportunity for Employer and Employee to Understand Each Other," *Craftsman* 10 [1906]: 492).

6. William Howe Tolman, *Social Engineering* (New York: Macmillan Co., 1909), pp. 255-56; U.S., Congress, Senate, Committee on Education and Labor, *Hearings, Investigation of Strike in Steel Industries,* 66th Cong., 1st sess., 1919, p. 261.

7. "Charity Cases 1920-21" folder, Amoskeag Manufacturing Company Records, case CD-1, Baker Library; U.S., Congress, House, *Hearings, United States Steel Corporation,* vol. 5, 62d Cong., 2d sess., 1912, p. 3398.

8. *Monthly Bulletin of the American Iron and Steel Institute* 5, no. 1 (January 1917): 5, and 5, no. 2 (March-April 1917): 59-61; Tolman, *Social Engineering,* p. 260.

9. Harriet Herring, *Welfare Work in Mill Villages: The Story of Extra-Mill Activities in North Carolina* (Chapel Hill: University of North Carolina Press, 1929), p. 302; *Monthly Bulletin of the American Iron and Steel Institute* 5, no. 2 (March-April 1917): 61.

10. *Monthly Bulletin of the American Iron and Steel Institute,* 5, no. 1 (January-February 1917): 28-29, and 5, no. 2 (March-April 1917): 59-61; letter of E. J. Barcalo, president of Barcalo Manufacturing Company, to James E. McKibben, 1 May 1913, Boston Chamber of Commerce Records, file 332-19, Baker Library; David J. Saposs, notes of interview with Deputy Sheriff Hagen, Cravens, Lousiana, 27 August 1914, Commission on Industrial Relations Records, box 2, National Archives, Washington, D.C.

11. Carrie B. Correll, "The Industrial Nurses' Club of Cleveland, Ohio," *Public Health Nurse* 12, no. 2 (February 1920): 118; letter of Martin F. Carpenter to Elsie M. Hood, 8 August 1927, Manufacturers' Research Association Records, file 432, case 2, Baker Library; U.S., Department of Labor Statistics, *Welfare Work for Employees in Industrial Establishments in the United States,* by Leifur Magnusson, Bulletin no. 250, 1919, p. 20; Willis Wisler, *A Plan for Handling Absenteeism in Industrial Plants,* U.S., Department of Labor, Working Conditions Service, Division of Labor Administration, Circular no. 3, 17 February 1919, p. 4; letter of Barcalo to McKibben, 1 May 1913, Boston Chamber of Commerce Records, file 332-19; Thomas Darlington, "The Trained Nurse in Welfare Work in the Iron and Steel and Allied Industries," *Monthly Bulletin of the American Iron and Steel Institute* 1, no. 2 (February 1913): 37; remarks of W. Irving Clark, M.D., service director, Norton Company, *Norton Service* (Worcester, Massachusetts: Norton Company, n.d.), New York Public Library.

12. Memorandum of Marshall to F. C. Holmes, 2 February 1922, Plymouth Cordage Company Records, file H, drawer 3, "Mr. Marshall's Reports" folder; National Civic Federation, *Conference on Welfare Work,* 1904, p. 115; Nelson and Campbell, "Taylorism Versus Welfare Work," p. 8.

13. "The Commonwealth Steel Company's Fellowship Work," *Monthly Bulletin of*

the American Iron and Steel Institute, 4, no. 4 (April 1916): 125; Florence Hughes, *Sociological Work, The New Jersey Zinc Co.* (Palmerton, Penn.: New Jersey Zinc Co., 1914), p. 24, New York Public Library.

14. Mary Barnet Gilson, "Relation of Home Conditions to Industrial Efficiency," *Annals of the American Academy* 65 (May 1916): 286.

15. Helen J. Ferris, "The College Graduate in Welfare Work," *Bookman* 43, no. 3 (May 1916): 289; *Employers and Employees,* pp. 164-65, 173.

16. Charles A. Lippincott, "Promoting Employee Team Work and Welfare Without Paternalism," *Industrial Management* 71, no. 3 (March 1926): 146.

17. *Employers and Employees,* p. 182; Elizabeth Lewis Otey, *Employers' Welfare Work,* U.S. Department of Commerce and Labor, Bulletin no. 123, 1913, p. 30.

18. Cranston, "Social Secretary," pp. 489-93; *Chicago Evening Post,* 4 April 1906, clipping in Cyrus H. McCormick, Jr., Papers, series 2C, box 42; *Journal of Social Forces* 3, no. 3 (March 1925): 506; Daniel Bloomfield, *Labor Maintenance: A Practical Handbook of Employees' Service Work* (New York: Ronald Press Co., 1920), p. 201; "Welfare Work in Company Towns," *Monthly Labor Review* 25, no. 2 (August 1927): 316. See also *Texaco Star* 8, no. 10 (October 1921): 11; Personnel Committee, Texas Company, *Health Maintenance,* 1936, sec. 2, p. 2; "The Texas Corporation and Subsidiaries: Employee Relations," typewritten report for the company committee on monopoly investigation, 1939, p. 48, all in Texaco Corporation Records, New York.

19. *Monthly Bulletin of the American Iron and Steel Institute* 5, no. 1 (January 1917): 5.

Chapter 13. Employee Representation

1. United Rubber, Cork, Linoleum & Plastic Workers, Education Department, "Labor Scrapbook" (Akron, Ohio, [1963]), p. 18.

2. Ibid.; William M. Leiserson, *Adjusting Immigrant and Industry* (New York: Harper & Brothers, 1924), pp. 126-27. Cf. Clarence Banks, "One Workman's View of Industrial Plan," *Industrial Relations* 5, no. 17 (22 January 1921): 562.

3. Paul H. Giddens, *Standard Oil Company (Indiana): Oil Pioneer of the Middle West* (New York: Appleton-Century-Crofts, 1955), p. 355; U.S., Congress, Senate, Committee on Interstate Commerce, *Hearings, Conditions in the Coal Fields of Pennsylvania, West Virginia, and Ohio,* 70th Cong., 1st sess., 1928, p. 1297.

4. Samuel Gompers, "The Company Union Fraud," *American Federationist* 19 (December 1922): 888-89; "Attitude of American Federation of Labor on Shop or Company Unions," *Industrial Relations* 1, no. 10 (20 December 1919): 78; Earl J. Miller, *Workmen's Representation in Industrial Government,* University of Illinois Studies in the Social Sciences, vol. 10, nos. 3, 4 (Urbana, 1924), p. 174.

5. B. Preston Clark, "The Present Unrest," typewritten notes for a speech to Plymouth Cordage Company executives, 18 November 1913, Plymouth Cordage Company Records, file H, drawer 3, "Labor-General" folder, Baker Library, Harvard University, Cambridge, Massachusetts.

6. Letter of Mackenzie King to John D. Rockefeller, Jr., 6 August 1914, reprinted in George P. West, *Report on the Colorado Strike,* pub. by the U.S. Commission on Industrial Relations, 1915, pp. 162-64.

7. Thomas W. Dyott, *An Exposition of the System of Moral and Mental Labor*

Established at the Glass Factory of Dyottsville (Philadelphia, 1833), p. 1; National Industrial Conference Board, *Work Councils in the United States,* Research Report no. 21 (Boston: National Industrial Conference Board, 1921), p. 5; Carroll E. French, *The Shop Committee in the United States* (Baltimore: Johns Hopkins Press, 1923), pp. 15-16.

8. H. F. J. Porter, "The Higher Law in the Industrial World," *Engineering Magazine* 29, no. 5 (August 1905): 646-47; National Industrial Conference Board, Report no. 21, pp. 5-6; French, *Shop Committee,* pp. 15-16.

9. Miller, *Workmen's Representation,* pp. 41-42.

10. Ibid.; John Leitch, *Man to Man: The Story of Industrial Democracy* (New York: B. C. Forbes Co., 1919); Joanna Farrell Sturdivant, "Employee Representation Plan of the Durham Hosiery Mills," *Social Forces,* March 1926, reprinted in Harriet L. Herring, *Welfare Work in Mill Villages: The Story of Extra-Mill Activities in North Carolina* (Chapel Hill: University of North Carolina Press, 1929), pp. 625-28; French, *Shop Committee,* pp. 16-17; Goodyear Tire & Rubber Company, *The Work of the Labor Division* (Akron, Ohio: By the author, 1920), p. 18, Paul W. Litchfield, "Future Factory Policy," *The Wingfoot Clan* 8, no. 25 (29 March 1929): 3; Goodyear Tire & Rubber Company, *Rules of Discipline* [Foreman's Manual, 1919], p. 29B; *Goodyear—A Family Magazine* 9, no. 5 (May 1920): 3. The Goodyear sources are in the Goodyear Archives, Akron, Ohio.

11. Sturdivant, "Durham Hosiery Mills," 625-28; Algie M. Simons, *Personnel Relations in Industry* (New York: Ronald Press Co., 1921), pp. 274-75; French, *Shop Committee,* pp. 16-17, remarks of Fred W. Climer, vice president for industrial relations, *Transcript, First Goodyear Industrial Relations Forum* (Akron, Ohio: Goodyear Tire and Rubber Company, 1949), p. 13, Goodyear Archives.

12. R. MacGregor Dawson, *William Lyon Mackenzie King: A Political Biography* (Toronto: University of Toronto Press, 1958), passim, esp. pp. 225-43.

13. H. S. Ferns and B. Ostry, *The Age of Mackenzie King: The Rise of the Leader* (London: William Heinemann, 1955), pp. 186, 194-98.

14. Letter of W. L. Mackenzie King to Charles W. Eliot, president of Harvard University, 12 July 1915, Eliot Papers, Harvard College Library, Cambridge, Massachusetts.

15. Dawson, *Mackenzie King,* p. 245; Ben M. Selekman and Mary Van Kleeck, *Employees' Representation in Coal Mines: A Study of the Industrial Representation Plan of the Colorado Fuel and Iron Company* (New York: Russell Sage Foundation, 1924), p. 352.

16. Selekman and Van Kleeck, *Employees' Representation in Coal Mines,* pp. 59-69.

17. Ibid., pp. 65-67.

18. Ibid., pp. 27, 80; Arthur H. Young, "Principle and Practice of Cooperation in Industrial Relations, As Embodied in Plans of Employee Representation," in U.S., Bureau of Labor Statistics, *Proceedings of the Sixth Annual Meeting of the International Association of Industrial Accident Boards and Commissions,* Bulletin no. 273, 1919, pp. 369-70.

19. French, *Shop Committee,* pp. 19-22.

20. Ibid.; National Industrial Conference Board, *Experience With Works Councils in the United States,* Research Report no. 50 (New York: Century Crofts., 1922), p. 15.

21. French, *Shop Committee,* p. 23.

22. National Industrial Conference Board, *Experience With Works Councils,* pp. 15-16; Young, "Cooperation in Industrial Relations," p. 369; Miller, *Workmen's Representation,* p. 45; A. B. Wolfe, *Works Committees and Joint Industrial Councils: A Report* (Philadelphia: United States Shipping Board, Emergency Fleet Corporation, Industrial Relations Division, 1919), pp. 245-46.

23. Miller, *Workmen's Representation,* pp. 43-46; National Industrial Conference Board, *Works Councils in the United States,* p. 1; National Industrial Conference Board, *Experience with Works Councils,* p. 1.

24. U.S., Department of Labor, Office of the Secretary, *Proceedings of the First Industrial Conference,* 6-23 October 1919, p. 144; Paul W. Litchfield, *The Industrial Republic: A Study in Industrial Economics* (Boston: Houghton Mifflin Co., 1920), pp. 2, 7.

25. French, *Shop Committee,* pp. 54-58.

26. National Industrial Conference Board, *Experience With Works Councils,* pp. 102-10, 347; "Employee Representation in Industry: Chamber of Commerce Reviews Plans in Cleveland," *Industrial Relations* 16, no. 2 (16 June 1923): 1564; Ben M. Selekman, *Sharing Management With the Workers: A Study of the Partnership Plan of the Dutchess Bleachery, Wappingers Falls, New York* (New York: Russell Sage Foundation, 1924), p. 129; Louis A. Boettiger, *Employee Welfare Work: A Critical and Historical Study* (New York: Ronald Press, 1923), pp. 226-27; Miller, *Workmen's Representation,* pp. 115-19; National Industrial Conference Board, Report no. 21, p. 112; Robert W. Bruére, "West Lynn," *Survey* 56 (1 April 1926): 23-26.

27. Miller, *Workmen's Representation,* pp. 134-39; "Employee Representation in Industry," p. 1564; Tom M. Girdler, *Boot Straps* (New York: Charles Scribner's Sons, 1943), p. 226.

28. Kimberly-Clark Company, *Co-operation,* May 1921, pp. 2-3, Kimberly-Clark Records, Neenah, Wisconsin; Selekman and Van Kleeck, *Employees' Representation in Coal Mines,* pp. 80-81, 150; Senate, *Conditions in the Coal Fields,* p. 1297; Sturdivant, "Employee Representation Plan," p. 206; Herbert Feis, *Labor Relations: A Study Made in the Procter and Gamble Company* (New York: Adelphi Co., 1928), p. 71; Robert Sidney Smith, *Mill on the Dan: A History of Dan River Mills, 1882-1950* (Durham, N.C.: Duke University Press), pp. 260-80, passim.

29. National Industrial Conference Board, *Experience With Works Councils,* pp. 79-85; Ben M. Selekman, *Employees' Representation in Steel Works: A Study of the Industrial Representation Plan of the Minnequa Steel Works of the Colorado Fuel and Iron Company* (New York: Russell Sage Foundation, 1924), pp. 77-89, 222.

30. George Sweet Gibb and Evelyn Knowlton, *The Resurgent Years, 1911-1927,* vol. 2 of the History of the Standard Oil Company [New Jersey], (New York: Harper and Brothers, 1956), pp. 588-93; Selekman, *Employees' Representation in Coal Mines,* pp. 96, 144; Mary Van Kleeck, "Sharing Management with the Workers," *Journal of Social Forces* 3, no. 3 (March 1925):509.

31. Goodyear Tire and Rubber Company, *Work of the Labor Division,* p. 63.

32. Giddens, *Standard Oil Company (Indiana),* pp. 342-43; National Industrial Conference Board, *Experience With Works Councils,* p. 85.

33. National Industrial Conference Board, *Experience With Works Councils,* p. 58; Robert W. Dunn, *Company Unions: Employers' "Industrial Democracy"* (New York: Vanguard Press, 1927), p. 62.

34. Selekman and Van Kleeck, *Employees' Representation in Coal Mines,* pp.

240-41; National Industrial Conference Board, *Experience With Works Councils*, p. 79.

35. Selekman and Van Kleeck, *Employees' Representation in Coal Mines*, p. 185.

36. National Industrial Conference Board, *Experience With Works Councils*, pp. 95, 127-29; National Industrial Conference Board, *Works Councils in the United States*, p. 109; Young, "Cooperation in Industrial Relations," pp. 371-75; John Calder, "Experience with Employees' Representation During Business Depression," *Industrial Management* 64, no. 2 (August 1922): 114.

37. Selekman and Van Kleeck, *Employees' Representation in Coal Mines*, p. 77.

38. David Brody, *Steelworkers in America: The Nonunion Era* (Cambridge: Harvard University Press, 1960), p. 235.

39. Raymond B. Fosdick, *John D. Rockefeller, Jr.: A Portrait* (New York: Harper and Brothers, 1956), pp. 177-78.

40. "Attitude of American Federation of Labor on Shop or Company Unions," p. 78.

Chapter 14. Response and Decline

1. Louis A. Boettiger, *Employee Welfare Work: A Critical and Historical Study* (New York: Ronald Press, 1923), pp. 142-45; *ACIPCO: A Story of Modern Industrial Relations*, 3d ed. (Birmingham, Ala.: American Cast Iron Pipe Co., 1920), pp. 72-74; letters of George H. Simons to Augustus P. Loring, 19 August 1918, and Charles P. Marshall to F. P. Holmes, 7 December 1922, Plymouth Cordage Company Records, file H, drawer 3, "Group Insurance" folder, Baker Library, Harvard University; Glenn Gilman, *Human Relations in the Industrial Southeast: A Study of the Textile Industry* (Chapel Hill: University of North Carolina Press, 1956), pp. 136-37.

2. Martin D. Gehris, remarks before the Philadelphia Chamber of Commerce, 17 November 1921, *Proceedings of the Coal Mining Institute*, 1921, p. 66; Robert Sidney Smith, *Mill on the Dan: A History of Dan River Mills, 1882-1950* (Durham, North Carolina: Duke University Press, 1960), p. 243; "The Mutual Interest Work of the American Rolling Mill Company, Middletown, Ohio," *Monthly Bulletin of the American Iron and Steel Institute* 4, nos. 6, 7 (June-July 1916): 187.

3. Letters of W. S. Thomas, Wagner Electric Manufacturing Company, and Acme White Lead and Color Works, Detroit, Michigan, to James A. McKibben, 9 April 1913, Boston Chamber of Commerce Records, file 332-19, Baker Library; Charles W. Moore, *Timing a Century: History of the Waltham Watch Company* (Cambridge: Harvard University Press, 1945), p. 183.

4. Abraham Epstein, "Industrial Welfare Movement Sapping American Trade Unions," *Current History Magazine, New York Times* 24, no. 4 (July 1926): 520.

5. See, for example, Irving Bernstein, *The Lean Years: A History of the American Worker, 1920-1933* (Boston: Houghton Mifflin Co., 1960).

6. David Brody, "The Rise and Decline of Welfare Capitalism," in John Braeman et al., *Change and Continuity in Twentieth-Century America: The Twenties* (Columbus: Ohio State University Press, 1968), pp. 160-61, 171.

7. Ibid., pp. 148, 178.

8. R. E. Phillips, "The Betterment of Working Life," *World's Work* (December 1900): 165; William M. Leiserson, *Adjusting Immigrant and Industry* (New York: Harper and Brothers, 1924), pp. 126-27; Ida M. Tarbell, *New Ideals in Business: An*

Account of Their Practice and Their Effects Upon Men and Profits (New York: Macmillan Co., 1916), p. 227; J. David Houser, *What the Employer Thinks: Executives' Attitudes Toward Employees* (Cambridge: Harvard University Press, 1927), pp. 23, 42; R. MacGregor Dawson, *William Lyon Mackenzie King: A Political Biography, 1874-1923* (Toronto: University of Toronto Press, 1958), p. 239.

9. Philip Taft, "Violence in American Labor Disputes," *Annals of the American Academy of Political and Social Science*, September-November 1966, passim; National Civic Federation, *Conference on Welfare Work, 1904* (New York: Press of Andrew H. Kellogg, 1904), p. 119; Robert Ozanne, *A Century of Labor-Management Relations at McCormick and International Harvester* (Madison: University of Wisconsin Press, 1967), pp. 104-6; H. G. Lee, "Welfare Work Conducted by Representative Employers throughout the United States," report to the U.S. Commission on Industrial Relations Records, State Historical Society of Wisconsin, pp. viii-x; Smith, *Mill on the Dan*, p. 319; James Myers, *Representative Government in Industry* (New York: George H. Doran Company, 1924), p. 19.

10. Epstein, "Industrial Welfare Movement," p. 521; Robert W. Dunn, *The Americanization of Labor: The Employers' Offensive Against the Trade Unions* (New York: International Publishers, 1929), p. 265; letter of "employees" to the Plymouth Cordage Company, 6 October 1917, Plymouth Cordage Company Records, file H, drawer 3, "Strike of 1916" folder, Baker Library; Federico López Valencia, *Instituciones patronales de previsión en los Estados Unidos,* Anales de la Junta para ampliación de estudios é investigaciónes científicas, vol. 16, no. 5a (Madrid, 1918), pp. 213-16.

11. Raynal C. Bolling, "United States Steel Corporation and Labor Conditions," *Annals of the American Academy* 42 (July 1912): 44; U.S., Bureau of Labor Statistics, *Proceedings of the Employment Managers' Conference, Philadelphia, Pa., April 2 and 3, 1917*, Bulletin no. 227, 1917, pp. 153, 156; Daniel Nelson and Stuart Campbell, "Taylorism Versus Welfare Work in American Industry: H. L. Gantt and the Bancrofts," *Business History Review* 46, no. 1 (Spring 1972): 9.

12. Algie M. Simons, *Personnel Relations in Industry* (New York: Ronald Press Co., 1921), p. 188; Stanley Buder, *Pullman: An Experiment in Industrial Order and Community Planning, 1880-1930* (New York: Oxford University Press, 1967), pp. 83-84, 93-99; Houser, *What the Employer Thinks,* pp. 51, 125.

13. Houser, *What the Employer Thinks,* pp. 179-80.

14. Ibid., p. 35; F. Ray Marshall, *Labor in the South* (Cambridge: Harvard University Press, 1967), p. 74.

15. *Monthly Bulletin of the American Iron and Steel Institute* 3, no. 10 (October 1915): 289; letter of B. Preston Clark, vice president, Plymouth Cordage Company to H. F. Baker, 25 May 1913, Plymouth Cordage Company Records, file H, drawer 3, "General Welfare" folder, Baker Library.

16. Budgett Meakin, *Model Factories and Villages: Ideal Conditions of Labour and Housing* (Philadelphia: George W. Jacobs and Co., 1905), p. 58; George A. Stevens and Leonard W. Hatch, "Employers' Welfare Institutions," *Third Annual Report of the Commissioner of Labor,* 1903, pt. 4, in New York: *Assembly Documents, 1904* 22, no. 61 (Albany 1904): p. 304; remarks of Thomas G. Plant, minutes of meeting of the Committee on Industrial Relations, Boston Chamber of Commerce, 11 June 1909, Boston Chamber of Commerce Records, file 332-19, Baker Library.

17. Louis E. Van Norman, "Why Not More Beautiful Factories? Some Opinions of Manufacturers as to Attractive Business Plants," *Home and Flowers* 13, no. 1 (1902):

27; Oscar W. Nestor, "A History of Personnel Administration, 1890 to 1910" (Ph.D. diss., Department of Economics, University of Pennsylvania, 1954), pp. 40, 127; Mark M. Jones, "Development of the Health Department of Thomas A. Edison Interests," *Industrial Management* 55, no. 6 (June 1918): 491.

18. National Industrial Conference Board, *Industrial Relations: Administration of Policies and Programs* (New York: National Industrial Conference Board, 1931), pp. 84-86; Bernstein, *The Lean Years,* p. 183.

19. U.S., Public Health Service, "Summarized Report on the Sanitation of 124 Communities in the Bituminous Coal Districts of 9 States," report to the U.S. Coal Commission, 24 July 1923, Coal Commission Records, entry 13, box 7, Federal Records Center, Suitland, Maryland, p. 11; Bituminous Operators' Special Committee, *Maryland: The Campaign of Violence Conducted by the United Mine Workers of America Against the Open Shop Mines in the Georges Creek and Upper Potomac Fields,* Brief no. 10, submitted to the U.S. Coal Commission, 18 September 1923, Coal Commission Records, entry 8, box 4, p. 6; Marshall, *Labor in the South,* pp. 309-10; Harriet L. Herring, *Welfare Work in Mill Villages: The Story of Extra-Mill Activities in North Carolina* (Chapel Hill: University of North Carolina Press, 1929), p. 98.

20. Leiserson, *Adjusting Immigrant and Industry,* p. 65; Joseph H. White, *Houses for Mining Towns,* U.S. Bureau of Mines, Bulletin no. 87, 1914, pp. 7-8; Alexander M. Daly, "A Brief Survey of the Textiles in Massachusetts and Rhode Island," report to the U.S. Commission on Industrial Relations [1914?], Commission on Industrial Relations Records, box 5, National Archives, p. 7; John A. Garraty, "The United States Steel Corporation Versus Labor: The Early Years," *Labor History* 1, no. 1 (Winter 1960): 35-38; Moore, *Timing a Century,* pp. 176-78, 183.

21. Marshall, *Labor in the South,* p. 125; Arthur J. Todd, "Social Work and Industry," *Journal of Applied Sociology* 8, no. 6 (July-August 1924): 326.

22. National Industrial Conference Board, *What Employers Are Doing For Employees: A Survey of Voluntary Activities for Improvement of Working Conditions in American Business Concerns* (New York: National Industrial Conference Board, 1936), pp. 10, 26; Ozanne, *Century of Labor-Management Relations,* pp. 154-55; National Industrial Conference Board, *Effect of the Depression on Industrial Relations Programs* (New York: National Industrial Conference Board, 1934), pp. 8, 11.

23. National Industrial Conference Board, *Effect of the Depression,* pp. 4-8; National Industrial Conference Board, *What Employers Are Doing for Employees,* pp. 16-25.

24. John A. O'Donnell, Jr., "Company Housing," typescript report, Division of Review, National Recovery Administration, 15 November 1935, Records of the National Recovery Administration, Record Group 9, National Archives, Washington, D.C., pp. 2, 13, 36-37; Smith, *Mill on the Dan,* pp. 410-11; Ole S. Johnson, *The Industrial Store: Its History, Operations and Economic Significance* (Atlanta: Division of Research, School of Business Administration, University of Georgia, 1952), p. 79.

25. Joseph G. Rayback, *A History of American Labor* (New York: Free Press, 1966), p. 327.

26. National Industrial Conference Board, *Effect of the Depression,* p. 11; National Industrial Conference Board, *What Employers are Doing For Employees,* p. 10.

27. G. Herbert Duggins and Floyd R. Eastwood, *Planning Industrial Recreation* (Lafayette, Ind.: Purdue University, 1941), pp. 8-10.

28. Gilman, *Human Relations in the Industrial Southeast,* pp. 251, 278-79;

Milwaukee Journal, 11 March 1968; *Wisconsin State Journal* (Madison), 6 June 1968.

29. Andrew Hacker, ed., *The Corporation Take-Over* (Garden City, N.Y.: Anchor Books, 1965), p. 252; *Milwaukee Journal,* 17 May 1968, pt. 2, p. 26; Xerox copy of the sworn testimony concerning the Alabama operations of the American Can Company given at the hearing of the U.S. Commission on Civil Rights in Montgomery, Alabama, 30 April 1968, pp. 274–78, and U.S. Commission on Civil Rights, "Staff Report: Employment," Alabama Hearing, 27 April–2 May 1968, p. 9, in the author's possession.

30. Brody, "Rise and Decline of Welfare Capitalism," p. 148.

Essay on Sources

The manuscript sources used in this study include the records of American business companies, the personal papers of American businessmen, the records of governmental bodies, unpublished reports by governmental investigators, and unpublished theses and dissertations. Published sources include contemporary government reports as well as contemporary and recent books, articles, and pamphlets. The most useful sources are described below. Each source used in this study is also cited fully in each chapter in which it is used.

1. Company Records

The richest collection of business records in the United States is located in Cambridge, Massachusetts, in the Baker Library of the Graduate School of Business Administration of Harvard University. Of the records located there, the most useful collection is that of the Boston Chamber of Commerce, which includes results of a nationwide survey of welfare capitalism conducted in 1913. The records of the Plymouth Cordage Company, a very important welfare firm, are comprehensive and extremely useful. The records of the Amoskeag Manufacturing Company, the Dwight Manufacturing Company, the Manufacturers' Research Association, the Lyman Mills, and the Shawmut Coal Company are less important but still of value. The records of the following companies contain material on welfarism but are of little importance: Lawrence Manufacturing Company; American Steel and Wire Company; Conrey Placer Mining Company; Waltham Watch Company; Chace, Luther and Company; Pierson and Company, Ramapo Works; Pepperell Manufacturing Company; and the Slater Collection.

Of the extensive materials at the State Historical Society of Wisconsin in Madison, the voluminous records of the McCormick family and the International Harvester Company have been put to good use by Robert Ozanne in his *A Century of Labor-Management Relations at McCormick and International Harvester* (Madison: University of Wisconsin Press, 1967). Much good material remains, however, primarily in the Cyrus Hall McCormick, Jr., Papers and the Nettie Fowler McCormick Papers. These collections, like several of those in the Baker Library, contain material on other companies as well. The David Clark Everest Papers offer insights into the thinking of the president of the Marathon Paper Company, a welfare firm of secondary importance.

Business records retained in company archives are described in Society of American Archivists, Committee on Business Archives, *Directory of Business Archives in the United States and Canada,* preliminary ed., mimeographed, 1969. Many of them are closed to scholars, and searchers who visit those which are open are likely to be disappointed. Company archives which were of some use included those of Deere and Company, Moline, Illinois; Eli Lilly and Company, Indianapolis, Indiana; Procter and Gamble Company, Cincinnati, Ohio; Kimberly-Clark Corporation, Neenah, Wisconsin; Bennett Office, Inc., Minneapolis, Minnesota; Borden, Inc., New York, New York; Texaco, Inc., New York, New York; and Goodyear Tire and Rubber Company, Akron, Ohio. Searches at the following proved fruitless: Sears, Roebuck and Company, Chicago, Illinois; Hercules, Inc., Wilmington, Delaware; Black and Decker Manufacturing Company, Towson, Maryland; International Paper Company, New York, New York; B. F. Goodrich Company, Akron, Ohio. Inquiries at many other companies suggested that visits would be pointless.

2. Personal Papers

In addition to the McCormick and Everest Papers, some personal papers were of slight use. The J. Howard Nichols Papers in the Baker Library complement the Dwight Manufacturing Company Records. The Charles W. Eliot Papers in the Harvard College Library have some interesting correspondence with William Lyon Mackenzie King on the matter of employee representation. The Ethelbert Stewart Papers in the Bureau of Labor Statistics Records in the National Archives in Washington, D.C., are also of use.

3. Unpublished U.S. Government Records

A collection useful at every step in this study was that of the unpublished reports of investigators employed by the U.S. Commission on Industrial Relations, 1912–15. Often without revealing their identities, these men and women visited welfare companies throughout the United States, asking intelligent and often embarrassing questions and recording the answers at the time. Most of the manuscripts are located in the State Historical Society of Wisconsin, though the National Archives holds some of them. The National Archives has a complete set on microfilm.

The records of the U.S. Coal Commission in the Federal Records Center at Suitland, Maryland, are rich and complete. They are particularly good on housing and company stores. The records of the Bureau of Labor Statistics, the Department of Labor, and the National Recovery Administration, all in the National Archives, are, however, disappointing.

4. Theses

General studies include Oscar W. Nestor's "A History of Personnel Administration, 1890 to 1910" (Ph.D. diss., Department of Economics, University of Pennsylvania, 1954), which describes a wide variety of welfare practices but is weak on analysis. Gordon Maurice Jensen, "The National Civic Federation: American Business in an Age of Social Change and Social Reform" (Ph.D. diss., Department of History, Princeton University, 1956), is good on the National Civic Federation and thus helpful on the early years of welfare capitalism. Stephen J. Scheinberg, "The Development of Corporation Labor Policy, 1900-1940" (Ph.D. diss., Department of History, University of Wisconsin, 1966), concludes that employers were interested in guiding the development of the labor movement rather than in destroying it.

The best study of an individual company is Bernard M. Cannon, "Social Deterrents to the Unionization of Southern Cotton Mill Workers" (Ph.D. diss., Department of Sociology, Harvard University, 1951), which assigns welfarism an important role in retarding unionization in a South Carolina textile town. Richard Anderson Bowron, "American Cast Iron Pipe Company: A Study of an Industrial Democracy" (M.B.A. thesis, Wharton School, University of Pennsylvania), describes thoroughly an extremely interesting company. Howard K. Wilson, "A Study of Paternalism in the Colorado Fuel and Iron Company under John C. Osgood: 1892-1903" (A.M. thesis, Department of History, University of Denver, 1967), presents much information but unfortunately is not based on company records. The chief value of Ray E. Redmond, "A Study of Industrial Relations within the Colorado Fuel and Iron Company" (A.M. thesis, University of Denver, 1928), lies in its reprinting of the minutes of several meetings of committees of employee representatives.

5. Published Government Reports

Government publications contain a wealth of data for the student of welfare capitalism. The reports of the Bureau of Labor Statistics are particularly rewarding, as the bureau made four direct studies of welfare capitalism. They are Victor H. Olmstead, *The Betterment of Industrial Conditions,* Bulletin no. 31, 1900; Elizabeth Lewis Otey,

Employers' Welfare Work, Bulletin no. 123, 1913; *Welfare Work for Employees in Industrial Establishments in the United States,* Bulletin no. 250, 1919 (the most comprehensive); and *Health and Recreation Activities in Industrial Establishments, 1926,* Bulletin no. 458, 1928. Leifur Magnusson, *Housing by Employers in the United States,* Bulletin no. 263, 1920, is invaluable, and Bulletin no. 227, 1917, *Proceedings of the Employment Managers' Conference, Philadelphia, Pa., April 2 and 3, 1917,* is very useful. Boris Emmet, *Profit Sharing in the United States,* Bulletin no. 208, 1917, is excellent. The bureau's *Monthly Labor Review* presents much of the above data in concise form, as well as some important studies not reprinted elsewhere; for example, see G. W. W. Hanger, "Housing of the Working People in the United States By Employers," *Bulletin of the Bureau of Labor* 9, no. 54 (September 1904): 1191–1243.

Excellent studies of company towns made by other agencies of the federal government include W. S. Deffenbaugh, *Schools in the Bituminous Coal Regions of the Appalachian Mountains,* U.S. Bureau of Education, Bulletin no. 21, 1920; Nettie P. McGill, *The Welfare of Children in Bituminous Coal Mining Communities in West Virginia,* U.S. Department of Labor, Children's Bureau, Publication no. 117, 1923; Joseph H. White, *Houses for Mining Towns,* U.S. Bureau of Mines, Bulletin no. 87, 1914; and Dwight E. Woodbridge, *Sanitation at Mining Villages in the Birmingham District, Ala.,* U.S. Bureau of Mines, Technical Paper no. 33, 1913.

State labor bureaus made several studies of welfarism. The best include: Pennsylvania, Department of Internal Affairs, Bureau of Industrial Statistics, "Alleviation of Distress Among Workingmen," *Fifteenth Annual Report,* 1887, in *Annual Report of the Secretary of Internal Affairs* 15, pt. 3 (1888), the first study of welfarism made by any governmental body; New York, Department of Labor, *Third Annual Report of the Commissioner of Labor,* 1903, pt. 4: "Employers' Welfare Institutions," by George A. Stevens and Leonard W. Hatch, in New York, *Assembly Documents, 1904* 22, no. 61, 1904, a study of 110 companies having welfare work; Rhode Island, Commissioner of Industrial Statistics, *Nineteenth Annual Report, 1906,* "Welfare Work in Rhode Island"; and New Jersey, Bureau of Statistics of Labor and Industries, *Twenty-Seventh Annual Report, 1904,* "Industrial Betterment Institutions in New Jersey Manufacturing Establishments," perhaps the most complete case study.

6. Congressional Investigations

Material on every aspect of welfare capitalism may be found in the minutes of congressional investigating bodies. Of particular value to the student of industrial relations are House of Representatives,

Reports of the Industrial Commission, especially vols. 7, 12, 14, and 15, 1901; Senate, *Reports of the Immigration Commission,* vols. 6, 7, 9, 14, 16, and 19, 1911; and Senate, *Report on Conditions of Employment in the Iron and Steel Industry in the United States*, 4 vols., 1911-13. More specialized but still of great use are House of Representatives, *Report on the Miners' Strike in Bituminous Coal Field in Westmoreland County, Pa., in 1910-11,* 1912; House of Representatives, Committee on Labor, *Hearings, Peonage in Western Pennsylvania*, 1911, *Hearings, United States Steel Corporation*, vol. 5, 1911-12, and *Hearings, To Rehabilitate and Stabilize Labor Conditions in the Textile Industry of the United States,* 1936; Senate, Committee on Education and Labor, *Hearings, Investigation of Strike in Steel Industries,* 1919, *Hearings, Conditions in the Paint Creek District, West Virginia*, 1913, and *Hearings, West Virginia Coal Fields*, 1921; Senate, Committee on Interstate Commerce, *Hearings, Conditions in the Coal Fields of Pennsylvania, West Virginia, and Ohio,* 1928; and Senate, Committee on Manufactures, *Hearings, Conditions in Coal Fields in Harlan and Bell County, Kentucky,* 1932.

An interesting study by a state legislature which has good material on company stores is the Ohio, General Assembly, *Proceedings of the Hocking Valley Investigating Committee* (1893).

7. Books: Contemporary Works

Contemporary authors wrote frequently on welfare capitalism. The earliest general studies were Nicholas Paine Gilman, *Profit Sharing Between Employer and Employee: A Study in the Evolution of the Wages System* (Boston: Houghton, Mifflin and Co., 1889) and *A Dividend to Labor: A Study of Employers' Welfare Institutions* (Boston: Houghton, Mifflin and Co., 1899). The latter and William Howe Tolman, *Social Engineering* (New York: Macmillan Co., 1909) are still very useful. Probably better than either is Budgett Meakin, *Model Factories and Villages: Ideal Conditions of Labour and Housing* (Philadelphia: George W. Jacobs & Co., 1905), which has an encyclopedic quality. Federico López Valencia, *Instituciones patronales de previsiön en los Estados Unidos,* Anales de la Junta para ampliación de estudios é investigaciones científicas, vol. 16, no. 5a (Madrid, 1918), is factual and based on personal interviews. Some of the information is not obtainable elsewhere. Edwin L. Shuey, *Factory People and Their Employers* (New York: Lentilon & Co., 1900) has only fragmentary value.

Among those published later, the best were: Daniel Bloomfield, *Labor Maintenance: A Practical Handbook of Employees' Service Work* (New York: Ronald Press, 1920), basically a textbook for welfare capitalists; Louis A. Boettiger, *Employee Welfare Work: A Critical and Historical Study* (New York: Ronald Press, 1923), which emphasized European origins; William M. Leiserson, *Adjusting Immigrant and Industry* (New York: Harper and Brothers, 1924), which emphasized immigration problems; and J. David Houser, *What the Employer Thinks: Executives' Attitudes Toward Employees* (Cambridge: Harvard University Press, 1927). The latter remains one of the best books ever written about industrial relations in the 1920s.

The following general studies are less useful: Ida M. Tarbell, *New Ideals in Business: An Account of Their Practice and Their Effects Upon Men and Profits* (New York: Macmillan Co., 1916), whose laudatory tone proves again that there is no faith like that of a convert; Algie M. Simons, *Personnel Relations in Industry* (New York: Ronald Press, 1921), a text by a reconstructed Socialist; Harry Tipper, *Human Factors in Industry* (New York: Ronald Press, 1922); Lee K. Frankel and Alexander Fleisher, *The Human Factor in Industry* (New York: Macmillan Co., 1920), a textbook; Robert W. Dunn, *The Americanization of Labor: The Employers' Offensive Against the Trade Unions* (New York: International Publishers, 1927), a left-wing exposé; John R. Commons, *Industrial Goodwill* (New York: McGraw-Hill Book Co., 1919); Samuel Crowther, *Common Sense and Labour* (Garden City, N.Y.: Doubleday, Page and Co., 1920); Charles Richmond Henderson, *Citizens in Industry* (New York: D. Appleton and Co., 1915); Charles Cestre, *L'Usine et L'Habitation Ouvriere aux Etats-Unis* (Paris: Editions Ernest Leroux, 1921); and Edouard Maurel, *L'Ingenieur Social dans l'Industrie* (Paris: Librairie du Recueil Sirey, 1929).

The following review welfare work in Europe: Elinor T. Kelly, ed., *Welfare Work in Industry* (London: Sir Isaac Pitman and Sons, 1925), E. Dorothea Proud, *Welfare Work: Employers' Experiments for Improving Working Conditions in Factories* (London: G. Bell and Sons, 1916), and C. R. Fay, *Copartnership in Industry* (Cambridge, Eng.: Cambridge University Press, 1913).

Contemporary books on specific topics include Harriet L. Herring, *Welfare Work in Mill Villages: The Story of Extra-Mill Activities in North Carolina* (Chapel Hill: University of North Carolina Press, 1929), a first-hand description without embellishment of 322 North Carolina textile mills. See also her *Passing of the Mill Village; Revolution in a Southern Institution* (Chapel Hill: University of North Carolina Press, 1949) on the decline of welfarism. Jack Petrill, *After the Whistle Blows: A Guide to the Field of Recreation in Industry* (New York: William-Frederick Press for the Industrial Recreation Bureau, 1949), is a textbook for industrial recreation directors. Gorton James et al., *Profit Sharing and Stock Ownership for Employees* (New York: Harper and Brothers, 1926), a very thorough and thoughtful exposition, is the best available on the subject. Herbert Feis, *Labor Relations: A Study Made in the Procter and Gamble Company* (New York: Adelphi Co., 1928), is a laudatory study of a single company that is still of use because its author had access to all company records. Unfortunately, Edward George Hartmann placed little emphasis on industrial programs in *The Movement to Americanize the Immigrant* (New York: Columbia University Press, 1948).

There are several good books on employee representation. The most comprehensive is Ernest Richmond Burton, *Employee Representation* (Baltimore: Wilkins and Wilkins Co., 1926), but see also Earl J. Miller, *Workmen's Representation in Industrial Government* (Urbana: University of Illinois, 1924), James Myers, *Representative Government in Industry* (New York: George H. Doran Co., 1924), and Carroll E. French, *The Shop Committee in the United States* (Baltimore: Johns Hopkins Press, 1923). *American Shop Committee Plans,* compiled and published by the Bureau of Industrial Research (New York, 1919), is good on the particular characteristics of twenty of the major plans. Cleveland Chamber of Commerce, Committee on Labor Relations, *Employee Representation in Industry: Some Plans in Operation in Cleveland* (Cleveland: By the author, 1923), presents details of nineteen Cleveland plans in a favorable light.

Three series of books deserve special mention. Excellent in every respect are the studies made and published by the National Industrial Conference Board. The most useful are: *Works Councils in the United States,* Research Report no. 21 (Boston, 1919), *Practical Experience with Profit Sharing in Industrial Establishments,* Research Report no. 29 (Boston, 1920); *Experience with Works Councils in the United States,* Research Report no. 50 (New York, 1922); *Employee Magazines in the United States* (New York, 1925); *Employee Stock Purchase Plans in the United States* (New York, 1928); *Industrial Lunchrooms* (New York, 1928); *Industrial Relations in Small Plants* (New York, 1929); *The Present Status of Mutual Benefit Associations* (New York, 1931); *Industrial Relations: Administration of Policies and Programs* (New York, 1931); *Effect of the Depression on Industrial Relations Programs* (New York, 1934); and *What Employers Are Doing for Employees: A Survey of Voluntary Activities for Improvement of Working Conditions in American Business Concerns* (New York, 1936). Some of these are to a certain extent anti-union tracts, yet they still offer the best statistical evidence available on most aspects of welfare capitalism.

Publications of the National Civic Federation are slightly less valuable but less useful. Its *Conference on Welfare Work, 1904* describes welfare programs at many of the major plants. The proceedings of the ninth through twelfth annual meetings are also of use, the eleventh being the best. *Profit Sharing By American Employers* (New York, 1920) is thorough and lists profit sharing plans by employer.

Three books published by the Russell Sage Foundation attest to the power of the case study method. *Employees' Representation in Coal Mines* (New York, 1924) by Ben M. Selekman and Mary Van Kleeck and *Employees' Representation in Steel Works* (New York, 1924) by Selekman are careful studies of the employees' representation plan of the Colorado Fuel and Iron Company. Selekman's *Sharing Management With the Workers* (New York, 1924) studies the plan of the Dutchess Bleachery, Wappingers Falls, New York.

Books by welfare capitalists themselves include Samuel J. Jones, *Letters of Labor and Love* (Indianapolis: Bobbs-Merrill Co., 1905), one of the most extensive expositions of the thinking of a welfare capitalist; Paul Litchfield, *The Industrial Republic* (Boston: Houghton Mifflin Co., 1920), a classic presentation of the theory of welfarism; and Edward A. Filene, *The Way Out: A Forecast of Coming Changes in American Business and Industry* (Garden City, N.Y.: Doubleday, Page and Co., 1924), an analysis which argues for the liberalization of American business. Filene's brother, A. Lincoln Filene, wrote *A Merchant's Horizon* (Boston: Houghton Mifflin Co., 1924), which is a typical exposition of welfare capitalist ideas although the author is somewhat more idealistic than some of his colleagues. Washington Gladden, *Working People and Their Employers* (Boston: Lockwood, Brooks, and Co., 1876) is an early and extensive statement of the labor problem by the leading exponent of the "social gospel." John Leitch, *Man to Man: The Story of Industrial Democracy* (New York: B. C. Forbes Co., 1919) describes in glowing terms the accomplishments of the Leitch Plan.

Short accounts published by welfare companies are: Goodyear Tire and Rubber Company, *The Work of the Labor Division* (Akron, Ohio, 1920), the most useful, and *ACIPCO: A Study of Modern Industrial Relations,* 3d ed. (Birmingham, Ala.: American Cast Iron Pipe Co., 1920), which is nearly as good. Less important is Charles M. Ripley, *Life in a Large Manufacturing Plant* (Schenectady, N.Y.: Publication Bureau, General Electric Company, 1919). Pennsylvania Railroad Company, *Employee Representation on the Pennsylvania Railroad System* (Philadelphia, 1922), describes the plan in detail.

8. Books: Personal History

Two important figures in the field of industrial welfare work left memoirs. Lena Harvey Tracy's autobiography, *How My Heart Sang:*

The Story of Pioneer Industrial Welfare Work (New York: Richard R. Smith, 1950), is readable despite its title, and its greatest interest lies in her relationship to the Social Gospel movement. Clarence J. Hicks, who was a more important figure, left *My Life in Industrial Relations: Fifty Years in the Growth of a Profession* (New York: Harper and Brothers, 1941), which unfortunately underemphasizes Hicks's role in welfarism in favor of a denunciation of the New Deal.

The most useful biography of a welfare capitalist is Samuel Crowther, *John H. Patterson, Pioneer in Industrial Welfare* (Garden City, N.Y.: Doubleday, Page and Co., 1923), a laudatory life of the founder of the National Cash Register Company which nevertheless contains much information. Raymond B. Fosdick, *John D. Rockefeller, Jr.: A Portrait* (New York: Harper and Brothers, 1956), is an account by a lifelong associate which benefits by close acquaintance but suffers by adulation. Broadus Mitchell, *William Gregg, Factory Master of the Old South* (Chapel Hill: University of North Carolina Press, 1928), is a highly readable account of a domineering nineteenth-century employer but is of only peripheral use for this study. The autobiography of Tom M. Girdler, *Boot Straps* (New York: Charles Scribner's Sons, 1943), offers insights into the thought of a passionately anti-union executive. Gerald W. Johnson, *The Making of a Southern Industrialist: A Biographical Study of Simpson Bobo Tanner* (Chapel Hill: University of North Carolina Press, 1952) is brief but still valuable. John Brophy's autobiography, *A Miner's Life* (Madison: University of Wisconsin Press, 1964), edited and supplemented by John O. P. Hall, is a highly readable, informative, and judicious account of an important labor leader who spent his youth in company towns.

H. S. Ferns and B. Ostry, *The Age of Mackenzie King: The Rise of the Leader* (London: William Heineman, Ltd., 1955), argues that King did not conceive the Rockefeller Plan independently but rather did so with the conscious desire of serving Rockefeller interests. But R. MacGregor Dawson, *William Lyon MacKenzie King: A Political Biography, 1874-1923* (Toronto: University of Toronto Press, 1958) had access to the King diaries and makes him seem more disinterested.

9. Books: Company Histories

The most useful company biography is Robert Sidney Smith, *Mill on the Dan: A History of Dan River Mills, 1882-1950* (Durham, N.C.: Duke University Press, 1960), which contains an extensive and fascinating description of welfare practices at a very paternalistic textile company. Of the two volumes on the Standard Oil Company of New Jersey, George Sweet Gibb and Evelyn Knowlton, *The*

Resurgent Years, 1922-27 (New York: Harper and Brothers, 1956), which has an excellent analysis of Jersey Standard's employee representation plan, is more useful than Ralph W. Hidy and Muriel E. Hidy's *Pioneering in Big Business, 1882-1911* (New York: Harper and Brothers, 1955). A generally laudatory account of welfare practices at the Ford Motor Company is in Allan Nevins and Frank Ernest Hill, *Ford: Expansion and Challenge, 1915-1933* (New York: Charles Scribner's Sons, 1957). Paul H. Giddens has a good chapter on welfarism in his *Standard Oil Company (Indiana): Oil Pioneer of the Middle West* (New York: Appleton-Century-Crofts, 1955).

Boris Emmet and John E. Jeuck, *Catalogues and Counters: A History of Sears, Roebuck and Company* (Chicago: University of Chicago Press, 1950) is a valuable brief description of a typical welfare company. But Charles W. Moore, *Timing a Century: History of the Waltham Watch Company* (Cambridge: Harvard University Press, 1945) is less useful. William B. Gates, Jr., *Michigan Copper and Boston Dollars: An Economic History of the Michigan Copper Mining Industry* (Cambridge: Harvard University Press, 1951), is an excellent study but it devotes relatively little attention to the role of welfarism. Three Boswellian paeans by Alfred Lief have some information: *"It Floats": The Story of Procter & Gamble* (New York: Rinehart & Co., 1958) is more useful than either *The Firestone Story: A History of the Firestone Tire & Rubber Company* (New York: McGraw-Hill Book Co., 1951) or *Family Business: A Century in the Life and Times of Strawbridge & Clothier* (New York: McGraw-Hill Book Co., 1968). Robert Glass Cleland, *A History of Phelps Dodge, 1834-1950*, describes a company with a long-standing interest in the welfare of its employees.

10. Books: Recent General Studies

The most useful books for this study were Robert Ozanne, *A Century of Labor-Management Relations at McCormick and International Harvester* (Madison: University of Wisconsin Press, 1967), and Stanley Buder, *Pullman: An Experiment in Industrial Order and Community Planning, 1880-1930* (New York: Oxford University Press, 1967). Ozanne's is the only study devoted solely to labor policy within a single company based on extensive use of company records. The anti-union aspects of welfarism are emphasized to the extent that they constitute a major theme of the book. Buder's careful study of Pullman is very valuable, though it is more limited in time than Ozanne's. Almont Lindsey, *The Pullman Strike: The Story of a Unique Experiment and of a Great Labor Upheaval* (Chicago: University of Chicago Press, 1942; Phoenix Edition, 1964) is still useful. Milton Derber, *The American Idea of Industrial Democracy,*

1865-1965 (Urbana: University of Illinois Press, 1970), is a major survey of industrial relations which seeks to explain the development of the modern concept by comparing it to earlier ones.

James B. Allen, *The Company Town in the American West* (Norman: University of Oklahoma Press, 1966) has some good information but is an overall disappointment. Gerd Korman, *Industrialization, Immigrants, and Americanizers: The View from Milwaukee, 1866-1921* (Madison: State Historical Society of Wisconsin, 1967) has a curious organizing concept. There are useful chapters on welfare capitalism in Morrell Heald, *The Social Responsibilities of Business: Company and Community, 1900-1960* (Cleveland: Press of Case-Western Reserve University, 1970), and to a lesser degree in Charles R. Milton, *Ethics and Expediency in Personnel Management: A Critical History of Personnel Philosophy* (Columbia: University Press, 1970). Irving Bernstein, *The Lean Years: A History of the American Worker, 1920-1933* (Boston: Houghton Mifflin Co., 1960) includes an excellent survey of welfarism in the 1920s. David Brody, *Steelworkers in America: The Nonunion Era* (Cambridge: Harvard University Press, 1960), is a well-researched, well-written, and incisive study of labor relations in the steel industry. It may well be the best book available on industrial relations in the early twentieth century and includes a highly useful development of welfare work in the steel industry.

Books which are important but of less direct utility include: Edward Chase Kirkland, *Dream and Thought in the Business Community, 1860-1900* (Ithaca: Cornell University Press, 1956; Chicago: Quadrangle Paperbacks, 1964), which discusses businessmen's thinking; Jerold S. Auerbach, *Labor and Liberty: The La Follette Committee and the New Deal* (Indianapolis and New York: Bobbs-Merrill Co., 1966), which reacquaints us with violent anti-union methods of the 1930s; and Robert H. Wiebe, *Businessmen and Reform: A Study of the Progressive Movement* (Cambridge: Harvard University Press, 1962), which finds the business community to be fragmented rather than monolithic. Wiebe argues that businessmen made important contributions to economic regulation, but by broader definitions of progressivism, they do not qualify. James Gilbert devotes little attention to industrial welfare programs in *Designing the Industrial State: The Intellectual Pursuit of Collectivism in America, 1880-1940* (Chicago: Quadrangle Books, 1972), but the volume deals with the ideas in a peripheral way.

Specific aspects of labor relations are covered in Vernon H. Jensen, *Heritage of Conflict: Labor Relations in the Nonferrous Metals Industry up to 1930* (Ithaca: Cornell University Press, 1950), Gerald G. Eggert, *Railroad Labor Disputes: The Beginnings of Federal*

Strike Policy (Ann Arbor: University of Michigan Press, 1967), and F. Ray Marshall, *Labor in the South* (Cambridge: Harvard University Press, 1967). Of more direct use are John Coolidge, *Mill and Mansion: A Study of Architecture and Society in Lowell, Massachusetts, 1820–1865* (New York: Columbia University Press, 1942), an architectural history which includes keen insight into the social history of the city; Ole S. Johnson, *The Industrial Store: Its History, Operations and Economic Significance* (Atlanta: Division of Research, School of Business Administration, University of Georgia, 1952), a little-known study which shows that company store prices were higher than elsewhere; and George Korson, *Coal Dust on the Fiddle: Songs and Stories of the Bituminous Industry* (Hatboro, Penn.: Folklore Associates, 1965), which presents a good description of everyday life in mining camps. Alan R. Raucher, *Public Relations and Business, 1900–1929* (Baltimore: Johns Hopkins Press, 1968), ties welfare capitalism to the public relations movement.

11. Contemporary Articles

Several hundred articles on welfare capitalism appeared in dozens of journals. Their worth varied from extremely incisive to utterly devoid of meaning, but as a whole they did not offer as much useful information as most of the other sources. Those which described particular towns or other specific aspects of welfarism, which reported statistical evidence, or which presented forceful arguments for or against welfarism are described below. A few journals consistently yielded information on a broad spectrum of activities. The best of these was *Industrial Management,* which at various times was titled *Engineering Magazine* and *Factory and Industrial Management*. The *Monthly Bulletin of the American Iron and Steel Institute* sometimes devoted whole issues to a discussion of a particular welfare practice.

On specific company towns, see the following: Henry Loomis Nelson, "The Cheyneys' Village at South Manchester, Connecticut," *Harper's Weekly* 34, no. 1728 (1 February 1890): 87–88; I. W. Howerth, "Profit-Sharing at Ivorydale," *American Journal of Sociology* 2, no. 1 (July 1896): 43–57, on the Procter & Gamble Company; Leonora Beck Ellis, "A Model Factory Town," *Forum* 32, no. 1 (September 1901): 60–65, and Richard T. Ely, "An American Industrial Experiment," *Harper's Monthly* 105 (June 1902): 39–45, on Pelzer, South Carolina. George L. McNutt, "Real Profit Sharing and the Results," *Independent* 55, no. 2832 (12 March 1903): 619–22, describes A. S. Baker and Company of Evansville, Wisconsin, and George W. Eads, "N. O. Nelson, Practical Cooperator, and the Great Work He Is Accomplishing for Human Upliftment," *Arena* 36, no.

204 (November 1906): 463–75, describes Leclaire, Illinois. McNutt's "The Race Question Solved in Buxton," *Independent* 62, no. 3052 (30 May 1907): 1256–59, describes the coal mining town of Buxton, Iowa, whose population was 93 percent black.

George Romeyn Taylor, "Creating the Newest Steel City," *Survey* 22 (3 April 1909): 20–36, describes the early years of Gary, Indiana, and George H. Miller, "Fairfield, a Town with a Purpose," *American City* 9 (1913): 213–19, describes the steel town of Fairfield, Alabama. George Creel, "The Feudal Towns of Texas," *Harper's Weekly* 60, no. 3031 (23 January 1915): 76–78, describes Jasper and Kirbyville but is based on notes taken by Peter Speek of the U.S. Commission on Industrial Relations which are available in the National Archives. A. T. Luce, "Kincaid, Ill.: A Model Mining Town," *American City* 13 (1915): 10–13, is useful, as is G. Mortimer, "George F. Johnson and His 'Square Deal Towns,'" *American Magazine* 41 (January 1921): 36–37, a study of towns operated by the Endicott-Johnson Company. Robert W. Bruère, "West Lynn," *Survey* 56 (1 April 1926): 21–27, excellently describes the workings of an employee representation plan at a General Electric plant. Rhys G. Thackwell, "An Industrial Village of Home Owners," *American City* 36, no. 5 (May 1927): 669–71, describes Kohler, Wisconsin, and J. R. Snavely, "The Industrial Community Development at Hershey, Pennsylvania," *American Landscape Architect* 3, no. 5 (November 1930): 24–36, describes the chocolate city.

Other useful articles are Charles Buxton Going, "Village Communities of the Factory, Machine Works, and Mine," *Engineering Magazine* 21, no. 1 (April 1901): 59–74, and Charles W. Hubbard, "Some Practical Principles of Welfare Work," *Journal of Social Science* 42 (September 1904): 83–94. H. F. J. Porter, "Industrial Betterment," *Cassier's Magazine* 38, no. 4 (August 1910): 303–14, is an unusually thoughtful and coherent argument by a practitioner and exponent of welfare capitalism. Two articles by Donald Wilhelm, "Big Businessman as a Social Worker," *Outlook* 107 (22 August 1914): 1005–9, and 108 (23 September 1914): 196–201, present interviews with Elbert H. Gary and Cyrus H. McCormick, Jr., respectively. Joanna Farrell Sturdivant, "Employee Representation Plan of the Durham Hosiery Mills," *Social Forces* 4, no. 3 (March 1926): 625–28, is based on interviews with employers and employees in the plant. "Welfare Work in Company Towns," *Monthly Labor Review* 25, no. 2 (August 1927): 314–20, is only a hodgepodge of facts.

William Menkel applauds "'Welfare Work' on American Railroads," in *Review of Reviews* 38 (October 1908): 449–63. Louis E.

Van Norman, "Why Not More Beautiful Factories? Some Opinions of Manufacturers as to Attractive Business Plants," *Home and Flowers* 13, no. 1 (1902): 22-27, and Thomas Darlington, "Gardens in Connection with Workmen's Houses in Iron, Steel and Allied Industries," *Monthly Bulletin of the American Iron and Steel Institute* 1, no. 3 (March 1913): 67-99, discuss one of the most curious facets of welfarism. Richard T. Ely, "Industrial Betterment," *Harper's Monthly* 105 (September 1902): 548-53, takes a neutral attitude toward welfare companies in Cleveland, Ohio. Fred H. Rindge, Jr., "3,500 College Students Humanizing Industry," *World's Work* 27 (March 1914): 505-511, surveys the work of the YMCA Industrial Service Division.

Articles providing information on a large number of firms are Boyd Fisher, "Where Profit Sharing Fails and Where it Succeeds," *System* 39, no. 3 (March 1916): 233-39, and no. 4 (April 1916): 379-87, the results of an investigation of profit sharing at 125 companies; W. L. Chandler, "The Employees' Mutual Benefit Association," *Industrial Management* 55, nos. 1-4, 6 (January-June 1918): passim, the results of a study of 579 mutual benefit associations; "Shop Committees in Bridgeport: Survey of Employee Representation Plan Installed by War Labor Board," *Industrial Relations* 8, no. 1 (3 September 1921): 804-7, a study of 63 companies in Bridgeport, Connecticut, where 41 representation plans were installed with little success; and "Company Housing in the Cotton Textile Industry in Massachusetts," *Monthly Labor Review* 19, no. 2 (August 1924): 437-38, the results of a questionnaire sent to all Massachusetts textile companies in 1924.

Critics of welfarism penned their views in a series of highly interesting and informative articles. John R. Commons, " 'Welfare Work' in a Great Industrial Plant," *Review of Reviews* 28 (July 1903): 79-81, analyzes welfarism at McCormick's and gives heavily qualified approval. Samuel Gompers, in "The Good and Bad of Welfare Work," *American Federationist* 20, no. 12 (December 1913): 1041-43, finds more of the latter than the former. His "The Company Union Fraud," *American Federationist* 19 (December 1922): 888-89, is vitriolic. Zechariah Chafee, Jr., a Harvard professor, indicts the infringement of civil liberties in company towns in "Company Towns in the Soft Coal Fields," *Independent* 111, no. 3851 (15 September 1923): 102-4. A defense by a spokesman for the coal operators in W. C. Chanler, "Civil Liberties in the Soft Coal Fields: The Point of View of the Operators," *Independent* 111, no. 3853 (13 October 1923): 162-63.

Jeannette Paddock Nichols asks the question "Does the Mill Village Foster Any Social Types?" in the *Journal of Social Forces* 2, no. 3 (March 1924): 350-57, and finds that it did. A denunciation of company magazines is Jean Atherton Flexner, " 'Selling the Company' " *New Republic* 38 (9 April 1924): 171-74. Reinhold Niebuhr's answer to the question, "How Philanthropic is Henry Ford?" *Christian Century* 42 (9 December 1926): 1516-17, is: not very. One of the best articles is Abraham Epstein, "Industrial Welfare Movement Sapping American Trade Unions," *Current History Magazine, New York Times* 24, no. 4 (July 1926): 516-22. It presents the results of a survey of 1,500 of the largest companies in the United States. W. Fox, "The 'Company Community' in the American Coal Fields," *New Statesman* 30, no. 755 (15 October 1927): 6-8, is a sharply critical report by a British visitor.

12. Recent Articles

The most recent general survey of welfare capitalism is David Brody, "The Rise and Decline of Welfare Capitalism," in John Braeman et al., eds., *Change and Continuity in Twentieth-Century America: The 1920's* (Columbus: Ohio State University Press, 1968), pp. 147-78. Brody emphasizes the 1920s and argues that except for the Great Depression welfare capitalism might have continued to dominate industrial relations. See also Brody's essay, "The Emergence of Mass Production Unionism," in a book of similar title, John Braeman et al., eds., *Change and Continuity in Twentieth-Century America* (Columbus: Ohio State University Press, 1964), pp. 221-62. Homer J. Hagedorn tends to discount the importance of welfare capitalism in "A Note on the Motivation of Personnel Management," *Explorations in Entrepreneurial History* 10, nos. 3-4 (April 1958): 134-39. Henry Eilburt argues in "The Development of Personnel Management in the United States," *Business History Review* 33, no. 3 (Autumn 1959): 345-64, that welfarism was one of two sources of modern personnel management. Norman J. Wood surveys industrial relations policies with particular attention to changes arising within business itself in "Industrial Relations Policies of American Management, 1900-1933," *Business History Review* 34, no. 4 (Winter 1960): 403-20.

An excellent essay which treats welfarism in a single company is John A. Garraty, "The United States Steel Corporation Versus Labor: The Early Years," *Labor History* 1, no. 1 (Winter 1960): 3-38. Also good on specific companies are John N. Ingham, "A Strike in the Progressive Era: McKees Rocks, 1909," *Pennsylvania Magazine of History and Biography* 90 (July 1966): 353-77, on the Pressed Steel Car Company, and Howard M. Gitelman, "The Waltham System and the Coming of the Irish," *Labor History* 8, no. 3 (Fall 1967): 227-53, which argues that philanthropic motivations were minimal with regard to company housing. Eugene C. McCreary, "Social Welfare and Business: The Krupp Welfare Program, 1860-1914," *Business History Review* 42, no. 1 (Spring 1968): 24-49, is a good survey of the famous German welfare company. Daniel Nelson and Stuart Campbell skillfully discuss the clash between welfare capitalism and scientific management in "Taylorism Versus Welfare Work in American Industry: H. L. Gantt and the Bancrofts," *Business History Review* 46, no. 1 (Spring 1972): 1-16.

Two articles on recreation offer deep insight: Arthur H. Cole, assisted by Dorothy Lubin, "Perspectives on Leisure-Time Business," *Explorations in Entrepreneurial History,* 2d series, 1, no. 3, Supplement (1964), and Fritz Redlich, "Leisure-Time Activities: A Historical, Sociological, and Economic Analysis," *Explorations in Entrepreneurial History,* 2d series, 3, no. 1 (Fall 1965): 3-23. James O. Morris, "The AFL in the 1920's: A Strategy of Defense," *Industrial and Labor Relations Review* 11, no. 4 (July 1958): 572-90, describes the response of organized labor to company unions. Gaston V. Rimlinger, "Welfare Policy and Economic Development: A Comparative Historical Perspective," *Journal of Economic History* 26, no. 4 (December 1966): 556-71, analyzes the growth of welfare programs.

13. Photographs

The pictorial dimension of welfarism may be traced in a great many of the above sources. The best photographs are in Lena Harvey Tracy, *How My Heart Sang* (New York: Richard R. Smith, 1950); W. S. Deffenbaugh, *Schools in the Bituminous Coal Regions of the Appalachian Mountains,* U.S. Bureau of Education, Bulletin no. 21, 1920; Lawrence Lewis, "Uplifting 17,000 Employees," *World's Work* 9 (March 1905): 5939-50; Caroll T. Fugitt, "The Truce Between Capital and Labor," *Cassier's Magazine* 28 (September 1905): 339-59; and in the *Monthly Bulletin of the American Iron and Steel Institute,* vol. I. See also Bureau of Labor Statistics, *Welfare Work for Employees in Industrial Establishments in the United States,* Bulletin no. 250, 1919, and *Health and Recreation Activities in Industrial Establishments, 1926,* Bulletin no. 458, 1928.

Index